Perception of Prospective Teachers

ABOUT THE AUTHORS

PANNEER SELVAM is born in Salem - Valappady of Tamil Nadu. He started his career as school teacher in New Delhi in the year 1991. He joins as lecturer in DIET, perundurai of Erode in 2000. Bharathiyar University were gave the Philosophy in Doctorates in Language and Education. He is the seventh diploma holder from National University of Educational Planning and Administration (NUEPA), New Delhi in 2002. In 2005, the Tamil Nadu government was given the 'Excellence Award' for his unrivalled teaching activities and some organization also. He has published more than hundreds of Research Papers and books in the field of Education. At present he is working in the department of Education, Bharathidasan University, Tamil Nadu.

Mr. BABU THOMAS obtained his Master of Education and Master of Arts in Malayalam from Mahatma Gandhi University, Kottayam. He earned his Master of Science in Counsellingand Family Therapy (M.Sc-CFT) from IGNOU, New Delhi and in Applied Psychology from Bharathiar University, Coimbatore. He got his Post Graduate Diploma in Child, Adolescent and Family Counselling (PGD-CAFC) from Kerala University and Diploma in Training and Development (D-TD) from Indian Society for Training and Development (ISTD), New Delhi. He is a holder of UGC - NET (Education), SET, K-TET, Account Test & KER. He has 27 years of teaching experience in various reputed schools. At present working as a teacher in St. Ephrem's Higher Secondary School, Mannanam, Kottayam, Kerala. He received Air India – MalayalaManorama BOLT Award, All India AwardeeTeacher's Gurusreshta Award, MalankaraOrthodox Syrian Church Acharya Award. He is a Research Scholar in Education in Bharathidasan University, Tiruchirappalli, Tamil Nadu.

Perception of Prospective Teachers

Dr. S.K. Panneer Selvam
Assistant Professor, Department of Education
Bharathidasan University, T.N.,India

Babu Thomas
St. Ephrem's Higher Secondary School
Mannanam, Kottayam
Kerala

AMIGA PRESS INC.
DELHI (INDIA)

AMIGA PRESS INC.
H.O.: 28-A, Indra Park,
Chander Nagar, Delhi-110051 (India)
Tel.: 011-22504028, +91-98736-57000
E-mail: amigapress@gmail.com
amigaeditorial@gmail.com
amigapub@gmail.com
info@amigapress.co.in
Website : www.amigapress.co.in

This edition is published by Amiga Press Inc.

ISBN: 978-93-84533-71-7

First Published 2020

Printed and bound in India by Replika Press Pvt. Ltd.

Contents

1. **Moral Values and Student-Teacher Relationship of High School Students in Relation to Their Achievement in Mathematics** 1
Introduction; Need for the study; Objectives of the study; Hypotheses of the study; Statement of the problem; Tools used for the present study; Limitations of the study; Sample of the study; Achievement in Mathematics; Influence of gender on moral values; Influence of type of family on moral values; Major findings; Educational implications; Conclusion; References

2. **A Study on Guidance Needs of Higher Secondary Students in Relation to Certain Selected Variables** 7
Introduction; Need of the Study; Objectives of the Study; Hypotheses of the Study; Sample of the Study; Tool used for the Study; Statistical Techniques Used; Result and Discussion; Findings; Conclusion

3. **Study of Learning Difficulties among Higher Secondary Students in Biological Science** 10
Introduction; Need of the Study; Objectives of the Study; Hypotheses of the Study; Sample of the Study; Tool used for the Study; Statistical Techniques Used; Result and Discussion; Findings; Conclusion

4. **Opinion of College Students towards Role of Educational Institutions in Generating Knowledgeable Society** 13
Introduction; Need of the Study; Objectives of the Study; Hypotheses of the Study; Sample of the Study; Tool used for the Study; Statistical Techniques Used; Result and Discussion; Findings; Conclusion

5. **Study on Teacher Effectiveness of High School Teachers and their Attitude towards Teaching in Perambalur District** 18
Introduction; Need of the Study; Objectives of the Study; Hypotheses of the Study; Sample of the Study; Tool used for the Study; Statistical Techniques Used; Result and Discussion; Findings; Conclusion

6. **The Impact of Blended Learning Approach on ICT Readiness and Achievement in Teaching of Science at B.Ed Level** 23
Introduction; Need of the Study; Objectives of the Study; Hypotheses of the Study; Sample of the Study; Tool used for the Study; Statistical Techniques Used; Result and Discussion; Findings; Conclusion; References

7. **Attitude of B. Ed. Trainees towards Teaching With Reference to Social Maturity** 28
Introduction; Need of the Study; Objectives of the Study; Hypotheses of the Study; Sample of the Study; Tool used for the Study; Statistical Techniques Used; Result and Discussion; Findings; Conclusion; References

8. **Creating Path Collaboration for Successful Knowledge Transfer and Knowledge Exchange** 34
Introduction; Need of the Study; Objectives of the Study; Hypotheses of the Study; Sample of the Study; Tool used for the Study; Statistical Techniques Used; Result and Discussion; Findings; Conclusion; References

9. **Role of Higher Education Institutions in Generating Knowledgeable Society** 39
Introduction; Need of the Study; Objectives of the Study; Hypotheses of the Study; Sample of the Study; Tool used for the Study; Statistical Techniques Used; Result and Discussion; Findings; Conclusion; References

10. **Role of Higher Education Institution in Bridging among the Society** 45
Introduction; Need of the Study; Objectives of the Study; Hypotheses of the Study; Sample of the Study; Tool used for the Study; Statistical Techniques Used; Result and Discussion; Findings; Conclusion; References

11. Role of National Institutes on Creating Public Awareness for Rehabilitation of Persons with Disabilities **50**
Introduction; Need of the Study; Objectives of the Study; Hypotheses of the Study; Sample of the Study; Tool used for the Study; Statistical Techniques Used; Result and Discussion; Findings; Conclusion; References

12. Scientific Aptitude among the Arts and Science Students in Puducherry Region **56**
Introduction; Need of the Study; Objectives of the Study; Hypotheses of the Study; Sample of the Study; Tool used for the Study; Statistical Techniques Used; Result and Discussion; Findings; Conclusion; References

13. Development and Effectiveness of E-Content in Teaching of Biological Science Education for Knowledgeable Society **62**
Introduction; Need of the Study; Objectives of the Study; Hypotheses of the Study; Sample of the Study; Tool used for the Study; Statistical Techniques Used; Result and Discussion; Findings; Conclusion; References

14. Relationship of Academic Confidence and Academic Achievement of the Higher Secondary Students **67**
Introduction; Need of the Study; Objectives of the Study; Hypotheses of the Study; Sample of the Study; Tool used for the Study; Statistical Techniques Used; Result and Discussion; Findings; Conclusion; References

15. Technology Skill and Cognitive Skill of Teachers at High School Level **72**
Introduction; Need of the Study; Objectives of the Study; Hypotheses of the Study; Sample of the Study; Tool used for the Study; Statistical Techniques Used; Result and Discussion; Findings; Conclusion; References

16. Social Competency and Confidence Building of Disabled towards Knowledge Society **77**
Introduction; Need of the Study; Objectives of the Study; Hypotheses of the Study; Sample of the Study; Tool used for the Study; Statistical Techniques Used; Result and Discussion; Findings; Conclusion; References

17. **Role of Educational Institution in Generating Knowledgeable Society with Special Reference to D.Ed. Colleges of Mahabubnagar District of Telangana** 81
Introduction; Need of the Study; Objectives of the Study; Hypotheses of the Study; Sample of the Study; Tool used for the Study; Statistical Techniques Used; Result and Discussion; Findings; Conclusion; References

18. **Collaborating the Colleges of Education by Multi-Point Videoconference Teaching** 85
Introduction; Need of the Study; Objectives of the Study; Hypotheses of the Study; Sample of the Study; Tool used for the Study; Statistical Techniques Used; Result and Discussion; Findings; Conclusion; References

19. **Attitude of B.Ed. Trainees towards Teaching with Reference to Social Maturity** 90
Attitude - Meaning; Importance of Attitude towards Teaching; Definition of Social Maturity; Importance of Social Maturity; Need for the Study; Statement of the Problem; Objectives of the Study; Hypotheses of the Study; Method used in the study; Findings; Conclusion; References

20. **The Effect of CCE on Total Academic Achievement among High School Students** 97
Introduction; Need of the Study; Objectives of the Study; Hypotheses of the Study; Sample of the Study; Tool used for the Study; Statistical Techniques Used; Result and Discussion; Findings; Conclusion; References

21. **Scientific Aptitude among the Arts and Science Students in Puducherry Region** 103
Introduction; Need of the Study; Objectives of the Study; Hypotheses of the Study; Sample of the Study; Tool used for the Study; Statistical Techniques Used; Result and Discussion; Findings; Conclusion; References

22. **A study of Attitude of college and University Students towards Teaching Methods of their Teachers in relation their Academic Achievement** 108
Introduction; Need of the Study; Objectives of the Study; Hypotheses of the Study; Sample of the Study; Tool used for the Study; Statistical Techniques Used; Result and Discussion; Findings; Conclusion; References

23. Moral Values and Student-Teacher Relationship of High School Students in Relation to their Achievement in Mathematics **116**
Introduction; Need of the Study; Objectives of the Study; Hypotheses of the Study; Sample of the Study; Tool used for the Study; Statistical Techniques Used; Result and Discussion; Findings; Conclusion; References

24. Technology Skill and Cognitive Skill of Teachers at High School Level **123**
Introduction; Need of the Study; Objectives of the Study; Hypotheses of the Study; Sample of the Study; Tool used for the Study; Statistical Techniques Used; Result and Discussion; Findings; Conclusion; References

25. Effectiveness of Computer Based Multimedia Learning **128**
Introduction; Need of the Study; Objectives of the Study; Hypotheses of the Study; Sample of the Study; Tool used for the Study; Statistical Techniques Used; Result and Discussion; Findings; Conclusion; References

26. Hyper Diversed Teacher and Digital Skills **140**
Introduction; Need of the Study; Objectives of the Study; Hypotheses of the Study; Sample of the Study; Tool used for the Study; Statistical Techniques Used; Result and Discussion; Findings; Conclusion; References

27. An Assessment of Edu Digital Skills of Teachers in Namakkal District **149**
Introduction; Need of the Study; Objectives of the Study; Hypotheses of the Study; Result and Discussion; Findings; Conclusion; References

28. Implications of Multimedia in Teaching Economics with Special Reference to Higher Secondary Students in Chennai **157**
Introduction; Need of the Study; Objectives of the Study; Hypotheses of the Study; Sample of the Study; Tool used for the Study; Statistical Techniques Used; Result and Discussion; Findings; Conclusion; References

29. Effectiveness of Blended Learning Programme in Teaching Biology at Higher Secondary School Students **168**
Introduction; Need of the Study; Objectives of the Study; Hypotheses of the Study; Sample of the Study; Tool used for the Study; Statistical Techniques Used; Result and Discussion; Findings; Conclusion; References

30. Awareness of Educational Media among Higher Secondary Teachers of Thiruvannamalai District and their Perception of Media Based Education 173
Introduction; Need of the Study; Objectives of the Study; Hypotheses of the Study; Sample of the Study; Tool used for the Study; Statistical Techniques Used; Result and Discussion; Findings; Conclusion; References

31. Relevant Effectiveness of Computer Based Multimedia Learning Material 184
Introduction; Need of the Study; Objectives of the Study; Hypotheses of the Study; Sample of the Study; Tool used for the Study; Statistical Techniques Used; Result and Discussion; Findings; Conclusion; References

32. Perception of Prospective Teachers on Designing Learning 197
Introduction; Need of the Study; Objectives of the Study; Hypotheses of the Study; Sample of the Study; Tool used for the Study; Statistical Techniques Used; Result and Discussion; Findings; Conclusion; References

33. Awareness of Flip Teaching among School Teachers in and around Madurai District 206
Introduction; Need of the Study; Objectives of the Study; Hypotheses of the Study; Sample of the Study; Tool used for the Study; Statistical Techniques Used; Result and Discussion; Findings; Conclusion; References

34. Attitude of Prospective Teachers towards Blended Learning 211
Introduction; Need of the Study; Objectives of the Study; Hypotheses of the Study; Sample of the Study; Tool used for the Study; Statistical Techniques Used; Result and Discussion; Findings; Conclusion; References

35. Effectiveness of Continuous and Comprehensive Evaluation of Science 216
Introduction; Need of the Study; Objectives of the Study; Hypotheses of the Study; Sample of the Study; Tool used for the Study; Statistical Techniques Used; Result and Discussion; Findings; Conclusion; References

36. Effectiveness of Multimedia Programme in Perceiving Human Anatomy among Higher Secondary Students **223**
Introduction; Need of the Study; Objectives of the Study; Hypotheses of the Study; Sample of the Study; Tool used for the Study; Statistical Techniques Used; Result and Discussion; Findings; Conclusion; References

37. Usage of Internet for Education Purpose among Arts and Science College **232**
Introduction; Need of the Study; Objectives of the Study; Hypotheses of the Study; Sample of the Study; Tool used for the Study; Statistical Techniques Used; Result and Discussion; Findings; Conclusion; References

38. Students Attitude towards Audio-Visual Aids used by the Teachers **237**
Introduction; Need of the Study; Objectives of the Study; Hypotheses of the Study; Sample of the Study; Tool used for the Study; Statistical Techniques Used; Result and Discussion; Findings; Conclusion; References

1.

Moral Values and Student-Teacher Relationship of High School Students in Relation to Their Achievement in Mathematics

Introduction

Values are not absolute and they change from time to time. Moral values help every individual to form character with good habits. On his being a good habit is a good and useful member of the society and on his understanding the final purpose for which he courts is doing all activities with reason dictates, in order to achieve this purpose.Moral values refer to the genuine life principles in a person that make him a wholesome person. It focuses on values that motivate a person to pursue higher needs, the for self actualization. Teacher student relationship is a positive activity of "building a coalition among the multiple, shifting, intersecting and sometimes contradicting groups" for the all round development of the individual (Nicholas Burbules). Chaplin (1968) achievement defined as a specified level of attainment or proficiency in academic work as evaluated by the teachers or standard test or combination of both".

Need for the study

Academic achievement is an important aim in the field of education. A student's ambition can be fulfilled only if his achievement in school is high which is the basic attainment in judging the educational capacity of an individual. It is essential to raise the standard of achievement in education. Hence it is imperative to undertake research in this area. The students who are capable of learning well but do not perform well in mathematics need a little more individual attention. A proper study habit of the various factors which affect their performance will help the teacher to understand the students and give proper guidance. If this is not done in schools the world may have to lose a huge amount human resources. To reduce a large number of failures in mathematics at the high school level, high Student-Teacher relationship is necessary. If the pupils have good relationship with their teacher they can whine in their studies. So, here researcher made an attempt to know the importance and influence of these variables. 'Value Education' has become the latest trend in high school education. Today pupils are much worried about their behavior, attitude towards optimistic ideas. This study is conducted to analyze the students attitude towards 'moral values' students from different schools in Cuddalore district were taken into consideration for their study and two different categories of schools were selected to conduct the study and they are of Government schools, Government aided schools. In these different schools inculcation of moral values differ according to the school in which they study.

Objectives of the study

The following objectives have been set in the present study.

- To find out the level of Moral values of 9th standard students.
- To find out the level of student-teacher relationship of 9th standard students
- To find out the level of achievement in Mathematics of 9th standard students.
- To find whether there is any significant difference between the mean scores of Moral values of students studying in 9th standard with regard to (a) Gender (Male/Female) and (b) Type of family (Joint/Nuclear).
- To find whether there is any significant difference between the mean scores of personal values of students studying in 9th standard with regard to (a) Gender and (b) Type of family.

Hypotheses of the study

The following hypotheses have been set in the present study.

- The category of moral values of IX standard students is personal value innature
- The level of student – teacher relationship of IX standard students is averagein nature.
- The level of achievement in mathematics of IX standard students is average in nature.
- There is no significant difference between the mean score of moral values of IX standard students with regard to (a) Gender (Male/Female) and (b) Type of family (Joint/Nuclear).
- There is no significant difference between the mean scores of personalvalues

of students studying in IX standard with regard to (a) Gender and (b) Type of family.

Statement of the problem

The problem is stated as follows: Moral values and student-teacher relationship among high school students in relation to their achievement in Mathematics.

Tools used for the present study

The following are the tools selected for the present study.

- Moral judgement scale constructed by the investigator.
- Student-Teacher relationship inventory by the investigator.
- Marks scored by the students in mathematics paper in their quarterlyexamination held in September 2009.

Limitations of the study

The present investigation has the following limitations.

- The investigation is limited to 9th standard students only.
- The study is restricted to few schools in Cuddalore district.
- The sample size is restricted to 297 students due to lack of time.
- Student-teacher relationship with respect to teaching of mathematics alone has been considered in the present study.

Sample of the study

The present study is mainly concerned with the IX standard students studying in schools following the syllabus of Tamil Nadu boards of high school education. For the present study, the sample of 297, IX standard students studying in different management of the schools at Cuddalore district during the academic year 2009-2010 were chosen, using stratified random sampling technique. Out of the 10 schools in the sample six are government schools and four government aided schools. Among the 297 students in the samples 140 are boys and 157 are girls. The details of the sample composition with respect to the different characteristics are presented below

TABLE 4.1: Showing the criteria of classifying the sample into four categories based on their values.

Categories	No. of Students	Percentage
Personal	70	23.57
Family	62	20.88
Social	94	31.65
Spiritual	71	23.90
Total	**297**	**100.00**

From the table, it is seen that the category of moral values of IX standard students is social values in nature. Hence hypothesis I stating that "The category of moral values of IX standard students is personal values in nature" is rejected

Student-teacher relationship. Based on the information obtained from the IX standard students regarding their student-teacher relationship, the students are divided into three groups' namely low, moderate and high level of students – teacher relationship the details of which are presented below.

Table 4.2: Showing the criteria of classifying the sample into three groups of student – teacher relationship

Groups	Student-teacher relationship score range	**No. of students**	**Percentage**
Low	0 to 58	15	5.1
Moderate	59 to 79	57	19.2
High	80 to 100	225	75.8
Total		297	100.0

From the table, it is seen that the level of student-teacher relationship of IX standard students is high in nature. Hence hypotheses II stating that "The level of student-teacher relationship of IX standard students is average in nature is rejected.

Achievement in Mathematics

Based on the information obtained from the IX standard students regarding their achievement in mathematics, the students are divided into three groups namely low, moderate and high level of achievement in mathematics the detail of which are presented below.

Table 4.3: Showing the criteria of classifying the sample into three groups of achievement in Mathematics

Groups	**Achievement in Mathematics score range**	**No. of students**	**Percentage**
Low	2 to 34	98	33.0
Moderate	35 to 67	151	50.8
High	68 to 100	48	16.2
Total		297	100.0

From the table, it is seen that the level of achievement in mathematics of IX standard student is moderate in nature. Hence hypotheses III stating that "The level of achievement in mathematics of IX standard students is average in nature" is accepted.

Influence of gender on moral values

The scores of moral values of boys and girls have been analyzed as shown below

Table 4.4: Showing the significant difference between the mean scores of moral values of boys and girls

Group comparison	N	Mean	SD	SE	't' Value	Level of significance
Boys Girls	140 157	181.242357 185.161592	12.713 10.1546	1.074 0.810	2.92	0.01

From the above, table it is clear that girls are significantly higher than their counterparts with regard to moral values.Hence the hypothesis IV(a) stating that " There is no significant difference between the mean scores of moral values of IX standard students with regard to gender" is rejected.

Influence of type of family on moral values

The scores of moral values of students hailing from joint/nuclear families have been analyzed and the obtained results is presented below

Table 4.5: Showing the significant difference between the mean scores of moral values of students hailing from joint and nuclear families

Group comparison	N	Mean	SD	SE	't' Value	Level of significance
Joint Nuclear	233 64	183.6009 182.2500	11.3218 12.505	0.741 1.563	0.78	NS

The above table reveals that students from joint family do not differ much from that of nuclear ones in the case of moral values. Hence the hypothesis IV(b) stating that " There is no significant difference between the mean scores of moral values of IX standard students with regard to the type of family of the students" is accepted.

Major findings

A careful analysis of the data had resulted in the following findings:

- The category of moral values of IX standard students is social values in nature.
- The level of Student-Teacher relationship of IX standard students is high in nature
- The level of achievement in Mathematics of IX standard students is moderate in nature
- Girls are significantly higher than their counter parts with regard to moral values.
- Students from Joint family do not differ much from that of Nuclear ones in the case of moral values.

Educational implications

Education plays a vital role in understanding the importance of moral values in life. Proper education attempts to balance the frustration level and gradually inculcate the moral values in the life of an individual. The aim of education is to develop broadmindedness and universal outlook in the individuals with right wisdom. The Educational system must impart values in students such as tolerance, patience, understanding, truthfulness, gratitude, faith in God, self respect and also in the light of perspective, education should raise humanity and values such as brother hood, mercy, love etc. If a student becomes a good social citizen, it means he is morally well sound. Absence of this education results in disorder, distraction, exploitation, selfishness, aggression, hatred and frustration in the world. The objective of education should be for shaping and bringing out useful and self-dependent citizens with all good qualities.

Conclusion

The purpose of the present investigation is to investigate the relationships among the variables of moral values, student-teacher relationship and achievement in mathematics. The investigation is sure to find some usefulness in the field of education and findings of the investigation can serve as a database for further research.

References

- Burbules and Rice (1991), Difference, Authority and the Teacher Student Relationship by Clive Bieck.
- Clive Bieck, "Difference, Authority and the Teacher Student Relationship", Ontario Institute for studies in Education.
- Daniel, J.K and Selvamony Nirmal, "Value Education Today: Explorations in Social Ethics", All India Association for Christian Higher Education, New Delhi, 1990.
- Downie,R.S, "Roles and Values: An Introduction to Social Ethics", Methuen and Co, Ltd, London, 1971.
- Ignacimuth,S, "Values for Life", Better Yourself Books, Bombay, 1994.
- Kalra,M.Rajinder, "Value – Oriented Education in Schools: Theory and practices, "Shirpa Publications, Delhi, 2003.

❐

2.

A Study on Guidance Needs of Higher Secondary Students in Relation to Certain Selected Variables

Introduction

Guidance covers the whole process of education which starts from the birth of the child. As individuals need help throughout their lives, it is not wrong to say that guidance is needed from the cradle to the grave. Guidance is as old as the human civilization. In the primitive society, elders in the family offered guidance to the young and to persons in distress. Even today, in India, guidance, whether in educational, vocational or personal matters, is sought from family elders. Guidance -unorganized and informal -in all places and at all levels has been a vital aspect of the educational process. With the passage of time, revolutionary changes have taken place in the field of agriculture, industry, business and medicine. These changes in all walks of life coupled with extraordinary growth in our population has made the social structure very complex.

Need of the Study

Industrialization, urbanization, modernization and cybernation have deeply affected the traditional social structure such as family, kin, caste, religion etc. Among them education has brought a distinct psychological changes in attitudes, values and behaviors of the adolescents. Adolescence is period of storm and strife. He needs guidance in physical, social mental professional and vocational areas. Guidance in physical needs is required. Physiological changes result in growth spurt, which creates adjustment problems. Adolescents are often confronted with the problem of conforming or not conforming to group expectations and pressures. Hence he needs a social guidance. An adolescent tends to suffer from swinging moods and emotional instability. He oscillated from extreme optimism to absolute dependency. Sex urges cause anxiety and of guilt dealings. Hence he needs mental guidance.

Objectives of the Study

The following objectives were formulated to investigate the guidance needs

- To identify the guidance needs of higher secondary students.
- To study the guidance needs (physical, social, psychological, educational and vocational) of higher secondary students on the basis of gender and location of their residence.

Hypotheses of the Study

The study used the following hypotheses

- There exist varied guidance needs among secondary school students.
- There exists no significant difference between the guidance needs (physical, social, psychological, educational and vocational) of male and female higher secondary students.
- There exists no significant difference between the guidance needs (physical, social, psychological, educational and vocational) of urban and rural higher secondary students.

Sample of the Study

In the present study, samples of 250 higher secondary students were selected through purposive random sampling technique.

Tool used for the Study

Grewals guidance need inventory (1982) was used to by the the investigator for the collection of the data pertaining to this study.

Statistical Techniques Used

In order to testify hypotheses, statistical techniques Mean, S.D and t-test were used.

Result and Discussion

Table:1 Significance of difference in mean scores of guidance needs of male and female higher secondary students

Gender	N	Mean	SD	t-value	LS
Male	150	19.15	6.36	6.03	0.01 (S)
Female	100	13.94	5.84		

The result shows that the obtained t-value is significant at 0.01 level. So the null hypothesis is rejected and alternative hypothesis is accepted. Therefore it is concluded there is a significant difference for guidance needs of higher secondary student on the basis of gender.

Table:2 Showing Mean SD, and t-test for guidance needs of higher secondary student on the basis of locality

Locality	N	Mean	SD	t-value	LS
Urban	138	28.42	5.72	14.38	0.001 (S)
Rural	112	16.73	6.21		

From the above result, it is found that the obtained t-value is significant at 0.001 level. So the null hypothesis is rejected and alternative hypothesis is accepted. Therefore it is concluded there is a significant difference for guidance needs of higher secondary student on the basis of locality.

Findings

Result reveals that there is a significant difference for guidance needs of higher secondary student on the basis of gender.

Analysis proves that there is a significant difference for guidance needs of higher secondary student on the basis of locality.

Conclusion

The results from the study will help in throwing more light on the various guidance needs of male and female secondary school students. It will also help in studying the degree or extent of guidance needs of rural and urban secondary school students. In addition, it will provide information to teachers, education planners and school administrators about their responsibility in providing adequate facilities for guidance services in order that the students receive quality guidance. It will also reveal the various problematic areas in which secondary school students need guidance for the total development of their potentialities and proper adjustment in various areas of life.

❐

3.

Study of Learning Difficulties among Higher Secondary Students in Biological Science

Introduction

Learning difficulties aren't contagious, but they can be genetic. That means they can be passed down in families through the genes, like many other traits we get from our parents and grandparents. Someone with a learning disability probably has other family members who have had some learning troubles, too. Kids with learning problems are sometimes surprised to find out that one of their parents had similar troubles when he or she was in school. But kids today have an advantage over their parents. Learning experts now know a lot more about the brain and how learning works and it's easier for kids to get the help they need.

Significance of the Study

For the purpose of this, students with learning difficulties are defined as students who have significant difficulties in acquiring literacy and numeracy skills but excluding students who have an intellectual, physical or sensory impairment or whose learning difficulty is due to social cultural or environmental factors. Thus the group of students that are the subject of this digest includes (but is not limited to) those with learning disabilities, dyslexia, Attention Deficit Disorder/ Attention Deficit Hyperactivity Disorder and language and communication difficulties. Typically these students have memory and organization problems and have failed to make satisfactory progress with the regular classroom curriculum.

The surveys have indicated that 10 to 16 per cent of students are perceived by their teachers to have learning difficulties and have support needs, particularly in literacy, that go beyond those normally addressed by class teachers. These rates are similar to those reported in the UK and USA. Within the population of students with learning difficulties there is a smaller sub-set of students who show persistent and long lasting learning impairments and these are better identified as students with specific learning disabilities. Approximately 4 per cent of Australian students have a specific learning disability. Students in this smaller group have been identified as being more resistant to standard remedial intervention programmes because of assumed neurological dysfunction.

While estimates of the number of students experiencing numeracy difficulties are similar to those for literacy, one group of researchers noted that incidence studies of students with difficulties in numeracy are carried out less frequently and that the procedures used are less comprehensive than those used to identify those with literacy difficulties. Further, the assessment instruments that are available to identify numeracy difficulties are often unwieldy and outdated. In the same study, less than 30 per cent of schools assessed numeracy. In those schools that did assess numeracy, many used teacher-constructed instruments that did not adequately address the range of potential numeracy problems. Therefore, it is possible that the incidence of numeracy difficulties may be even higher than those reported for literacy.

Learning difficulties in numeracy and literacy reflect an enduring deficit rather than just a developmental lag, necessitating intervention programs of greater duration and intensity than those normally offered in the regular curriculum. Longitudinal studies have shown that 70 per cent of students with literacy difficulties at age 7 still have reading/literacy problems when aged 15. Therefore considering the above facts the present study is significant and needed one.

Objectives of the Study

To find out the significant difference in learning difficulties of higher secondary students in biological science with respect to their demographic variables.

Hypotheses of the Study

The level of learning difficulties of higher secondary students in biological science is average.

There is no significant difference in learning difficulties of higher secondary students in biological science with respect to their demographic variables.

Sample of the Study

In the present study, samples of 300 higher secondary school students were selected through purposive random sampling technique.

Tools Used for the Study

Learning difficulties (Nagarajan (2009)) tool was used by the investigator for the collection of the data pertaining to this study.

Result and Discussion

Table:1 Showing Mean SD, and t-test for learning difficulties higher secondary student on the basis of gender

Gender	N	Mean	SD	t-value	LS
Boys	138	16.34	5.62	1.161	0.246 (NS)
Girls	162	17.12	6.05		

From the above result that the obtained t-value is not significant at 0.01 level. So the null hypothesis is accepted and alternative hypothesis is rejected. Therefore it is concluded there is no significant difference between the learning difficulties among higher secondary student of male and female students.

Table:2 Showing Mean SD, and t-test for learning difficulties higher secondary student on the basis of location of the school

Locality	N	Mean	SD	t-value	LS
Urban	90	18.27	6.22	4.577	0.01 (S)
Rural	210	15.27	5.08		

From the above result, it is found that the obtained t-value is significant at 0.01 level. So the null hypothesis is rejected and alternative hypothesis is accepted.

Findings

Results show that there is no significant difference in Learning Difficulties of Higher Secondary students on the basis of gender.

Results exhibits that there is significant difference in Learning Difficulties of Higher Secondary students on the basis of school location.

Conclusion

On the completion of this present study the investigator has been prompted to conclude that the independent variable and the background variables included in the present study are not influential enough to alter the difficulties. Therefore the investigator feels that on the completion of the proposed topics of research given here, valid information with regard to difficulties may be obtained. Random sampling technique was used to select the sample.

❒

4.

Opinion of College Students towards Role of Educational Institutions in Generating Knowledgeable Society

Introduction

Economic development basically depends on knowledge availability. Globalisation and new information and communication capabilities provide opportunities as well as challenges for the sustainable consumption and production pattern. In this respect ICT is the modern driving force for economic development. New science breakthroughs and a technology driven pattern of innovation are the basic platform for economic development. It should be taken into a consideration that the achievements in science and technological innovations will not automatically bring about social, environmental and economic improvements.

The problem restated

To find out "Opinion of college students towards role of educational institutions in generating knowledgeable society

Need For Study

The emerging knowledge society has increased the priority of education and learning in society. In order to promote, support and organise activities leading to the development of the knowledge society, the organisation of platforms for a dissemination, transfer and utilisation approach, for society as a whole, of education and teaching of essential knowledge in support of a new social structure based on the new quality of life is of paramount importance. Universities are situated at the crossroads of research, education and innovation. In many respects they hold the key to the knowledge economy and society. They play an important role in the creation of the knowledge society. Besides their classical role as educational institutions, they are now a pool of knowledge and research institutions for knowledge generation. Close links between society and universities has generated interaction that proves to be an essential force in development. In addition, universities train an ever increasing number of students with increasingly higher qualifications, and thus contribute to strengthening the competitiveness of the Indian economy.

Background of the study

The knowledge economy and society stem from the combination of four interdependent elements: the production of knowledge, mainly through scientific research; its transmission through education and training; its dissemination through information and communication technologies; its use in technological innovation. The investigator has undertaken the study to find Opinion of college students towards role of educational institutions in generating knowledgeable society

Scope of the Study

It is of paramount importance for world, regional and state economic development to have broad access to the modern knowledge bases. In this respect it is imminent to the utilization of knowledge bases to have appropriate knowledge distribution systems. The education system is the basic means in the dissemination of knowledge. Close links between knowledge bases and education system promote knowledge transfer to all levels of human organisation. The essential component in invention and innovation is knowledge. The transfer and dissemination of knowledge increase ability to invent and innovate, that is to create new knowledge and new ideas that are then embedded in production, processes and organisation. Organisations and institutions capable of the creation and dissemination of knowledge are always part of the education system

Operational definitions

Opinion: Opinion is more generalized aspects of behaviour then process skills. It is learned predispositions towards aspects of our environment.

Knowledgeable Society: The role of the knowledge society in the future development of human society

Population variables

Gender: This refers to the male and female college students.

Type of colleges: This refers to the government and aided colleges.

Location of the College: This refers to the rural and urban areas.

Objectives of the study

To find out Opinion of college students towards role of educational institutions in generating knowledgeable society.

To find out the significance difference in Opinion of college students towards role of educational institutions in generating knowledgeable society with respect to Gender, Type of college, Location of the college.

Hypotheses

Opinion of college students towards role of educational institutions in generating knowledgeable society is high

There is significant difference between the Opinion of college students towards role of educational institutions in generating knowledgeable society with reference to Gender, Type of college and Location of the college.

Methodology

Survey method was used for data collection and the stratified representative sampling technique is used. The size of the sample was 60 college students, with due, representation given to the variables namely Gender, Type of the college, and Location of the college. Opinionnionaire prepared and validated by the investigator was used for this study. The tool has 20 items. The collected data was analyzed statistically by using following techniques, The Mean (X), The Standard Deviation (σ) and The 't' test.

Delimitation

Among the various colleges in Tamil Nadu the samples are taken from the district of Madurai.

Among the various colleges in Madurai, the samples are taken from few colleges.

Hypothesis testing

Hypothesis 1:

Opinion of college students towards role of educational institutions in generating knowledgeable society is high

Table 1: The Opinion of college students towards role of educational institutions in generating knowledgeable society.

Sample	Sample(N)	Theoretical Mean	Obtained Mean
College students	60	10	12.5

The above table shows that the obtained mean score of the Opinion of college students towards role of educational institutions in generating knowledgeable society is 12.5, which is found to be greater than the theoretical mean 10, which is the frame of reference. The analysis shows that the Opinion of college students towards role of educational institutions in generating knowledgeable society is high.

Hypothesis 2: There is significant difference between the Opinion of college students towards role of educational institutions in generating knowledgeable society with reference to Gender, Type of college and Location of the college

Table 2: Comparison of Male and Female college students' opinion towards role of educational institutions in generating knowledgeable society

Variable	Sub-Variables	N	Mean	S.D	't' value	Level of Significance at 0.05
Gender	Male	30	12.93	1.390	0.238	Not Significant
	Female	30	12.3636	1.329		

The obtained't' value 0.238 is lesser than the table value 1.96 at 0.05 level of significance. Hence there is no significant difference between male and female college students opinion towards role of educational institutions in generating knowledgeable society. Both variables mean scores are indicating that there is high opinion towards the role of educational institutions in generating knowledgeable society

Table 3: Comparison of Government and Aided college students' opinion towards role of educational institutions in generating knowledgeable society

Variable	**Sub-Variables**	**N**	**Mean**	**S.D**	**'t' value**	**Level of Significance**
Type of The college	Government college	30	12.03	1.455	0.789	Not Significant
	Gov - Aided college	30	11.9667	1.29943		

The obtained't' value 0.789 is lesser than the table value 1.96 at 0.05 level of significance. This shows that there is no significant difference between Government and Aided college students' opinion towards role of educational institutions in generating knowledgeable society. They had understood the important role of educational institutions in generating knowledgeable society but no significant difference between two.

Table 4: Comparison of Urban and Rural college students' opinion towards role of educational institutions in generating knowledgeable society.

Variable	Sub-Variables	N	Mean	S.D	't' value	Level of Significance
location	Urban	30	12.33	1.268	0.9778	Not Significant
	Rural	30	11.8667	1.22		

The obtained 't' value 0.9778 is lesser than the table value 1.96 at 0.05 level of significance. This shows that there is no significant difference between Urban and Rural college students' opinion towards role of educational institutions in generating knowledgeable society. They had understood the role educational institutions in generating knowledgeable society but no significant difference between two.

Conclusion

The capacity for information transformation into knowledge is represented by the ability of the cultural system to convert available information into scientific and technological values used in everyday life. It strongly depends on the cultural and social system. The notion "knowledge society" emerged toward the end of the 90s and is particularly used, by some in academic circles, as an alternative to the "information society". UNESCO, in particular, has adopted the term "knowledge society", or its variant, "knowledge societies", within its institutional policies. There has been a great deal of reflection on the issue, which strives to incorporate a more integral conception that is not only related to the economic dimension. The investigator wanted to know opinion of college students towards the role of educational institutions in generating knowledgeable society.

❐

5.

Study on Teacher Effectiveness of High School Teachers and Their Attitude towards Teaching in Perambalur District

Introduction

In any educational pyramid, the teaching personnel are considered as an architect. Teacher is the one under whose supervision and guidance the destiny of future rests. The success of any educational system depends beyond doubt on his requisite qualities. Kothari Commission (1964-66) recommended, "….of all the factors which determine the quality of education and its contribution to national development, the teacher is undoubtedly the most important. It is on his personal qualities and character, his educational qualifications and professional competence that the success of all educational endeavors must ultimately depend." The role of teacher is assuming new dimensions due to technological progress and new vistas of knowledge resulting from scientifically verified innovations. The teacher in modern society is very important in social reconstruction and transmission of wisdom, knowledge and experiences. The role and responsibilities of a teacher are infinite and limitless.

Statement of the Problem

"Study on Teacher Effectiveness of High School Teachers and their Attitude towards Teaching in Perambalur District".

Objectives of the Study

To Measure the Level of Teacher Effectiveness of High School Teachers and their Attitude towards Teaching in Perambalur District.

To Measure the Level of teacher effectiveness with respect to the demographic variables such as Gender, Locality, Type of management, Qualification.

Hypotheses of the Study

The Level of Teacher Effectiveness of High School Teachers and their Attitude towards Teaching is high.

There is no significant difference on the Mean Values towards teacher effectiveness of High School Teachers and their Attitude towards teaching with respect to their Gender.

There is no significant difference on the Mean Values towards teacher effectiveness of High School Teachers and their Attitude towards teaching with respect to their locality.

There is no significant difference on the Mean Values towards teacher effectiveness of High School Teachers and their Attitude towards teaching with respect to their Type of School.

There is no significant difference on the Mean Values towards teacher effectiveness of High School Teachers and their Attitude towards teaching with respect to their qualification of Teacher.

Sampling Procedure

The samples for the present study consist of 250 high school teachers in Perambalur District. The Investigator got Prior Permission from the Head of the school approached the teacher of each school for getting necessary co-operation. I am Explain the purpose of Research Title "Study on Teacher Effectiveness of High School Teachers and their Attitude towards Teaching in Perambalur District". I am provided to the tool Xerox copies. In order to present confutation investigator explained about the tool and the Way of answering questions before administering the questionnaire. The questionnaire was administered individual to all the students.

Analysis and interpretation of the data

Hypothesis – 1 : The Level of Teacher Effectiveness of High School Teachers and their Attitude towards Teaching is high.

Table -1: Mean and the standard deviation scores on the level of teacher effectiveness of high school teachers and their attitude towards teaching in Perambalur district

S. No	Variables	N	Mean	SD
01.	Total	250	142.33	13.93

Table 1 shows that Mean and SD of the total sample Teacher Effectiveness of High School Teachers and their Attitude towards Teaching score were 142.33 and 13.93. It shows that the level is high. Analysis of the Mean and Standard Deviation Scores towards teacher effectiveness of high School Teachers and their Attitude towards teaching with respect to their Gender.

Hypothesis – 2: There is no significant difference on the Mean Values towards teacher effectiveness of High School Teachers and their Attitude towards teaching with respect to their Gender.

Table 2: 'T' Values Between The Mean Scores Towards Their Teacher Effectiveness Of High School Teachers And Their Attitude Towards Teaching With Respect To Their Gender

S. No	Gender	N	Mean	SD	't' value
01.	Male	60	141.53	12.28	0.55**
02.	Female	190	142.58	14.44	

From the above Table 2 it is seen that the't' value, 0.55 is not significant at 0.05 level. It is understood from the result that there is no significant difference between male and female high school teacher towards their teacher effectiveness and their Attitude towards teaching. Female and male teacher are having similar level towards their teacher effectiveness of high school teachers and their Attitude towards teaching and hence the framed null hypothesis is found to be accepted. Analysis of the Mean and Standard Deviation Scores towards teacher effectiveness of High School Teachers and their Attitude towards teaching with respect to their locality .

Hypothesis – 3: There is no significant difference on the Mean Values towards teacher effectiveness of High School Teachers and their Attitude towards teaching with respect to their locality.

Table 3: 'T' Values Between The Mean Scores Towards Their Teacher Effectiveness of High School Teachers And Their Attitude Towards Teaching With Respect to Their Locality.

S. No	LOCALITY	N	Mean	SD	't' value
01.	Rural	108	141.62	13.99	0.70**
02.	Urban	142	142.87	13.92	

It is understood from the above Table 3 it is seen that the't' value, 0.70 is not significant at 0.05 level. It is understood from the result that there is no significant difference towards teacher effectiveness of High School Teachers and their Attitude towards teaching with respect to their locality are having similar level towards their hence, the framed null hypothesis is found to be accepted. Analysis of the Mean and Standard Deviation Scores towards their teacher effectiveness of High School Teachers and their Attitude towards teaching with respect to their Type of School.

Hypothesis – 4: There is no significant difference on the Mean Values towards teacher effectiveness of High School Teachers and their Attitude towards teaching with respect to their Type of School.

Table 4: 'T' Values Between The Mean Scores Towards Their Teacher Effectiveness Of High School Teachers And Their Attitude Towards Teaching With Respect To Their Type Of School

S. No	Type of School	N	Mean	SD	't' value
01.	Government School	75	141.63	11.79	0.57**
02.	Private School	175	142.63	14.78	

** - Not Significant at 0.05 level

It is seen from the Table 4 that the't' value, 0.57 is not significant at 0.05 level. It is understood from the result that there is no significant difference between Government School and Private School towards teacher effectiveness of High School Teachers and their Attitude towards teaching are having similar level. Hence the framed null hypothesis is found to be accepted. Analysis of the Mean and Standard Deviation Scores towards their teacher effectiveness of High School Teachers and their Attitude towards teaching with respect to their Educational Qualification.

Hypothesis – 5: There is no significant difference on the Mean Values towards teacher effectiveness of High School Teachers and their Attitude towards teaching with respect to their qualification of Teacher.

Table 5: 'T' Values between the Mean Scores towards Their Teacher Effectiveness of High School Teachers and Their Attitude towards Teaching with Respect to their Educational Qualification

S. No	Educational Qualification	N	Mean	SD	't' value
01.	UG	171	141.75	13.01	0.90**
02.	PG	79	143.59	15.76	

Table 5 revels that the't' value, 0.90 is not significant at 0.05 level. It is understood from the result that there is no significant difference between UG and PG qualified B.Ed. teacher towards their teacher effectiveness of High School Teachers and their Attitude towards teaching. UG and PG qualified B.Ed. teacher are having similar level towards their teacher effectiveness of High School Teachers and their Attitude towards teaching. Hence the framed null hypothesis is found to be accepted.

Findings and Conclusion

In the study of correlation aspects it was observed that teacher effectiveness was low positively correlated to their attitude towards teaching. Hence the hypothesis that there would be a significant positive relationship between the teacher effectiveness and attitude towards teaching of high school teacher is accepted.

There is no significant difference between male and female high school teacher towards their teacher effectiveness and their Attitude towards teaching. Female and male teacher are having similar level towards their teacher effectiveness of high school teachers and their Attitude towards teaching and hence the framed null hypothesis is found to be accepted.

There is no significant difference towards teacher effectiveness of High School Teachers and their Attitude towards teaching with respect to their locality are having similar level towards their hence, the framed null hypothesis is found to be accepted.

There is no significant difference between Government School and Private School towards teacher effectiveness of High School Teachers and their Attitude towards teaching are having similar level. Hence the framed null hypothesis is found to be accepted.

There is no significant difference between UG and PG qualified B.Ed. teacher towards their teacher effectiveness of High School Teachers and their Attitude towards teaching. UG and PG qualified B.Ed. teacher are having similar level towards their teacher effectiveness of High School Teachers and their Attitude towards teaching. Hence the framed null hypothesis is found to be accepted.

Bibliography

1. Good, Carter, V.S 1966 'Elements of Educational Research' Newyork, 296-302.
2. Best,John(1989), "Research in Education", Prentice Hall of India Private Limited, NewDelhi.
3. Yadav(1983), "Effect of Training and Teaching Competence", Ph.D. Edu., Meerut University.
4. Singh(1986), " Preparing Better Teachers", Journal of Indian Education. 12(2):3.
5. Kulbir Single Siddu (1987) 'Methodology of Educating Research' NewDelhi.

❐

6.

The Impact of Blended Learning Approach on ICT Readiness and Achievement in Teaching of Science at B.Ed Level

Introduction

In this type attempts are made for making use of a combination of traditional and ICT enhanced a learning practices. Blended learning describes the learning environment that either combines teaching methods, delivery methods, media formats or mixture of all these. It also refers to the integrated learning activities such as mixture of on line, off line and face to face learning. In other words blended learning is a mixture of traditional and e learning strategies. It is the combination of face to face learning with web based on line approaches the combination of media, methods and pedagogical approaches, to enhance control over learning, critical thinking and assessment.

As per the words of Graham, C.R. (2005) blended learning is a blending of different learning methods, techniques and resources and applying them in an interactively meaningful learning environment. Learners should have easy access to different learning resources in order to apply the knowledge and skills they learn under the supervision and support of the teacher inside and outside the classroom. This approach will combine face-to-face instruction with computer-mediated instruction. It also applies science or IT activities with the assistance of innovative educational technologies using computer, cellular or I-phones, Sky TV channels and other electronic media. Purnima Valiathan (2002) has defined as "The term blended learning is used to describe a solution that combines several different delivery methods, such as collaboration software, Web-based courses, EPSS, and knowledge management practices. Blended learning also is used to describe learning that mixes various event-based activities, including face-to-face classrooms, live e-learning and self-paced instruction."

Objectives of the Study

The following are the objectives of the study.

- To identify the level of achievements through blended learning modules in science subjects.
- To analysis the achievements of student teachers through blended learning.
- To evaluate the effectiveness of blended learning modules in science subjects.
- To study the ICT readiness of student teachers learning through blended learning.

Hypotheses of the Study

The following hypotheses were formulated based on the objectives of the study

There is no significant difference in the post test achievement in science between the control and experimental group student teachers.

There is no significant difference in the post test ICT readiness scores between the control and experimental group student teachers.

The blended learning strategy in not effective in improving the post test achievement of student teachers in science.

There is no significant relationship between the achievement and ICT readiness of student teachers.

Method

To study the effectiveness of blended learning strategy, the pre-test, Post-test equivalent group experimental design was adopted in the study.

Sample

A sample of 20B.Ed student teachers comprising Physical science, Biological science and Computer science optional subjects were selected for the study from M.S.P college of Education, Virudhunagar as the control group subjects and 20 B.Ed. student teachers comprising Physical science, Biological science and computer science optional subjects from Sri Vidya college of Education, Virudhunagar were selected as the experimental group subjects. They were selected through purposive sampling technique.

Tools

The following tools were used in the study

- Tool 1: Achievement test in science education constructed and validated by the investigator.
- Tool 2 : ICT readiness scale constructed and validated by the investigator.

Statistical Techniques Followed in the Study

In differential analysis the significant difference between groups were studied by using mean, standard deviation and 't' test. The co-efficient of correlation was determined by using Pearson product moment method.

Analysis of Data

The analysis of data using the't' test is shown in Tables.

Showing the Significant difference between the means of control and exp erimentalgrouphighschoolstudentsintheirpre-testachievementinscience and ICT readiness.

Table: 1

Variables	Group	N	M	SD	't'	Pvalue	S/NS
Achievement	Pre-test Control group	20	7.7	3.05	1.312	0.197	NS
	Pre-test Experimental group	20	7.67	3.20			
ICT readiness	Pre-test Control group	20	22.6	7.49	1.320	0.195	NS
	Pre-test Experimental group	20	20.96	8.06			

NS–Not significant at 0.01levels

The calculated value of't' is not significant at 0.01 level of significance. It is concluded that the control and experimental group student teachers do not differ in their achievement in science, ICT readiness in Pre-test.

Showing the Significant difference between the means of control and experim entalgrouphighschoolstudentsintheirpre-testachievementinscience,ICT readiness.

Table: 2

Variables	Group	N	M	SD	't'	Pvalue	S/NS
Achievement	Post-test Control group	20	20.12	4.40	22.389	0.000	S
	Post-test Experimental group	20	36.72	4.93			

ICT readiness	Post-test Control group	20	40.72	12.56	26.358	0.000	S
	Post-test Experimental group	20	96.57	10.87			

NS–Not significant at 0.01levels

The calculated value of 't' is significant at 0.01 level of significance. This makes it obligatory to reject the null hypothesis. It is concluded that the significant difference between the experimental and control group of student teachers in their achievement in science and ICT readiness. The experimental groups of students are at a higher level than the control group of student teachers in their achievement in science and ICT readiness.

Gain Score Analysis

The gain score analysis of the control group and experimental group student teachers in achievement science shown in table 3.

Showing the gain score analysis for achievement in science of the student teachers.

Table: 3

	Group	N	M_1	M_2	Mean gain	Gain percentage
Achievement	Control group	20	14.55	36.07	21.52	21.52
	Experimental group	20	13.64	73.53	59.62	59.62

Correlation Analysis

The Correlation analysis of the control group and experimental group student teachers in achievement in science and ICT readiness shown in table 4. Significance of correlation between the variables.

Table: 4

Variables	N	'r'
Achievement Vs ICT Readiness	109	0.694**

**Correlation is significant at the 0.01 level.

The calculated 'r' value between achievement in science education and ICT readiness is 0.694 and significant at 0.0t level. These significant 'r' values make it obligatory to reject the above said null hypotheses. It is inferred that achievement and ICT readiness are having significant correlation in blended learning strategy.

Finding of the Study

The 't' test analysis showed that

The control group and Experimental group students differ in their achievement in science. The experimental group students are at a higher level than the control group of student teachers.

The experimental group and control group students differ in their ICT readiness. The experimental group students are at a higher level than the control group of student teachers.

The gain of the experimental group is more than the gain of the control group student teachers in their achievement and ICT readiness. Show the Blended learning approach is appreciably effective in teaching of science than the conventional lecture method.

There is a significant positive correlation between Achievement and ICT readiness of student teachers.

Educational Implications

The study reveals that the blended learning approach is appreciably effective in teaching of science Education than the conventional lecture method. S h o w the blended learning approach can be adopted by the teacher to teach science for the B.Ed college students. This method will motivate the students to ask higher order questions during the learning of science education. It will develop the critical thinking among the students it also develop the problem solving skill among the students. Show the blended learning approach will enhance the achievement of the student teachers in science and their ICT readiness.

References

- ArifAltun. (2008). Use of Content Management system for Blended learning: Perception of Pre-service Teachers. Turkish Online Journal of Distance Education, 9(4).
- Best, John W., Research in Education. Prentice Hall Pvt Ltd, New Dehli.1990.
- Bruce Joyce and Marsha Weil. (!985), Models of Teaching. New Delhi: Prentice Hall of India Pvt Ltd.
- Joy Coleen, 1991, The effect of cooperative learning on selected student variables (cooperative Integrated Reading and Composition on academic achievement in reading comprehension, vocabulary and spelling and on student self esteem). Washington State University. DAI, vol. 52, No. 10, April 1992. P.3516.
- Mohanasundaram, K., and Murugesan, S. (2000). A study of personality, scientific creativity and achievement of higher secondary students. Indian journal of psycho metry and education, vol.31, No 1, 25-28.

❐

7.

Attitude of B. Ed. Trainees towards Teaching With Reference to Social Maturity

Introduction

The destiny of India is being shaped in the class room in which a teacher plays a significant role as per the Kothari commission report on Education (1964-66). The basic personality pattern of the teacher's behavior and attitudes are important factors in building an emotionally balanced classroom climate that promotes the mental health of school children.

Attitude - Meaning

According to modern psychological literature, an attitude represents individual feelings for against something. We may also define an attitude as the degree of acceptance given by an individual for something. Edwards (1969) "An attitude may be defined as a learned emotional response set for or against something."

Importance of Social Maturity

Maturity assures accountability, constantly asset, judge and takes appropriative decisions. Maturity develops a balanced emotional outlook, helping the individual to accept himself his talents and limitations and accept others as they are. It helps towards progressive advancement in spiritual growth, impelling the individual to adapt himself to change life without emotional crisis.

Need for the Study

The word social maturity is comprised of two words social and maturity. Social means 'Living in Communities' and Maturity means 'Adjust himself to the social world around him. Thus social maturity refers to attaining maturity in social relationships i.e. to establish good relations with family, friends, neighbours and all other persons living in our society. Parents and teachers must be very particular in maintaining interpersonal relationship with the young students in order to channelize their energy in right direction. Teaching includes all the activities of providing education to other. Teacher Education Colleges play significant role in developing not only intellectual but also social maturity. Therefore, the B.Ed. trainees have social maturity as a part of their training. Hence, the present study is under taken.

Statement of the Problem

The problem stated for the present study has been given as *"Attitude of B.Ed. Trainees towards Teaching with reference to Social Maturity"*.

Objectives of the Study

The researcher has framed the following objectives for the present study,

- To find out the significance of mean difference in their attitude towards teaching and social maturity with reference to gender.
- To find out the significance of mean difference in their attitude towards teaching and social maturity with reference to locality.
- To find out the significance of mean difference in their attitude towards teaching and social maturity with reference to parents educational qualification.
- To find out the relationship between the attitude towards teaching and social maturity of B.Ed. Trainees.

Hypotheses of the Study

For the present study, the researcher has framed the following hypotheses.

There is no significant difference in their attitude towards teaching and social maturity with reference to gender.

There is no significant difference in their attitude towards teaching and social maturity with reference to locality.

There is no significant difference in their attitude towards teaching and social maturity with reference to parents' educational qualification.

There is no relationship between the attitude towards teaching and social maturity of B.Ed. Trainees.

Method used in the study

Normative survey method has been used in the present study to collect the data from the B.Ed. trainees in the selected colleges of Education of Ariyalur

District in Tamilnadu. Using Random Sampling 200 samples has been collected from the Colleges of Ariyalur District in Tamil Nadu for the present study.

Tools used in the study

The following tools are used in the present study.

Scale of Attitude towards Teaching - constructed and standardized by the researcher and R. Muthaiyan.

Social Maturity scale - constructed and standardized by Nalini Rao.

Testing of the Hypothesis

Hypothesis - 1 : There is no significant difference in their attitude towards teaching and social maturity with reference to gender. The hypothesis was tested using 't' test

Attitude towards teaching					
Gender	**N**	**Mean**	**Standard Deviation**	**'t' value**	**Level of Significance**
Male	100	159.5347	18.6524	0.4487	NS
Female	100	158.4343	15.8114		
Social maturity					
Male	100	257.8020	29.0852	3.431*	0.01
Female	100	263.3737	27.1546		

The above table shows that the computed value of 't' 0.4487 is less than the critical values of 2.58 and 1.96 at 0.01 and 0.05 levels respectively and hence it is not significant. Consequently, the null hypothesis is not to be rejected and it can be said that there is no significant difference between B.Ed. trainees in their attitude towards Teaching with reference to gender.

The second part of the table shows that the computed value of 't' 3.431 is greater than the critical value of 2.58 at 0.01 level and hence it is significant. Consequently, the null hypothesis is to be rejected and it can be said that there is a significant difference between B.Ed. trainees in their Social Maturity with reference to gender. It is also inferred from the above table that the female trainees are socially matured than the male trainees.

Hypothesis - 2: To find out the significance of mean difference in their attitude towards teaching and social maturity with reference to locality. The hypothesis was tested using 't' test.

Attitude towards teaching					
Locality	**N**	**Mean**	**Standard Deviation**	**'t' value**	**Level of Significance**
Rural	136	158.4426	17.0010	0.5286	NS
Urban	64	159.8462	17.7572		
Social maturity					

Rural	136	262.4590	28.7225	2.951*	0.01
Urban	64	257.5897	27.3194		

The above table shows that the computed value of 't' 0.5286 is less than the critical values of 2.58 and 1.96 at 0.01 and 0.05 levels respectively and hence it is not significant. Consequently, the null hypothesis is not to be rejected and it can be said that there is no significant difference between B.Ed. trainees in their attitude towards Teaching with reference to locality.

The second part of the table shows that the computed value of 't' 2.951 is greater than the critical value of 2.58 at 0.01 level and hence it is significant. Consequently, the null hypothesis is to be rejected and it can be said that there is a significant difference between B.Ed. trainees in their Social Maturity with reference to locality. It is also inferred from the above table that the rural trainees are socially matured than the urban trainees.

Hypothesis -3: There is no significant difference in their attitude towards teaching and social maturity with reference to parents' educational qualification. The hypothesis was tested using 'F' test.

Attitude towards teaching					
Source of Variation	**Sum of Squares**	**df**	**Mean Variance of Squares**	**'F' value**	**Level of Significance**
Between groups	2793.131	3	931.044	3.125**	0.05
Within groups	58391.34	196	297.915		
Social maturity					
Between groups	21036.600	3	7012.200	8.947*	0.01
Within groups	153610.688	196	783.728		

The above table shows that the computed value of 'F' 3.125 is less than the critical value of 3.78 at 0.01 level and greater than the critical value of 2.60 at 0.05 level and hence it is significant at 0.05 level. Consequently, the null hypothesis is to be rejected and it can be said that there is a significant difference between B.Ed. trainees in their attitude towards Teaching with reference to parent's educational qualification.

The second part of the table shows that the computed value of 'F' 8.947 is greater than the critical value of 3.78 at 0.01 level and hence it is significant at 0.01 level. Consequently, the null hypothesis is to be rejected and it can be said that there is a significant difference between B.Ed. trainees in their social maturity with reference to parent's educational qualification.

Hypothesis-4: There is no relationship between the attitude towards Teaching and Social Maturity of B.Ed. Trainees. The hypothesis was tested using Karl Pearson's Product Moment Coefficient of Correlation.

Correlations			
		Attitude towards Teaching	Social Maturity
Attitude towards Teaching	Pearson Correlation	1	0.137*
Social Maturity	Pearson Correlation	0.137*	1

The above table shows that the computed value of 'r'(0.137) is greater than the critical values of 0.081 at 0.01 level and hence, it is significant. Consequently, the null hypothesis is to be rejected and it can be said that, there is a relationship between the attitude towards Teaching and Social Maturity of B.Ed. Trainees. Even though the value of 'r' is positive, the relationship is negligible.

Summary of findings

The following are the findings of the present study.

There is no significant difference between B.Ed. Trainees in their attitude towards Teaching with reference to gender.

There is no significant difference between B.Ed. Trainees in their attitude towards Teaching with reference to locality.

There is a significant difference between B.Ed. Trainees in their attitude towards Teaching with reference to parent's educational qualification. It is also inferred that trainees whose parents' educational qualification is 1st Standard to 10th Standard (161.4231) have high level of attitude than the trainees whose parents' educational qualification is 11th Standard to 12th Standard (158.1832), the trainees whose parents' educational qualification is Under Graduate Degree (160.8108) and trainees whose parents' educational qualification is Post Graduate Degree and above (154.8333).

There is a significant difference between B.Ed. Trainees in their Social Maturity with reference to gender. It is also inferred that the Female trainees are socially matured than the male trainees.

There is a significant difference between B.Ed. Trainees in their Social Maturity with reference to locality. It is also inferred that the rural trainees are socially matured than the urban trainees.

There is a significant difference between B.Ed. Trainees in their social maturity with reference to parent's educational qualification. It is also inferred that the trainees whose parents' educational qualification is Post Graduate Degree and above (276.3333) are socially matured than the trainees whose parents' educational qualification is 1st Standard to 10th Standard (257.6923), trainees whose parents' educational qualification is 11th Standard to 12th Standard (258.7023) and the trainees whose parents' educational qualification is Under Graduate Degree (266.5946).

There is a relationship between the attitude towards Teaching and Social Maturity of B.Ed. Trainees. Even though the value of 'r' is positive, the relationship is negligible.

Conclusion

The present study has investigated the Attitude of B.Ed. Trainees towards Teaching with reference to Social Maturity. From the findings of the study, it is concluded that the B.Ed. trainees attitude towards teaching do not differ significantly with reference to gender and locality. But, the B.Ed. trainees attitude towards teaching differs significantly with reference to Parent's Educational Qualification. It is also concluded that the B.Ed. trainees Social Maturity differs significantly with reference to gender, locality and Parent's Educational Qualification.

References

- Affizal Ahmad & Rafidah Sahak (2009). Teacher-Student Attachment and Teachers' Attitudes Towards Work. *Jurnal Pendidik dan Pendidikan, Jil. 24,* 55–72.
- Bhalla, A., Jajoo, U.N. & Kalantri, S.P. (2002). Attitude of teachers towards teaching. Journal Association Physicians India, 50:1405-8.
- Buch, M.B. (ed). (1991). Fourth Survey of research in Education. New Delhi: National Council of Educational Research and Training
- Keisham Shitaljit Singh (2012). Teachers' Attitude Towards Information and Communication Technology (ICT). *Shodh Sanchayan, 3(2),* 1-4.
- Nalini Rao (1986). Manual for Rao's Social Maturity Scale. Agra: National Psychological Corporation.

❐

8.

Creating Path Collaboration for Successful Knowledge Transfer and Knowledge Exchange

Introduction

Knowledge creation is the key to an adaptive and innovative organisation. Leveraging knowledge in an organisation faces many barriers as well as acting as a catalyst for growth in strategic and operational environments. Burke (Burke 2000) defines knowledge recursively as "meaning derived from information and other knowledge". This renewed attention on knowledge is driven by the observation that the world is moving into a 'knowledge age' where the importance of knowledge calls for a shift in the thinking in society and in large organisations. This study focuses on the acquisition of knowledge through path collaboration.

Significance of the Study

The education system is quite challenging to the various stakeholders while there is a great demand to build it to global quality. The plans most of the time are not executed and even if done only fail due to various reasons. Knowledge transfer is the practical problem of transferring knowledge from one part of the organization to another. Like knowledge management, knowledge transfer seeks to organize, create, capture or distribute knowledge and ensure its availability for future users. It is considered to be more than just a communication problem. Knowledge transfer is more complex because (1) knowledge resides in organizational members, tools, tasks, and their sub networks and (2) much knowledge in organizations is tacit or hard to articulate. Since the investigator is involved in education which is transferring of knowledge through various modes has decided to conduct this study on the students population of higher education in Madurai.

Objectives of the Study

To find out the level of collaboration in transferring knowledge to the students in higher education

To find out the significant differences in the path collaboration for transferring knowledge among students in higher education in terms of: i) Gender: Male / Female, ii) location of institution: Rural/Urban, iii) Level of study: UG/PG and iv) Knowledge exposure: Traditional methods of learning/ Digital.

Hypotheses of the Study

There is average level of collaboration in transferring knowledge to the students in higher education.

There is significant differences in the path collaboration for transferring knowledge among students in higher education in terms of i) Gender: Male / Female, ii) location of institution: Rural/Urban, iii) Level of study : UG/PG and iv) Knowledge exposure: Traditional methods of learning/ Digital.

Methodology

The investigator adopted Survey method for the present study. The population of the current study consisted of female students (UG & PG) in Madurai. Random Sampling technique was adopted. 100 students (UG & PG) and in Madurai were selected randomly as samples of the study. The investigator used a self constructed tool for the present study. The items were framed under three dimensions as follows: 1. Techno centric 2. Organisational 3. Community collaboration, Statistical Techniques used arc Mean, Standard Deviation and 't' test.

Variables Studied

In the present study the socio demographic variables considered were: i) Gender: Male /Female ii) location of institution: Rural/Urban iii) Level of study: UG/PG iv) Knowledge exposure: Traditional methods of learning/ Digital

Analysis and Interpretation

Hypothesis 1: There is average level of collaboration in transferring knowledge to the students in higher education.

Table 1: Mean and SD of students population in the level of collaboration in transferring knowledge to the students in higher education.

Sl. No	Students	N	Mean	S.D
1.	Male	50	66.3	4.25
2.	Female	50		

The above table indicates that the mean of the students population in the level of collaboration in transferring knowledge to the students in higher education is 66.3 and standard deviation is 4.25. Hence the hypothesis "There is average level of collaboration in transferring knowledge to the students in higher education" is accepted.

Hypothesis 2 (a): There is a significant difference among students in their view on the path collaboration for transferring knowledge among students in higher education in terms of Gender .

Table 2: Difference among students in their view on path collaboration for transferring knowledge among students in higher education in terms of Gender.

S. No	Gender	N	Mean	S.D	't' Value	Level of significance	Result
1.	Male	50	45.2	4.716	0.358	0.05	NS
2.	Female	50	59.2	4.86			

The above table shows that the 't' value (0.358) is less than the table value 1.96 at0.05 level. Therefore the research hypothesis "There is a significant differences in the path collaboration for transferring knowledge among students in higher education in terms of Gender" is rejected.

Hypothesis 2 (b): There is a significant difference among students in their view on the path collaboration for transferring knowledge among students in higher education in terms of Location of institution.

Table 3: Difference among students in their view on Path Collaboration for transferring knowledge among students in higher education in terms of Location of institution

S. No	Location	N	Mean	S.D	't' Value	Level of significance	Result
1.	Rural	60	59.6	4.039	0.489	0.05	NS
2.	Urban	40	53.6	3.286			

The above table shows that the 't' value (0.489) is less than the table value 1.96 at0.05 level. Therefore the research hypothesis: "There is a significant difference among students in their view on path collaboration for transferring knowledge among students in higher education in terms of Location of institution" is rejected.

Hypothesis 2 (c): There is a significant difference among students in their view on the path collaboration for transferring knowledge among students in higher education in terms of Level of study .

Table 4: Difference among students in their view in the path collaboration for transferring knowledge among students in higher education in terms of Level of study.

S. No	Level of study	N	Mean	S.D	't' Value	Level of significance	Result
1.	UG	70	46.86	3.401	0.344	0.05	NS
2.	PG	30	44.60	3.209			

The above table shows that the 't' value (0.344) is less than the table value 1.96 at0.05 level. Therefore the research hypothesis, "There is a significant difference among students in their view on the path collaboration for transferring knowledge among students in higher education in terms of Level of study" is rejected.

Hypothesis 2 (d): There is a significant difference among students in their view on the path collaboration for transferring knowledge among students in higher education in terms of Knowledge exposure .

Table 5: Difference among students in their view in the path collaboration for transferring knowledge among students in higher education in terms of Knowledge exposure

S. No.	Knowledge Exposure	N	Mean	S.D	't' Value	Level of significance	Result
1.	Traditional	50	45.03	5.131	0.231	0.05	NS
2.	Digital	50	47.40	4.829			

The above table shows that the 't' value (0.231) is less than the table value 1.96 at0.05 level. Therefore the research hypothesis "There is a significant difference among students in their view on the path collaboration for transferring knowledge among students in higher education in terms of knowledge exposure" is rejected.

FINDINGS OF THE STUDY

The level of collaboration in transferring knowledge to the students in higher education is above average.

There is significant difference among students in their view on the path collaboration for transferring knowledge among students in higher education in terms of

i) Gender: Male /Female
ii) Location of institution: Rural/Urban
iii) Level of study: UG/PG
iv) Knowledge exposure: Traditional methods of learning/ Digital

Conclusion

In conclusion, the paper has summaries the findings and recommendations of a knowledge transfer study for the students of Madurai in higher education. The particular findings are relevant for educational institutions seeking to implement knowledge transfer strategies for building a flexible and innovative educational system.

References

Broadbent, M. (1998). The phenomenon of knowledge management: what does it mean to CIOs and the IS organisation?, Gartner Group.

Burke, M. (2000). Thinking together: new forms of thought system for a revolution in military affairs,

Defence Science and Technology Organisation.

Davenport, T. H. (1997). Information Ecology: Mastering the information and knowledge environment.

New York, Oxford University Press.Fransman, M. (1998). Information, knowledge and vision theories of the firm. Technology, organization,and competitiveness: perspectives on industrial and corporate change. G. Dosi, D. J. Teece.

❐

9.

Role of Higher Education Institutions in Generating Knowledgeable Society

Introduction

Higher education is of vital importance for the country, as it is a powerful tool to build knowledge-based society of the 21st Century. The higher education is a 'key factor' in the revitalization of urban communities and rural areas and serves prominent roles in competitive strategies of regions, states and nations. The research function of academia remains a prime source of knowledge and innovation at national, regional and international levels. Yet, over the past decade, most industrialized states have been obliged to address the double challenge of providing wider access to postsecondary education and training and ensuring adequate investment in high-level research. This is proving to be a delicate balancing act, which hinges on visionary policies and a more diversified funding base. Governments pursue reforms to build world-class systems of higher education, which assure quality in both research and teaching.

Objectives of The Study

The objectives of the study are i) to measure the level of opinion of Student- Teachers towards Role of Higher Education Institutions in Generating Knowledgeable Society ii) to measure the significant difference between the Role of Higher Education Institutions in Generating Knowledgeable Society among Male and Female, Arts and Science Student- Teachers and Student- Teachers Parent Qualification.

Hypotheses

The Null hypotheses were formulated to realize the above objectives.

Nature of The Research

As the study aimed to measure the level of opinion of Student- Teachers towards Role of Higher Education Institutions in Generating Knowledgeable Society among Student- Teachers in Colleges of Education, it is a Normative Survey Research.

Sample Selection

Investigators randomly selected Student- Teachers from 4 Self Finance Colleges of Education out of 32 colleges of education in Trichy District as samples. The samples were given to the 110 student- Teachers. The filled – in questionnaires were received from them were 110. The total sample has been classified further on the basis of Gender, Subject and Parents Qualification.

Table 1: Sample distribution

S.No	Category	Size	Percentage
01.	Male Student- Teachers Female Student- Teachers	40 70	45.45 54.54
02.	Arts Student- Teachers Science Student- Teachers	49 61	44.54 55.45
03	School Level Parent Qualification College Level Parent Qualification	62 48	49.09 50.90

Development of Tool

The investigators developed a Five Point Scale to measure the opinion of Student- Teachers towards Role of Higher Education Institutions in Generating Knowledgeable Society. It consists of Strongly Agree, Agree, Undecided, Disagree and Strongly Disagree with various Dimensions such as Generating Quality (GQ), Generating Knowledge(GK) and Generating Mankind(GM). There were 25 statements in this questionnaire. The developed questionnaire was given to the Teacher Educators and Voluntaries who are involved in Education field to verify whether the instruments are really aimed to measure the Role of Higher Education Institutions in Generating Knowledgeable Society in midst of Student- Teachers. Their valuable suggestions were incorporated. Moreover, test – retest method was followed to find out the reliability among the Student- Teachers. The obtained 'r' value 0.81 shows that the tool is highly valuable. Thus the Validity and Reliability of the tool were established.

Data Analysis

Thus the data collected in this manner undertake analysis by using different statistical technique. Mean and SD were calculated for each Variables to calculate 't' values which is the test of significance of the difference between two Means.

Table 2: Mean and SD of the Student- Teachers towards the Role of Higher Education Institutions in Generating Knowledgeable Society in Student- Teachers with different Category

Sl.No	COMPONENTS		N	MEAN	SD
01.	Total		110	68.28	6.95
02.	Gender	Male Female	54 56	66.7 69.2	6.11 7.27
03.	Subject	Arts Science	47 63	65.8 70.3	6.37 6.79
04.	Parents Qualification	School Level College Level	72 38	67.4 69.4	5.63 8.28

From the above Table 2 it is revealed that the average Mean Score of opinion of Student- Teachers towards Role of Higher Education Institutions in Generating Knowledgeable Society Score is 68.28. Moreover the minimum score is 65.8 and the maximum score is 70.3. This reveals opinion of Student- Teachers towards Role of Higher Education Institutions in Generating Knowledgeable Society was good among Student- Teachers.

Table 3: Significance Difference on the Mean Scores of Student- Teachers towards the Role of Higher Education Institutions in Generating Knowledgeable Society with different Category

Component	Dimension	Sex	Mean	SD	t test	Remarks
Gender	**Total**	Male Female	66.7 69.2	6.11 7.27	1.95	S
	GQ	Male Female	66.9 67.3	11.18 7.72	0.217	NS
	GK	Male Female	65.9 67.3	7.87 9.32	0.852	NS
	GM	Male Female	67.9 73.0	7.94 13.38	2.44	S
Subject	**Total**	Arts Science	65.8 70.3	6.37 6.79	3.56	S
	GQ	Arts Science	64.9 69.0	10.90 6.82	2.26	S
	GK	Arts Science	64.5 68.6	8.04 9.05	2.50	S
	GM	Arts Science	68.5 73.3	13.06 6.79	2.29	S

Parents Qualification	**Total**	SL CL	67.4 69.4	5.63 8.28	1.33	NS
	GQ	SL CL	68.1 66.0	8.15 10.14	1.10	NS
	GK	SL CL	65.5 68.4	7.04 10.53	1.52	NS
	GM	SL CL	69.3 73.6	8.70 14.85	1.64	NS

GQ: Generation Quality **GK:** Generating Knowledge

GM: Generating Mankind

NS: Not Significant **S:** Significant

The 't' value of the above table shows that the is no significant difference at 5% level for the Male and Female Student- Teachers towards various dimensions such as GQ and GK. With respect to GQ and GK the opinion of Male and Female Student- Teachers towards Role of Higher Education Institutions in Generating Knowledgeable Society is same.

The 't' value 1.95 and 2.44 from the above table reveals that there exist a significant difference at 5% among Male and Female Student- Teachers towards Total and various dimension such as GM. With respect to Total and GM the opinion of Female Student- Teachers are higher than the Male Student – Teacher towards Role of Higher Education Institutions in Generating Knowledgeable Society. Expect Total and GM the stated Null Hypothesis is accepted.

The table 3 shows that the 't' value is significant difference at 5% level for the Total as well as various dimensions such as GQ,GK and GM. From the above Table it can be understood that the opinion of Science Student- Teachers towards Role of Higher Education Institutions in Generating Knowledgeable Society is higher than the Arts Student – Teachers. Hence with respect to Total as well as various dimensions such as GQ, GK and GM the stated Null Hypothesis is rejected.

From the above table 3, the calculated 't' value reveals that there is no significant difference at 5% level for the Total as well as various dimensions such as GQ,GK and GM. Thus with respect to Total as well as GQ,GK and GM the opinion of School Level Parent Qualification Student – Teachers and College Level Parent Qualification Student-Teachers towards Role of Higher Education Institutions in Generating Knowledgeable Society is same. Hence with respect to Total as well as GQ, GK and GM the stated Null Hypothesis is accepted.

Findings

The salient findings of the study are i) all the Student- Teachers are having positive opinion towards Role of Higher Education Institutions in Generating Knowledgeable Society ii) With respect to GQ and GK the opinion of Male and Female Student- Teachers towards Role of Higher Education Institutions in Generating Knowledgeable Society is same and with respect to Total and GM the opinion of Female Student- Teachers are higher than the Male Student - Teacher iii) the opinion of Science Student-Teachers towards Role of Higher Education Institutions in Generating Knowledgeable Society is higher than the Arts Student-Teachers. with respect to Total as well as various dimensions such as GQ,GK and GM and iv) with respect to Total as well as GQ,GK and GM the opinion of School Level Parent Qualification Student -Teachers and College Level Parent Qualification Student -Teachers towards Role of Higher Education Institutions in Generating Knowledgeable Society is same.

Conclusions & Discussions

The results shows that all the Student- Teachers are having higher opinion towards Role of Higher Education Institutions in Generating Knowledgeable Society it is the positive trend. The above result also infers the mean scores of Female Student-Teachers are having higher Mean Score than Male student-teachers towards their opinion in Role of Higher Education Institutions in generating knowledgeable society with respect to Total as well as the dimensions Generating Mankind (GM). This is because the Female student-teachers may believe Higher Education Institutions is the only tool to generate the knowledgeable society. But the Male student-teachers do not depend only on Higher Education Institutions. Moreover regarding the dimension Generating Mankind (GM) the Female student teachers are having higher opinion than the Male student-teachers. This may be due to Female student teachers may felt that Higher Education Curriculum will develop not only the knowledge but also the mankind, moral and ethical values. By considering the subject Science Student-Teachers are having higher mean scores than the Arts Student-Teachers towards the opinion on the Role of Higher Education Institutions in generating knowledgeable society with respect to Total as well as all dimensions GQ,GK,GM. This may be due to the Science Student-Teachers may equipped with recent trend in their subject therefore they may satisfied with the quality, knowledge and mankind. But the Arts student teachers may not satisfied with their Higher Education Curriculum and they gave lesser opinion than the Science student teachers.

Education Implications

The present Survey research shows that Student-Teachers are having higher opinion on the role of higher Education institution in generating knowledgeable society. This positive trend is certainly help the quality of higher education in India. The higher education departments have great responsibility by maintaining this positive opinion by introducing various innovations and modifications while framing the curriculum. The statuary bodies like UGC and NAAC must have constant touch with the students who are the stack holders of higher education departments to maintain the constant improvement in the quality, Knowledge and Mankind.

References

- Best,J.W, Research in Education, Prentice – Hall of India (P) Ltd., New Delhi.
- Lokesh koul.(2005). Methodology of Educational Research, Vikas Publishing House (P) Ltd, New Delhi.

❐

10.

Role of Higher Education institution in Bridging among the Society

Introduction

The role of higher education is to be, response to the challenge of an active future contribution to human and social development. A good balance must be reached in the basic functions of Education. While focusing only on the transformative function of education may pose dangers to the human dimension and development, unilateral concentration on responsible development aspects it may generate reactive approaches and delay economic benefits. Disregarding the inclusiveness function may lead to slower development and even isolationism and focusing on short-term issues is not good for long-term goals and future generations. We must reinforce Education networks between 'Southern' and 'Northern', rich and poor, and developed and developing institutions in order to bridge the gap between Society and institutions.

Objectives of the Study

The objectives of the study are i) to measure the level of Role of Higher Education Institution bridging the society among Student- Teachers in Colleges of Education. ii) to measure the level of significant difference Role of Higher Education Institution bridging the gap in the society among Male and Female, Married and Unmarried Student -Teachers, Arts and Science Student- Teachers ,Locality, Qualification and Student- Teachers Parent Qualification.

Hypotheses

The Null hypotheses were formulated to realize the above objectives.

Nature of the Research

As the study aimed to measure the level of Role of Higher Education Institution bridging the among the society Student- Teachers in Colleges of Education, it is a Normative Survey Research.

Sample Selection

Investigators randomly selected Student- Teachers from 4 Self Finance Colleges of Education in Trichy District as samples. The samples were given to the 110Student- Teachers. The filled – in questionnaires were received from them were 110. The total samples have been classified further on the basis of Gender, Subject, Qualification, Locality and Parents Qualification.

Table 1: Sample distribution

S.No	Category	Size	Percentage
01.	Male Female	54 56	49.09 50.90
02.	Arts Science	47 63	42.72 57.27
03.	School Level College Level	72 38	65.45 34.54

Development of Tool

The investigators developed a Five Point Scale to measure the role of Higher Education Institution in Bridging among the Society in Colleges of Education. It consists of Strongly Agree, Agree, Disagree and Strongly Disagree with Various Dimensions Such as Generation Gap (GG),Socio Economic Gap(SEG) , Emotional Gap(EG).. There were 24 statements in this questionnaire. The developed questionnaire was given to the Teacher Educators and Voluntaries who are involved in Education field to verify whether the instruments are really aimed to measure the role of Higher Education Institution in Bridging Among the Society in midst of Student- Teachers. Their valuable suggestions were incorporated. Moreover, test – retest method was followed to find out the reliability among the Student- Teachers. The obtained 'r' value 0.81 shows that the tool is highly valuable. Thus the Validity and Reliability of the tool were established.

Data Analysis

Thus the data collected in this manner undertake analysis by using different statistical technique. Mean and SD were calculated for each Variables to calculate 't' values which is the test of significance of the difference between two Means.

Table 2: Mean and SD of the Student- Teachers towards role of Higher Education Institution in Bridging among the Society in Student- Teachers with different Category

Sl.No	COMPONENTS		N	MEAN	SD
01.	Total		110	70.50	9.16
02.	Gender	Male Female	46 64	65.45 73.36	8.81 7.96
03.	Subject	Arts Science	47 63	69.72 7.30	9.26 9.16
06.	Parents Qualification	School Level College Level	62 48	71.72 67.90	8.86 9.19

From the above Table 2 it is revealed that the average Mean Score of role of Higher Education Institution Score is 84.06 Moreover the minimum score is 69.66 and the maximum score is 87.11. This reveals Awareness Student- Teachers towards role of Higher Education Institution was good among Student- Teachers.

Table 3: Significance Difference on the Mean Scores of Male and Female Student- Teachers

S.No	Dimension	Sex	Mean	SD	t test	Remarks
1.	**Total**	Male Female	65.45 73.36	8.81 7.96	5.90	S
2.	**GG**	Male Female	70.38 76.52	13.63 7.59	2.49	S
3.	**SG**	Male Female	60.20 68.40	10.49 10.70	3.92	S
4.	**EG**	Male Female	69.70 78.90	12.78 11.07	3.36	S

GG: Generation Gap **SG:** Socio Economic gap **EG :** Emotional Gap
NS: Not Significant **S:** Significant

The Table 3 shows that the 't' value is significant difference at 5% level for the Total Student- Teachers as well as various dimensions such as Total, GG, SG and EG. From the above Table it can be understood that the Awareness on role of Higher Education Institution among Male and Female Student- Teachers are similar. With respect to GG,EG the mean value of Female Student- Teachers was higher than the Male Student Teacher towards Awareness on role of Higher Education Institution Hence the stated Null Hypothesis is accepted.

Table 4: Significance Difference on the Mean Scores of Arts and science Student- Teachers

S.No	Dimension	Subject	Mean	SD	t test	Remarks
1.	**Total**	Arts Science	69.72 70.30	9.26 9.16	0.18	NS
2.	**GG**	Arts Science	73.35 74.40	12.23 9.92	0.44	NS
3.	**SG**	Arts Science	64.50 65.30	11.82 11.03	0.32	NS
4.	**EG**	Arts Science	75.90 74.40	13.41 12.03	0.49	NS

GG: Generation Gap **SG:**Socio Economic gap **EG :** Emotional Gap
NS: Not Significant **S:** Significant

The Table 4 shows that the 't' value is not significant difference at 5% level for the Total Student- Teachers as well as various dimensions such as Total, GG, SG and EG. From the above Table it can be understood that the Awareness on role of Higher Education Institution among Male and Female Student- Teachers are similar. With respect to GG,SG the mean value of Science Student- Teachers was higher than the Arts Student Teacher towards Awareness on role of Higher Education Institution Hence the stated Null Hypothesis is rejected.

Table 5: Significance Difference on the Mean Scores of Parents Qualification at School level and college level Student- Teachers

S.No	Dimension	Parents **Qualification**	**Mean**	**SD**	**t test**	**Remarks**
1.	**Total**	SL CL	71.72 67.90	8.86 9.19	1.26	NS
2.	**GG**	SL CL	75.20 72.34	10.55 11.21	1.3	NS
3.	**SG**	SL CL	65.70 64.10	11.31 11.41	0.33	NS
4.	**EG**	SL CL	78.20 71.00	10.34 14.14	2.46	NS

GG: Generation Gap **SG:** Socio Economic gap **EG :** Emotional Gap
NS: Not Significant **S:** Significant

The Table 5shows that the 't' value is not significant difference at 5% level for the Total Student- Teachers as well as various dimensions such as Total, GG, SG and EG. From the above Table it can be understood that the Awareness on role of Higher Education Institution among Students –Teachers Parents Qualification at School Level and College level Student- Teachers are similar. With respect to GG,SG, EG the mean value of Student- Teachers Parents qualification at School level was higher than the Student- Teachers Parents qualification at College level towards Awareness on role of Higher Education Institution Hence the stated Null Hypothesis is rejected

Findings

With Respective to Gender the mean scores of Female Student –Teachers are higher than the male Student –Teachers towards awareness on the role of higher Education Institution in bridging among the society. In total as well as all the dimensions, this may due to the female student teachers aims the higher education Institutions to act as a bridging among the society. This is because even though higher education institutions conducted women empowerment programs. They are still associated with the society. The above data also infers the mean scores of the student teachers whose parental qualification in school level is higher than the college level parental qualification among Emotional Gap (EG) towards Awareness on the role of higher Education Institution in bridging among the society. This is because of student teachers of school the level qualified parents have higher perception towards higher education institution in bridging among the society. But, the student- teachers whose parents qualification at college level are having educations in bridging among the society. Hence their awareness level is low.

Educational Implications

There are some expectations from Government and parents for the development o f the society through higher education. Student –Teachers education and women empowerment programme are given more emphasis in the curriculum then the women can more empowerment and develop themselves as well the society through higher education. To increase the quality of higher education the Govt. encourage more self-financing institutions to encourage higher education. The government should follow the world class education syllabus to increase the standards in higher education. Public –Private Partnership is most essential to bring women education in the higher education programme.

References

- Akermarks,S.S,(1998). *Higher Education – Achievements and Challenges*, Paris, UNESCO.
- Best,J.W, *Research in Education,* Prentice – Hall of India (P) Ltd., New Delhi.
- Lokesh Koul.(2005). *Methodology of Educational Research*, Vikas Publishing House (P) Ltd, New Delhi.
- Rama, J.M,(1997).*Human Rights and Indian Values,* New Delhi, NCTC.

11.

Role of National Institutes on Creating Public Awareness for Rehabilitation of Persons with Disabilities

Background

The constitution of India ensures equality, freedom, Justice and dignity of all individuals and implicitly mandates an inclusive society for all including persons with disabilities. As Dr.Abdul Kalam rightly declared that the persons with disabilities are the great human resource assets in the society it is universally recognized now that persons with disabilities constitute valuable human resources for societies. As we all know that Education plays an important role for the development of any nation, meaningful education alone can enable the persons with disabilities to face the challenges of life effectively and participate in meaningful activities in the society.

The section 26 of Persons with Disabilities (Equal Opportunities Protection of Rights and Full Participation) Act 1995, clearly directs and encourages the appropriate government and non government organizations to ensure that every child with a disability has access to free education in an appropriate environment till he attain the age of Eighteen Years. The Article 24 in UN Convention of Rights of Persons with Disabilities clearly specified the rights of persons with disabilities to get appropriate education. The quality of free and compulsory education is ensured through the Rights of Children to Free and Compulsory Education Act 2009. Educating the public on persons with disability is also addressed in all the above acts through awareness creation. The responsibilities of creating awareness on the area of persons with multiple disabilities is directed to the Government and Non Government organizations especially through National Institutes established for persons with disabilities.

National Institute for Visually Handicapped (NIVH)

National Institute for the visually handicapped is established in the year 1982 at Dehradun UP, to cater the needs of persons with visual impairments. NIVH provides services for persons with visual impairment, develops human resources to rehabilitate the persons with visual impairments and undertakes research and developments. The entire above programme include the creation of public awareness.

National Institute for Orthopedically Handicapped (NIOH)

National Institute for the orthopedically handicapped is established in the year 1978 to cater the needs of persons with orthopedically handicapped. NIOH provides services for persons with orthopedically impaired, develops human resources to rehabilitate the persons with orthopedically impaired and undertakes research and developments. The entire above programme include the creation of public awareness.

Ali Yavar Jung National Institute for the Hearing Handicapped (AYJNIHH)

Ali Yavar Jung National Institute for the hearing handicapped is established in the year 1983 at Mumbai to cater the needs of persons with hearing impairments. AYJNIHH provides services for persons with hearing impairment, develops human resources to rehabilitate the persons with hearing impairments and undertakes research and developments. The entire above programme include the creation of public awareness.

National Institute for the Mentally Handicapped (NIMH)

National Institute for the mentally handicapped is established in the year 1984 to cater the needs of persons with intellectual impairments. NIMH provides services for persons with intellectual impairment, develops human resources to rehabilitate the persons with intellectual impairments and undertakes research and developments. The entire above programme include the creation of public awareness.

National Institute for Rehabilitation Training and Research (NIRTAR)

National Institute for Rehabilitation Training and Research is established in the year 1984at Cuttak Orisa to cater the needs of persons with locomotor impairments. NIVH provides comprehensive services for persons with locomotor impairment, develops human resources to rehabilitate the persons with locomotor impairments and undertakes research and developments. The entire above programme include the creation of public awareness.

Institute for Physically Handicapped (IPH)

Institute for Physically Handicapped is established in the year 1975 to cater the needs of persons with physically challenged. IPH provides services for persons with physically challenged, develops human resources to rehabilitate the persons with physically challenged and undertakes research and developments. The entire above programme include the creation of public awareness.

National Institute for Empowerment of Persons with Multiple Disabilities (NIEPMD)

National Institute for Empowerment of Persons with Multiple Disabilities is established in the year 2005 at Chennai to cater the needs of persons with multiple disabilities. NIEPMD provides services for persons with multiple disabilities, develops human resources to rehabilitate the persons with multiple disabilities and undertakes research and developments. The entire above programme include the creation of public awareness. All the above National Institute is working under the ministry of social justice and empowerment, Government of India. There are thousands of NGOs working for the persons with disabilities also creating awareness under the guidance of ministry of social justice and empowerment and the above National Institutes.

Aim

To find out the magnitude of awareness created in the area of rehabilitation of persons with disabilities in our country

Objectives

To understand the needs of persons with disabilities enumerated in the Policies and Acts of Government of India

To prepare the list of various resource centers of rehabilitation of persons with disabilities

Method

The study method is survey type. The National Institutes and its activities to create public awareness either directly or indirectly working for persons with disabilities were collected for this study.

Results

The programme conducted by the National Institutes is given in Table 1:

	No of courses conducted	No of services provided	No of Short term programme conducted	No of schemes and benefits guided	No of Publications made	No of awareness materials made
NIVH	5	17	146	13	92	19
AYJNIHH	15	21	98	13	94	21
NIMH	10	10	60	13	58	18
NIOH	5	18	10	13	28	8
NIRTAR	5	18	22	13	25	7
IPH	3	10	10	13	17	4
NIEPMD	8	15	100	13	06	10
Total 7	51	109	456	91	330	87

One year certificate courses , two years diploma courses in teacher training programme, none year degree courses in teacher training programme, 3 - 4 1/2years professional degree courses, one year master degree in teacher training programme , one year Post Graduate Diploma programme, two years master degree programme in professional courses on the respective field is given.

Two years master degree programme in the area of visual impairment is not introduced so far. The services provided by the National Institutes are clinical or hospitals, schools, community programmes. The nature of short term training programme are in-service training programme, training to other departments such as administrative staffs, medical professionals, allied medical professionals, general education teachers, Anganwadi workers, transport staff. The guidance provided to persons with disabilities to avail thirteen schemes and benefits are common in all the institutes. The important schemes and benefits are scholarships, Income Tax exemption, train pass, subsidies, transfer facilities where the service is available for persons with disabilities. The common awareness materials prepared by National Institutes to educate the public are hand bills, notice, posters, Short films,Videos, and hoardings.

Publications are made to educate the student trainees undergoing courses, parents to understand the procedure of training their children, other professionals to understand the complication of training the persons with disabilities and to take appropriate measures. The major activity of human resource development programme undertaken in our country are tabulated and compared below in Table 2:

Table 2: Comparison of manpower on different levels of life cycle

Sl No	Name of the programme	No of programme available	Percentage
1	Early Intervention	9	1.5
2	Preschool programme	31	3.5
3	Primary Education programme	368	41.0
4	Secondary Education Programme	179	20.0
5	Post secondary Education programme	37	3.5
6	Theraputics	170	20.0
7	Vocational programme	17	1.5
8	Community programme	52	5.5
9	Management programme	29	3.5
	Total	892	100

Discussion

There are 892 courses offered for rehabilitation of persons with disabilities in our country. Manpower development at primary level education programme is 41 % which is relatively more than that of other program. The Man power development at Early Intervention programme and the vocational programme are meager 1.5% when compare to other programme. The man power development is relatively increased in school programme and therapeutic programme. I t is may be due to the employment available on those aspects

Conclusion and Recommendation

It is evidence that the objectives of National Institutes established for persons with disabilities are mainly to develop service delivery models, to develop human resources to provide services for persons with disabilities and to conduct research and developments are undertaken well by the National Institutes established for rehabilitation of persons with disabilities. As part of the above programme creation of awareness in the public is also carried out with varying degree from institute to institute. This is mainly from the directions which the institute gets from the government Acts and Policies as well as the directions which they get from ministry

In order to prevent the incident the materials prepared is yet to reach at all level that is from macro to micro level. Training programme for other departmental staff is weak due to the interest which the public shows on rehabilitation of persons with disabilities.

In order to overcome such problem the Government of India should bring out a schedule of activities in each department in which the awareness programme on prevention, early detection and intervention of persons with disabilities should be a part of the programme. The HRD programme should be an integrated one. The Curricular content on persons with disability may be introduced from the secondary level onwards.SSA programme and IEDSS programme draws attention to provide the school education compulsory. In order to empower the persons with disabilities at all level the projects on Early Intervention level preschool level and at vocational level may be seriously launched so that the total rehabilitation will take place at a time in a chain of activities.

References

- Gowtham Banerjee (2004). Rehabilitation Council of India. Legal Rights of persons with Disabilities New Delhi. Retrieved from http://socialjustice.nic.in/pdf/ar 08eng.pdf
- National Institute for Visually Handicapped (2013). Annual report Dehradun. retrieved from https://www.nivh.gov.in
- National Institute for Mentally Handicapped (2013). Annual report Secunderabad.
- Retrieved from http://www.nimhindia.org
- AliYavur Jung National Institute for Hearing Handicapped (2013). Annual report Mumbai. Retrieved from http://ayjnihh.nic.in/annual%20report%20 (2012-13).pdf
- Government of India (1995). Persons with Disabilities (Equal Opportunity Protection of Rights and Full Participation Act (1995). retrieved from http://socialjustice.nic.in/pwd act (1995).php
- Government of India (2000). National Trust (Welfare of Persons with Autism Cerebral Palsy Mental Retardation and Multiple disabilities) Act (1995). Retrieved from http://socialjustice.nic.in/pdf/nt act (1999).pdf
- IGNOU –MHRD (2006). Hand book of inclusive education government of India project. Retrieved from http://www.ignou.ac.in/ignou.

❐

12.

Scientific Aptitude among the Arts and Science Students in Puducherry Region

Introduction

The modern world of ours is certainly different from the ancient world or the middle ages. This breakthrough is largely due to science and its advancements. Science is the investigation and interpretation of events in the natural and physical environment of man. Science as a core subject develops the personal and social responsibility and competency needed by all youth to serve the needs of democratic society. Perceiving the problem, relating the problem to previous experience, formulating hypothesis after testing, deriving conclusions and arriving at generalizations are the scientific aptitudes. The study of scientific aptitude among the college students is a mandatory work to estimate scientific knowledge, problem solving skills and scientific attitude of college students in order to improve scientific aptitude of students to serve in this technological world.

Purpose of the Study

Since the students are not opting the subjects only because of their interest in it, and there are various external forces that are driving the students to opt a subject in which they are not interested, it is realized that a study to find out whether the students really get the necessary aptitude towards the subjects they are studying. The main purpose of this study is to determine whether the science students have scientific aptitude or not. It also determines the scientific aptitude of arts students.

The arts students may be selected their study for various reasons. This study is used to find the scientific aptitude of interested arts students in colleges. This research will enable to find out the scientific aptitude among the college students in Puducherry region.

Objectives of the Study

The present investigation has been undertaken in order to find out the following

- To study the levels of scientific aptitude among the arts and science students in Puducherry region.
- To study the difference between male and female college students in respect of their scientific aptitudes.
- To study the difference between urban and rural college students in respect of their scientific aptitudes.
- To study the difference between government and private college students in respect of their scientific aptitudes.
- To study the difference between students of English and Tamil medium of instruction at school level in respect of their scientific aptitudes.

Hypotheses of the Study

There is no significant difference between arts and science students towards scientific aptitude.

There is no significant difference between male and female students towards scientific aptitude.

There is no significant difference between urban and rural students towards scientific aptitude.

There is no significant difference between government and private college students towards scientific aptitude.

There is no significant difference between Tamil and English medium students towards scientific aptitude.

Method of Study

In the present investigation, the investigation is forms using Descriptive Survey Method.

Sample of the Study

Sampling is the process by which a relatively small number of individuals or measure of individuals objects or events selected and analyzed in order to find out something about entire population from which it was selected. The sample for the study consists of college students of Puducherry region. 400 samples taken for this present research study. The selection of the sample is made by simple Random sampling technique and the method is adopted to achieve the objectives of the study is Normative Survey Method.

Tool

For the purpose of data collection, the investigator adopted scientific aptitude test for college students' constructed by A.K.P.Sinha & L.N.K.Sinha (2000). This test aim to measure the scientific aptitude among the college students. There are 34 items in seven areas. There is no time limit for the test, but usually it takes 30 minutes to conduct the test. The areas of scientific aptitude are as follows. Experiment Bent, Detection of inconsistencies or illogical conclusions, Ability to deduce conclusion from the data provided, Accuracy of interpretation, Ability to reason and solve problems, Caution and thoroughness and Accuracy of observation.

Reliability and Validity of the Tool

Reliability is the degree of consistency that the instrument or procedure demonstrate whatever it is measuring it does so consistently. Since reliability is the most essential and significant feature of the test, the split half test have been calculated for this test .The test-retest reliability for the sample of 58 is found 0.81. Total scores of the test were used for accessing temporal stability; the retest period was 3 weeks approximately. Validity is that quality of the data gathering instrument on procedure that enables it to measure what it is supposed to measure. Reliability is a necessary but not sufficient condition for validity.

Data Collection

The scores of the scientific aptitude for college students have been calculated from 400 college students studied English or Tamil medium in their higher secondary level. Clear instructions have been given to the respondents and their earnest co-operation was sought. Sufficient time was given to all the respondents and they were asked to freely register their responses for all the items without omitting any, under the direct supervision of investigation.

Statistical Technique Used

Analysis of the data in the present study is done in such a way as to give focus on the comparison among given objectives. The data is descriptively analyzed by computing mean, median, standard deviation and t-test

Analysis of the Data

Objective Test: To study the levels of scientific aptitude among the arts and science students in Puducherry region.

Table 1: Level of Scientific Aptitude among Arts and Science Students

Variable	Low		Moderate		High	
	F	%	F	%	F	%
Scientific Aptitude	75	18.75	265	66.25	60	15

Hypothesis Test

Null Hypothesis.1: There is significant difference between arts and science students towards scientific aptitude.

Table 2: The significance of the difference between the means of Arts and Science students

Course	N	Mean	SD	t - value	DF	Remarks
Arts	155	67.72	9.38	2.21	398	Significant
Science	245	87.41	13.71			

The t value is found to be 2 and it is significant at 0.05 levels. Therefore the Null hypothesis is rejected and it is concluded that there is significant difference between arts and science towards scientific aptitude.

Null Hypothesis.2: There is no significant difference between Male and Female students towards scientific aptitude.

Table 3: The significance of the difference between the means of Male and Female Science students

Gender	N	Mean	SD	t - value	DF	Remarks
Male	185	79.84	15.38	0.06	398	Not Significant
Female	215	79.73	15.69			

The t value is found to be 0.069 and it is not significant at 0.05 levels. Therefore the Null hypothesis is retained and it is concluded that there is significant difference between Male and Female students towards scientific aptitude.

Null Hypothesis.3: There is no significant difference between Urban and Rural students towards scientific aptitude.

Table 4: The significance of the difference between the means of Urban and Rural Science students

Residence	N	Mean	SD	t - value	DF	Remarks
Urban	261	80.87	15.59	0.06	1.97	Significant
Rural	139	77.73	15.25			

The t value is found to be 1.967 and it is significant at 0.05 levels. Therefore the Null hypothesis is rejected and it is concluded that there is significant difference between the Urban and Rural students towards scientific aptitude.

Null Hypothesis.16: There is no significant difference between Government and Private College students towards scientific aptitude.

Table 5: The significance of the difference between the means of Government and Private students

College	N	Mean	SD	t - value	DF	Remarks
Government	146	78.14	16.28	0.06	1.98	Significant
Private	254	80.72	15.03			

The t value is found to be 1.98 and it is significant at 0.05 levels. Therefore the Null hypothesis is rejected and it is concluded that there is significant difference between the Government and Private college students towards scientific aptitude.

Null Hypothesis.17: There is no significant difference between Tamil and English medium students towards scientific aptitude.

Table 6: The significance of the difference between the means of Tamil and English medium students

College	N	Mean	SD	t - value	DF	Remarks
Tamil	117	73062	14.22	5.27	398	Significant
English	283	82.33	15.35			

The t value is found to be 5.275 and it is significant at 0.05 levels. Therefore the Null hypothesis is rejected and it is concluded that there is significant difference between the Tamil and English medium students towards scientific aptitude.

Suggestions for Further Research

A research study can be undertaken to study the scientific aptitude among the college students in Puducherry in order to suggest the suitable measures to improve their scientific aptitude.

A similar may be undertaken on a large sample covering all the colleges in Puducherry and colleges in other areas also.

The present study is limited to only arts and science students of 400 numbers. Further it has been observed that in this study only few variables are considered to make the suggestions.

Recommendations

This work is very helpful for guidance and counseling in the area of scientific research. With the help of these findings the investigator wants to emphasize that the rural students, female students, government college students and arts college students are in a low level compared with their competitors in scientific aptitude. These persons compulsorily have to take guidance and counseling to improve their scientific aptitude.

Conclusion

Based upon research conduct, we conclude that the boys and girls have the same scientific aptitude. Here the sex has no play role in describing the level of aptitude.

❐

13.

Development and Effectiveness of E-Content in Teaching of Biological Science Education for Knowledgeable Society

Introduction

Teacher is considered to be the architect of the nation. Owing to knowledge explosion and tremendously fast changing ICT, the teachers sometimes find it rather difficult to cope with the new intellectual challenges being thrown up by the changed global and local context. Therefore, they need to acquire new knowledge, and reliable and authentic information. The current system of teacher education is working to enhance the quality and effectiveness of teacher preparation programs at the pre-service level and also through in-service programs for serving teachers throughout the country.

Statement of the Problem

Kothari commission says 'destiny of the country was decided inside the class rooms'. So, to attain this destiny, the classrooms should be more effective. Academic input alone is the prime cause in establishing the quality of teaching. The efficiency of the teaching depends on the technology (e-content) input given by the teacher in the Colleges of Education. Hence the investigator would like to probe in finding the appropriate measure to the problem. So, the investigator has intended to study "Development and Effectiveness of E-content in Teaching of

Biological Science Education for knowledgeable Society".

Need and Significance of the Study

The traditional lecture method and black board were not interesting. The traditional lecture method makes less effective for the learning of the students. With the fast paced changes in education and training methodology, E-content is now the most preferred solution for learning effectively, whilst the e-learning through interactive content offers unique advantage. Hence the development of e-content in educational technology can bc faster and effective and it maintains sustained interest in students and avoids boredom. Hence, keeping all these in views the investigator attempted an experiment to develop an e-content in Teaching of Biological Science Education for B.Ed., student teachers. So the investigator decided to study the Development and Effectiveness of E-content in Teaching of Biological Science Education.

Objectives of the Study

The following objectives have been framed by the researcher in the study

To develop and validate an e-content package on the subject unit in Teaching of Biological Science Education at B.Ed., level.

To develop and validate an achievement test in Teaching of Biological Science Education to assess the achievement of student teachers in Biological Science Education

To Study the effectiveness of the developed e-content in Teaching of Biological Science Education at B.Ed. level.

Hypotheses of the Study

The following hypothesis was formulated based on the objectives of the study:

E-content method of teaching is not effective in improving the achievement of student teachers in Teaching of Biological Science Education.

Methodology

The present study used pre test- post test –two group experimental design. The student teachers of control group were taught by traditional lecture method which includes verbal discourse, chalk and talk and text only. The students of experimental group were taught through e-content and the measures were taken to control or minimize the threats to internal and external validity to a reasonable degree. A variable of the study is Achievement of student teachers in Teaching of Biological Science Education.

Sample : A sample of 25 B.Ed. student teachers comprising Biological Science optional subject were selected from Oxford College of Education, Trichy as the control group and 25 B.Ed student teachers comprising Biological Science optional subject were selected as experimental group from J. J. College of Education, Trichy. They were selected through Purposive Sampling technique.

Tools: The following tools were used in the study: The pre and post achievement tests were constructed and validated by the investigator.

Data Collection

The present investigator directed to handle all the six instructional classes and taught the selected subject unit to the control group on the prefixed days. The total subject unit was divided into two sub units. (Parallel to e-content modules) and each sub units was taught in two instructional hours. Thus all the two sub units were completed in a week long programme without affecting the routine work of the concerned college. The student teachers who had attended all the two instructional classes completely have been taken for the final analysis. Thus the final data were collected from 50 student teachers who had been selected by Purposive Sampling technique.

Data Analysis

Descriptive statistics was used to describe the sample with reference to the variable taken for the study. The differential analysis, the significance of difference between groups was studied using M, S.D,'t' test.,Gain Score Analysis and Effect Size Analysis.

Hypothesis Testing: Gain Score Analysis and Effect Size Analysis

The above hypothesis was tested by using the gain score analysis and effect size analysis.

Gain Score Analysis

Gain score analysis was carried out to find out the relative effectiveness of the treatment strategy over the traditional method of teaching. The instructional objectives were same for the Pre-test and Post-test. The gain scores are the measures to study the effectiveness of treatment strategy in improving the achievement of the student teachers in Teaching of Biological Science Education. The mean scores of the control and experimental group are shown in table 1.

Table 1 Mean gain and gain percentage scores of the Pre-test and Post-test scores.

Group	N	Pre-test M1	Post-test M2	Mean Gain Score	Gain Percentage
Control	25	21.60	22.52	0.91	0.91
Experimental	25	23.72	32.60	8.88	8.88

The table 1 indicates that the gain percentage in the achievement of the student teachers in Teaching of Biological Science Education. The mean gain score of Experimental group (8.88) is greater than the Control group (0.91). Therefore, teaching through e-content is effective in enhancing the achievement of the student teachers in Teaching of Biological Science Education.

Effect Size Analysis

Effect size analysis was carried out using pooled standard deviation to find out the relative effectiveness of the treatment strategy over the traditional method. Effect size and cohen's d for the achievement of the student teachers in Teaching of Biological Science Education are shown in the table 2.

Table 2 showing the difference between the Pre-test and Post-test scores due to treatment for the experimental group.

Group	Mean Scores	SD	Cohen's d	r value	Effect size
Control	22.52	5.705	1.796	0.668	Large
Experimental	32.60	5.515			

The effect size analysis showed that, the Cohen's d value is 1.796 and 'r' value is 0.668. The effect is large. So the null hypothesis is rejected. It is concluded that the effectiveness of e-content method of teaching in the achievement of student teachers in Teaching of Biological Science Education is very large. This result is due to E- Content method of teaching which made teaching learning process more interesting and helped the learners to achieve high.

Major findings of the Study

E- content method of teaching is effective in improving the achievement of student teachers in Teaching of Biological Science Education. The mean gain score of Experimental group (8.88) is greater than the Control group (0.91).

The effect size analysis showed that, the Cohen's d value is 1.796 and 'r' value is 0.668. The effect is large. It infers that the effectiveness of e-content method of teaching in the achievement of student teachers in Teaching of Biological Science Education is very large.

Discussion

The effect size analysis showed that the effectiveness of e-content method of teaching in the achievement of student teachers in Teaching of Biological Science Education is very large. This result is due to E- Content method of teaching which made teaching learning process more interesting and helped the learners to achieve high. The outcome of the study is a clear pointer to the fact that e-content package presentation is more effective in Teaching of Biological Science Education at B.Ed., level than the traditional lecture method.

Educational Implications

The study reveals that e-content method of teaching is more effective than the traditional method of teaching in improving the achievement in Teaching of Biological Science Education at B.Ed., level. Findings of the present study reveal that e-content material has observed an effective tool in teaching learning process.

E-content method of teaching will help our young teachers confident in facing the challenges of this technology world. Besides, the e-content approach can be effectively used to meet the individual differences of the learners.

References

- Aggarval J.C. (2002). Education Research an introduction Aryu Book Depot, New Delhi.
- Angadi.G.R (2011). "Development and validation of Multimedia package in Biology",GCTE Journal of Research and Extension in Education, Government collage of Teacher Education, Kerala. Vol-6(1) Jan-(2011).
- Jeya Shanmuga Raja. J, E-Content Development on Teaching method of Zoology at B.Ed Level., Paper presented at the International conference on Quality Enhancement in Distance Education for LifeLong Learning 26-27 March (2011). Bharathidasan University.
- Udayakumar.P, Impact of Multimedia Technology in Learning Biological Science on B.Ed. Trainees, http://www.languageinindia.com/feb2013/udayakumarfinal.pdf saved on 14.5.13.

❒

14.

Relationship of Academic Confidence and Academic Achievement of the Higher Secondary Students

Introduction

Academic confidence stem from the following four sources. (i) Mastery experience (ii) Vicarious experience (iii) Verbal persuasion and (iv) Physiological states. Most of the higher secondary students who go for professional degree in merit have a high level of confidence in their academics. Also, the students who scores more but choosing the arts and science degree according to their willingness have the highest confident level in their academic then the other students. Hence the academic confidence plays a vital and significant role in any students life for the better academic achievement. Sander, P and Sander, L (2006) studied the understanding Academic confidence. The relationship between academic confidence and self-efficacy is discussed elsewhere and it has been suggested that it stems from the same four sources proposed for self-efficacy; mastery experience, vicarious experience, verbal persuasion and physiological states. Lalage sanders and Paul. Sander (2007) developed the Academic Behavioural confidence A comparison of medical and Psychology students there was a significant difference between the ABC scores for the two groups (P<.05) in line with the prediction. Further examination of data showed that the ABC scores of the medical students as a group were more varied than those of the psychologists whilst the latter showed more variation across the elements of this scale. The academic confidence is conceptualized as how far the students are having a strong belief and trust on their academic side. As now a day the higher education has been distributed by various social and technological courses the students were introduced with all brand new inventions which affect them physically and also psychologically. Above all when their academic confidence is at their highest they will have a high level of academic achievement. The investigator was very much interested in knowing the relationship between the academic confidence and academic achievement of the higher secondary students.

Objectives

The following were the objectives formulated by the investigators for the present investigation.

To study if there is any significant relationship between the academic confidence and academic achievement of the female higher secondary students.

To study if there is any significant relationship between the academic confidence and academic achievement of the higher secondary students studying in the schools located in the urban area.

To study if there is any significant relationship between the academic confidence and academic achievement of the higher secondary students studying in the schools located in the rural area.

To study if there is any significant relationship between the academic confidence and academic achievement of the higher secondary students residing in the urban area.

To study if there is any significant relationship between the academic confidence and academic achievement of the higher secondary students residing in the rural area.

Hypotheses

The following were the hypotheses framed by the investigators from the formulated objectives.

- There is no significant relationship between the academic confidence and academic achievement of the male higher secondary students.
- There is no significant relationship between the academic confidence and academic achievement of the female higher secondary students.
- There is no significant relationship between the academic confidence and academic achievement of the higher secondary students studying in the schools located in the urban area.
- There is no significant relationship between the academic confidence and academic achievement of the higher secondary students studying in the schools located in the rural area.

- There is no significant relationship between the academic confidence and academic achievement of the higher secondary students residing in the urban area.
- There is no significant relationship between the academic confidence and academic achievement of the higher secondary students residing in the rural area.

Sample: Normative survey method has been used in the present investigation. Random sampling technique has been used in the selection of the sample of as many as 760 higher secondary students studying in higher secondary schools situated in the Tanjore district, Tamilnadu, India.

Tool : Academic confidence scale (ACS) constructed and validated by sna has been used in the present study. This scale consists of 30 statements, which were only positive statements. Each statement have five options, namely "strongly agree", "agree", "undecided", "disagree", "strongly disagree". The responses of the subjects were scored by assigning numerical values or arbitrary weights to the items. The statements were having the scoring as 5,4,3,2 and 1 for the responses from 'strongly agree' to 'strongly disagree'. An individual score is the sum of all the score of the 30 items. The score ranges from 30 to 150. The maximum score that one can get in this is 150. For the academic achievement the half yearly exam marks has been taken and were converted in to percentages and utilized for the computation.

Statistical Techniques Employed

The means and standard deviation for academic confidence scores and academic achievement scores of the sub-sample were calculated. The 'r' test was used in order to study the significant relationship between the means of the academic confidence score and academic achievement score.

Analysis and Interpretation

The following inferences are drawn from the Table – 1. In respect of the sub-samples of the higher secondary school students, all of them have a high level of academic confidence and academic achievement as their mean scores were above the average level i.e., the mid value.

Table 1: The mean, Standard Deviation and 'R' Value of Academic Confidence Scores and Academic Achievement Scores of the Sub-Samples

variable	n	academic confidence scores		academic achievement scores		'r' value	level of significance
		mean	sd	mean	sd		
male students	361	113.56	19.26	72.88	14.08	0.211	significant at 0.01 level
female students	399	127.34	16.02	73.61	13.90	0.156	significant at 0.01 level
students residing in the urban areas	374	119.87	20.52	75.22	11.09	0.118	significant at 0.05 level
students residing in the rural areas	386	121.27	17.85	72.01	16.01	0.231	significant at 0.01 level
students studying in the schools located in the urban areas	324	121.46	20.26	75.09	10.74	0.190	significant at 0.01 level
students studying in the schools located in the rural areas	436	120.13	17.82	71.81	16.57	0.184	significant at 0.01 level

Important Findings

The following were the important findings obtained from the present investigation.

- There is a significant relationship between the academic confidence and academic achievement of the higher secondary school male students at the 0.01 level of significance.
- There is a significant relationship between the academic confidence and academic achievement of the higher secondary school female students at the 0.01 level of significance.
- There is a significant relationship between the academic confidence and academic achievement of the higher secondary school students residing in the urban areas at the 0.05 level of significance.
- There is a significant relationship between the academic confidence and academic achievement of the higher secondary school students residing in the rural areas at the 0.01 level of significance.
- There is a significant relationship between the academic confidence and academic achievement of the higher secondary school students studying in the schools located in the urban areas at the 0.01 level of significance.
- There is a significant relationship between the academic confidence and academic achievement of the higher secondary school students studying in the schools located in the rural areas at the 0.01 level of significance.

Conclusion

The present investigation revealed that the higher secondary students studying in the Tanjore district of Tamilnadu, India, were found to have a high level of academic confidence and academic achievement which in turn gives a very low level of the below average students. So it can be revealed from the investigation that academic confidence plays a vital role in higher secondary students academic achievement.

References

- Acito, Frank, McDougall, Patrica M and Smith, Daniel C, (2008). One hundred years of excellence in business education: What we learned? Science Direct, Business Horizons (2008). 51,5-12.
- Additional Opportunities for MBA Students, Stanford Graduate School of Business, http://www.gsb.stanford.edu/programs/mba/financial-aid/types/fellowships, retrieved on October (09). 2013.
- Alvi, Khalid, (2005). Islam KaMoasharatiNizam, Al-Faisal Nashran, Lahore, Pakistan.
- Amer, Shaukat, (2007). In Search of a Binding Force-Society at the Top", American Association of Behavioral and Social Sciences Perspectives, Fall-(2007).

❐

15.

Technology Skill and Cognitive Skill of Teachers at High School Level

Introduction

Technological advancement has contributed greatly to the acceleration of human progress in the past several centuries. The information and communication technology has been a tremendous force for human development by providing information rich environment and raising standards of living. Technology globalizes communication. Globalization and its new rules are also shaping the path for new technologies. The demand for more open and accessible learning has started increasing since the early 1950s. Many factors are contributing to this changing educational culture. The most important of which are economic, social and technological forces. Education and training are not limited to only the fortunate few now. It has spread far and wide. It has reached all levels of society due to technological advancements.

Cognitive skill

Cognitive functioning is a term referring to a human's ability to process to that should not deplete on a large scale in healthy individuals. Cognition mainly refers to things like memory, the ability to learn new information, speech, and understanding of written material. The brain is usually capable of learning new skills in the aforementioned areas, typically in early childhood, and of developing personal thoughts and beliefs about the world.

Statement of the Problem

The investigator has selected the present study with the aim of knowing the technological skill and cognitive skill of teachers at high school level. Therefore it has been entitled as "Technology Skill and Cognitive Skill of Teachers at High School Level".

Definition of the Terms

Technology Skill: It refers to technological proficiency of teachers in handling hardware and software of educational technology.

Cognitive Skill: It refers to things like memory, the ability to learn new information, speech, and understanding of written material.

High School Level

The 9th and 10th STD level in 10+2+3 system of education.

Objectives

To find out the level of technology skill of teachers at high school level.

To find out the difference in technology skill among teacher in terms of sex.

To find out the difference in technology skill among teacher in terms of experience.

To find out the relationship between technology skill and cognitive skill of teachers at high school level.

Hypotheses

The level of technology skill of high school teachers is average.

There is no significant difference in technology skill among teachers at high school level in terms of sex.

There is no significant difference in technology skill among teachers at high school level in terms of experience.

There is no relationship between technology skill and cognitive skill among teachers at high school level.

Methodology

Construction of tool is an essential part in any research work. A valid tool will give the needed findings more specifically. Hence, designing a tool is very important. The researcher has collected 38 items on awareness and knowledge on educational technology was prepared by the investigator. The investigator based on his experience and after a thorough review of literature on technology skill prepared the questionnaire. There were 30 items on cognitive skills developed and validated by the investigator. The investigator had discussion personally with the teacher educators and the persons knowledgeable in the field of educational technology.

Establishment of reliability and validity of the tool

The questionnaires were administered among the 50 high school teachers and re-administered among the same 50 high school teachers after a gap of 15 days. The correlation found between the two tests was 0.86. It is a high level of correlation. Thus the reliability was ensured. The investigator has consulted experts for the preliminary form of the questionnaire on Technology skill and cognitive skill of Teachers. The consultation had with subject experts ensures face and content validity of the tool. According to Garret, H.E (1967, P.365) the index of reliability is sometimes taken as a measure of validity. The test is found to be having reliability, hence it may be considered as having validity.

Scoring

For the purpose of scoring, the response given by the high school teachers were calculated. The correct response was given 1 mark. Thus the maximum score in the questionnaire on educational technology would be 38 and the maximum score in the cognitive skill would be 30.

Sample Design

The investigator has followed simple random sampling method for the present study. The investigator has collected a sample of 303 high school teachers in Madurai district for the present study.

Analysis and Interpretation of Data

The investigator has tested the hypothesis one by one.

Hypothesis1: The level of technology skill of high school teachers is average.

Score	Technology skill of high school teachers	No. Of students	**Percentage**
81-100	V.Good	0	0
61-80	Good	2	0.66
41-60	Average	65	21.45
21-40	Poor	186	61.38
0-20	V.Poor	50	16.5
	Total	303	100

It is evident from the table 1 that 61.38 % of high school teachers are having poor technology skill. 21.45 % of teachers are having average level of technology skill. 16.5% of teachers are having very poor technology skill. 0.66% of teachers are having good technology skill. However, there is no one in the sample selected have Very good level of technology skill. Hence the hypothesis stated is rejected.

Hypothesis 2: There is no significant difference in technology skill among teachers at high school level in terms of sex.

Table 2. Mean, S.D and 't' value for the significant difference in technology skill among high school teachers in terms of sex.

Gender	N	Mean	S.D.	't'	Critical value	Level of significance
Male	84	12.09	4.83	0.062	1.986 for df of 301 at 0.05 level	N.S.
Female	219	13.23	4.39			

It is evident from table 2 that the obtained 't' value is 0.062. It is lesser than the critical value of 1.986 for degrees of freedom at 0.05 level. It is not significant. Hence the hypothesis stated is rejected. It can be concluded from the above finding that there is no significant difference in technology skill among high school teachers in terms of sex.

Hypothesis 3: There is no significant difference in technology skill among teachers at high school level in terms of experience.

Table 3. Mean, S.D and 't' value for the significant difference in technology skill among high school teachers in terms of experience.

Teaching Experience	N	Mean	S.D.	't'	Critical value	Level of significance
Below 5 years	31	11.19	5.24	0.079	1.986 for df of 232 at 0.05 level	N.S.
5 years to 10 years	203	12.98	4.37			
Below 5 years	31	11.19	5.24	0.038	1.986 for df of 98 at 0.05 level	N.S.
10 years and above	69	13.50	4.54			
5 years to 10 years	203	12.98	4.37	0.403	1.986 for df of 270 at 0.05 level	N.S.
10 years and above	69	13.5	4.54			

It is evident from table 3 that the obtained 't' value is 0.079. It is lesser than the critical value of 1.986 for degrees of freedom at 0.05 level. It is not significant. Hence the hypothesis stated is rejected. It is evident from table 3 that the obtained 't' value is 0.038. It is lesser than the critical value of 1.986 for degrees of freedom at 0.05 level. It is not significant. Hence the hypothesis stated is rejected. It is evident from table 3 that the obtained 't' value is 0.403. It is lesser than the critical value of 1.986 for degrees of freedom at 0.05 level. It is not significant. Hence the hypothesis stated is rejected. It is concluded from the above finding that there is no significant difference in technology skill among high school teachers in terms of experience.

Hypothesis 4: There is no correlation between technology skill and cognitive skill among teachers at high school level.

Table 4. Correlation between technology skill and cogntive skill among teachers at high school level

S.No.	Variable	N	Df	"r"	Significance level 0.05
1	Technology Skill Cognitive Skill	303	301	0.17951	.088

It is evident from Table 4 that 'r' value is 0.179. It exceeds the critical value of .088 at 0.05 levels. Hence it can be interpreted that there exists significant positive correlation between technology skill and cognitive skill among teachers at high school level. It can be surmised that the technology skill and cognitive skill are positively correlated. Hence the hypothesis stated as there is no correlation between technology skill and cognitive skill is rejected.

Findings of the Study

61.38 % of high school teachers are having poor technology skill. 21.45 % of teachers are having average level of technology skill. 16.5% of teachers are having very poor technology skill. 0.66% of teachers are having good technology skill. However, there is no one in the sample selected have Very good level of technology skill.

There is no significant difference in technology skill among high school teachers in terms of sex.

There is no significant difference in technology skill among high school teachers in terms of experience.

There is a positive correlation between technology skill and cognitive skill among teachers at high school level.

Reference

- Arul Sekar, J.M and Thiyagu.K (2007). 'Information and Communication Technology', Prophet publishers, Trichi.
- Alexis Leon and Mathews Leon (1999). "The Fundamentals of Information Technology, Leon Vikas publications, New Delhi.
- Bimal ghosh (1979). "Profiles of social change", oxford publication, New Delhi.

❐

16.

Social Competency and Confidence Building of Disabled towards Knowledge Society

Introduction

'Blindness separates us from things, Deafness separates us from people' – Immanuel Kant. Hearing impaired refers to individuals with permanent hearing loss or decrease in hearing. Hearing impairment affects a person in many ways, including their confidence level. Lack of confidence leads to communication barriers and makes insecurity in their social life. Optimistic collaboration with others is one achievable way to increase their confidence level. Inclusive education provides opportunities for academic and social benefits for all students. Salamanca Statement (1994) states that every child has a fundamental right to education, and must be given the opportunity to achieve and maintain an acceptable level of learning. The philosophy behind inclusive education is all children to participate learn and have an equal treatment irrespective of their mental and physical ability. The Government of India has played a key role in making policies to provide education for children with disabilities. National Policy on Education (1986) has taken an initiative steps in the area of inclusive education which recommended as 'to integrate the handicapped with the general community at all levels as equal partners, to prepare them for normal growth and to enable them to face life with courage and confidence'.

Inclusive education for Hearing Impaired students

The benefits of inclusive education for hearing impaired students are noticeable one.

Hearing impaired students who have been included in regular classroom shown stronger academic results and it leads to interaction with higher achieving students and desire to take challenges.

It leads to develop the valuable communication skills, problem solving skills and both individual and group work skills.

It helps to identify and understand what others are feeling so that they can respond appropriately

It develops the skill of social competence with their peers and also share and gain heir knowledge towards them with confidence.

Objectives

To find the relationship between level of confidence and social competency among hearing impaired adolescence students.

To predict the linear combination of level of confidence and dimensions of social competency among hearing impaired adolescence students.

Hypotheses

Level of confidence and social competency of hearing impaired adolescence students is moderate.

A linear combination of the variables namely self-management, interpersonal skill and academic skill significantly predicts Level of confidence of hearing impaired adolescence students.

Methodology

Tools were constructed by the investigators. The reliability was found to be 0.9 for Level of confidence and 0.7 for Social competency. The validity of Level of confidence and Social competency was 0.95 and 0.84 respectively. Correlation and Regression were computed for analysing the data.

Analysis and Interpretation

Table 1:Correlation between Level of confidence and Social competency

Description	Sample size	r	Significant Level
Level of Confidence and Social Competency	256	0.431	0.01

The above table shows that the 'r' value of level of confidence towards social competency is 0.431 which indicates positive relationship between level of confidence and social competency. Hence we conclude that when level of confidence increases social competency also increases at 0.01 level of significance.

REGRESSION

Table 2: Model Summary

Model	R	R-Square	Adjusted R-Square	Standard Error of the Estimate
1	0.248	0.061	0.050	6.320

Table 3: ANOVA

Model		Sum of Squares	df	Mean Square	F	Sig.Level
1	Regression	658.047	3	219.349	5.492	0.001
	Residual	10063.953	252	39.936		
	Total	10722.000	255			

Table-4: Regression Co- efficient to show the effect of Self-management, Interpersonal skill and Academic skill on level of confidence

Model	Unstandard zed co-efficient		Standardized co-efficient	't' -test	Significant
	B	Std. Error	B		
Constant	70.638	3.670		19.248	0.000
Self-management	-.094	.150	-.038	-.626	.532
Interpersonal	0.500	.132	.231	3.778	0.000
Academic skill	0.315	.283	.068	1.114	.267

The result of regression analysis reveal highly significant 'F' value (F= 5.492, P<0.01) indicates that the linear combination of all the variables taken together contribute towards level of confidence and significantly predicts confidence level of hearing impaired students. A comparison of B co-efficient and rank indicates that interpersonal skill is the most important predictor of level of confidence of hearing impaired students.

Regression Equation

$$Y = 70.638 +-.094X_1 +0.500X_2 + 0.315X_3$$

When Y is the level of confidence score that is predicted and X_1, X_2, and X_3 are the raw scores of independent variables.

Educational Implications

Towards a knowledge exchange.,

The teachers and parents of hearing impaired should be given an orientation programme and regular workshops on issues faced by hearing impaired students. In order to enhance self-confidence in them a few guidelines like,

- Let the child speak
- Treat the child same as normal child
- Teach into needs of the child
- Discover the child's interest and develop them
- Acknowledge both attempts and success

Conclusion

Quality in education for all, freedom of speech and expression, Universal access to everyone and their participation, access to information and knowledge and inclusive social welfare these are the central pillar of the society to meet knowledge sharing and retention. To construct collaboration path into knowledgeable society, all policies must seek ways to address inequality and social injustice to promote knowledgeable society. To develop and strengthen the competitiveness in global economy, our Government also needs to develop policies which foster inclusive participation by citizens through their critical thinking and creativity.

References

- Dodge, K. A. (1985). Facets of social interaction and the assessment of social competence in children. New York: Springer-Verlag.
- Education Commission (1966): Education and National Development: *Report of the Education Commission 1964-66,* Government of India: New Delhi.
- Individual with Disabilities Education Act of 1990, Pub. L. No. 101-476, 104 Stat.1142 (1991).
- Ladd, G. W., Munson, H. L., and Miller, J. K. (1984). Social Integration of deaf adolescents in secondary level mainstreamed programs. *Exceptional children*, 50(5), 420-428.

❒

17.

Role of Educational Institution in Generating Knowledgeable Society with Special Reference to D.Ed. Colleges of Mahabubnagar District of Telangana

Introduction

Educational institution has a strong impact on the society may be it is formal or non-formal education system and provide great knowledge to the society. The existing societies have deeply designed by the concern educational institutions and its practices. Role of the educational institution is heavy when it comes to shaping up of the society by means of preaches or practices. An Educational institution has comes with its conventional or modern methods but it has enormous effect on the society to transform it to the knowledgeable one. The present paper demonstrates how the educational institutions are the major flagpoles that dictate in developing the society into the well-informed one. To know educational institutions effect on society I have gone through with the staff and students of Diploma in education (D.Ed.) of Mahabubnagar district and the ten districts of New budded Telangana state. It laid its foundation in the ancient times of the education systems where the people flourished and notified throughout the world with their intellect property and prosperity in the society which was blessed with great intellectuals of the society. Even today we have reputed institutions but have not shown its impacts on the present society where it has to show. There are many reasons for this where, we discussed in this paper.

Main objective of the paper

1. The main objective of the paper is to know how the educational institutions have the major role in developing the society into the well-informed one.

2. To know the status of Education in Mahabubnagar.

3. To know the role of the Educational Institutions in bringing knowledgeable society.

4. To bring possible steps in the way of providing the solution for the problems.

The table shows present scenario of Govt.DIETs.

Sl.No.	Name of the DIET	Number of posts Sanctioned	Number of posts filled
1	Govt.DIET.Mahabubnagar	32	9
2	Govt.DIET.Neredmet, Hyderabad	32	0
3	Govt.DIET.Vikarabad, Ranga Reddy District	32	9
4	Govt.DIET.Medak	32	3
5.	Govt.DIET.Karimnagar	32	6
6.	Govt.DIET.Adilabad	32	0
7.	Govt.DIET.Khammam	27	5
8.	Govt.DIET.Nizamabad	32	6
9.	Govt.DIET.Warangal	32	14
10.	Govt.DIET.Nalgonda	27	6
	Total	310	58

In the private D.Ed. colleges the Lecturers are recruited and their certificates are procured and other locally available teachers are conducting the classes or 2 lecturers are dealing with 10 subjects (5 strategic and 5 methodologies).

Significance

The pilot study is carried out only for the purpose to get the knowledge regarding the role of the educational institutions and its effects on the society which is the vital one to drive Mahabubnagar district into enlightenment and provide knowledge of various sectors to the people.

Universe or Population

The universe/population for this study is students and teachers of various institutions in the entire Telangana state.

Sample: 100 students of Telugu medium and 50 students of Urdu medium Govt. DIET college, 35 students of Private D.Ed. colleges of Mahabubnagar, 9 Lecturers of Govt. DIET. Mahabubnagar and information regarding the vacancies of the Govt. DIET. are collected from websites and GTEA diaries.

Methodology

Information collected through a questionnaire from 150 teacher trainees of Govt. DIET. Mahabubnagar plus 35 private D.Ed. teacher trainees and 9 lecturers from Govt. DIET. Mahabubnagar, approached websites of TSSA and from "Chatropadyaya Darshini" magazine published by Govt. DIET. Mahabubnagar regarding this study.

Tools Applied

Questionnaire of students having 14 statements
Questionnaire of Teachers having 13 statements

Statistical Tools

For the statistics I have use arithmetic means for further analysis of the data.

Administration of the Questionnaire

The survey has conducted by administering the questionnaires with 14 items in the students and 13 in the lectures to all 150 D.Ed. teacher trainees of Telugu and Urdu medium and 9 Telugu and Urdu lecturers of the Govt. DIET. Mahabubnagar and the results are tabulated for statistics purpose and drawn the arithmetic means for further analysis.

Findings

Maximum number of students said that the institution haven't provides any scope for honesty.

- They said in a few occasions of Independence and Republic Day they have an opportunity to hear about the National heroes and they said that they did not have information regarding Indian legendary personalities regularly.
- There are very few occasions provided to play sports and games and listening extension lecturers on the beliefs and myth.
- They said that they did not have any guidance pertaining to vocation and education.
- There is no educational competition which was conducted by the DIETs.
- They said no NSS program has conducted.
- Very few lecturers provide skilled practice by means of demos.

- The college has provided an atmosphere to celebrate once religious festival such as Ramzan.

The institution did not provide other subjects rather than curricular prescribed subjects.

All Private D.Ed. college students said that they are forced to give extra amount (college maintenance fee) other than regular fee.

All Private D.Ed. college students said that they have paid amount for the supply of records.

Many Private D.Ed. students said the institutions have demanded for the amount for the attendance.

Conclusion

The main social objective of education is to complete the socialization process. The family gets the child, but the modern family tends to leave much undone in the socialisation process. The other institutions have come into being in place of family to complete the socialization process. Now, the people fell that it is "the institution's business to train the whole child even to the extent of teaching him honesty, fair play, consideration for others and a sense of right and wrong". The Educational institution devotes much of its time and energy to the matter such as co-operation, good citizenship, doing one's duty and upholding the law. But is needed the government mechanism to make it successful by taking timely action in fostering them.

References

- Chatropadyaya Darshini – of Govt.DIET.Mahabubnagar, 2013-14.
- Web site of TSSA, Web site of Board of SSC examinations., King, K. & McGrath, S. (2002)
- Globalisation, Enterprise and Knowledge. Education, Training and Development in Africa.
- Oxford, Symposium Books., King, R. (2003) The Growth of Private Higher Education:
- Regulating for Diversity or Homogeneity? ACU Inaugural Visiting Fellow's public Lecture.

❐

18.

Collaborating the Colleges of Education by Multi-Point Videoconference Teaching

Introduction

Toda collaborative learning is possible for students and instructors across geographies to participate in live classes, record the entire classroom experience including lectures, audiovisual and text materials. Teaching by video conferencing is a unique method of providing real time face -to – face interaction that enables immediate peer and teacher interaction. Multi-point video conferencing is an expansion of classroom video conferencing to involve three or more institutions.

Need of the Study

Over the years there have been significant changes in learning environment of students. It reflects the changing nature of students' life with students facing many competing demands in their time and requiring flexibility in learning. Because of this increase in demand, it has been necessary to introduce and foster innovative approaches and structures and make the most effective use of new technology in higher education. Basically, inter-institutional collaboration is essential to enhance a users' learning experience. It allows students to interact with information in new ways, change context and even create their own visualizations. The investigator wants to discuss the effective instruction in physical science education by employing multi site-to-site video conference as a delivery mode to the student teachers in Colleges of Education to serve the fast growing educational need and compare the effectiveness of the instruction with that of conventional method.

Objectives of the Study

- To find out the Effectiveness of Instruction in Physical science education through Video Conference to the student teachers
- To find out the difference between the control and experimental group in post-test performance of physical science education.
- To find out the gap closures in the performance of physical science education in the control and the experimental group
- To draw the profile showing the difference between the post test performance of control and experimental group.

Hypotheses

There is a significant difference between the control group and experimental group in pre test performance of physical science education.

There is a significant difference between the control and experimental group in post test performance of physical science education

Gap closures in the experimental group are greater than the control group in the performance of physical science education.

Methodology

The entry behavior test consisting of 150 multiple choice items was constructed and administrated by the investigator on the content of the B.Sc. degree course chemistry to 90 student teachers of previous year for the purpose of validation. After validation, the refined tool consists of 100 multiple choice items administrated to 150 B.Ed. student teachers 30 from Mangayarkarasi College of Education for women, 20 from KAPI college of Education, 16 from KAPI College of Education for women, 34 from Shakthi College of Education, 15 from Charles College of Education, 18 from Aurobindomira College of Education, 17 from A.S. college of Education affiliated to TamilNadu Teachers Education University. Based on the performance of student teachers, the sample is divided into two groups control group and experimental group by applying matching technique within the five points of the entry behavior test scores. The investigator selected 90 student teachers 45 for Control, 45 for Experimental. The design of the study is pre-test / post test equivalent group design.

Instructional Strategy

Two lessons Taxonomy of Educational Objectives, Methods of Teaching were taught to the Control Group through Traditional Method. For this experimental group, the investigator has prepared lessons using Multimedia delivered through video conference Pre/Post test consists of 48 multiple choice items after validation. The investigator at Mangayarkarasi College of Education for Women Madurai District(main location) has taught student teachers who are sitting in front of her while simultaneously teaching student teachers who are sitting at geographically distanced sites of SAKTHI College of Education, Ottanchatram, Dindigul District, KAPI College of Education and KAPI College of Education for women , Nagamalai using video conferencing equipment. A digital camera and a video card are used to capture images at each site. A microphone, a sound card and speakers are used to capture and project voices at each site. The vendor Tandberg Video Conferencing system at the internet broadband capacity of 1mbps transmits instruction delivered by the investigator at Mangayarkarasi College of Education to the student teachers at SHAKTHI and KAPI college of Education via Polycomm Mobile Video Conferencing system at the internet broadband capacity 512 kbps.

DATA ANALYSIS AND INTERPRETATIONS

Table 1- Pretest performance of control group and experimental group

Unit	GROUPS	MEAN	S.D	t value	L.S
Taxonomy of educational objectives	Control Group	7.02	1.32	0.39	N.S.
	Exp. Group	6.91	1.53		
Methods of teaching	Control Group	6.73	1.81	0.11	N.S
	Exp. Group	6.69	2.10		

From table 1, it is inferred that there is no significant difference between the pre-test mean scores of the Control Group , Experimental Group. Therefore two groups were similar in terms of their pre-test performance before the application of the treatment. Hence hypothesis 1 is rejected.

Table 2 - Posttest performance of control group and experimental group

Unit	GROUPS	MEAN	S.D	t value	L.S
Taxonomy of educational objectives	Control Group	15.91	1.58	16.36	0.001
	Exp. Group	26.96	4.30		
Methods of teaching	Control Group	15.84	2.20	18.84	0.001
	Exp. Group	27.00	2.86		

From the table 2, it is inferred that there is significant difference between the post-test mean scores of the Control Group and Experimental Group student teachers in the units Taxonomy of Educational Objectives and Methods of Teaching. Hypothesis 2 is accepted. It shows that Video Conferencing was interesting for the student teachers. Results on media richness suggested that the student teachers could feel the presence of other college student teachers in the remote place and could get replies quickly from remote places. Use of sound, video, animation and graphics in the subject matter of Unit I and Unit 2 stimulated auditory and visual senses to encourage interaction.

Table 3 - Gap closure of control group and experimental group

Unit	Control group			Exp. Group		
	Pre test	Post test	Gap Closure	Pre test	Post test	Gap Closure
Taxonomy of edu. objectives	7.02	15.91	26.96	6.91	26.96	60.59
Methods of teaching	6.73	15.84	27.38	6.69	27.00	60.97

The table 3 reveals that the Gap Closure in the unit Taxonomy of Educational Objectives and Methods of teaching for the Control Group and Experimental Group student teachers. The higher level of post test scores than pre test scores is due to teaching through traditional and video conferencing. The gap closure of Experimental group is greater than control group. In Video conferencing face-to -face instruction is crucial in enhancing interactivity given the situation where teacher and student teachers are separated by distance. Media richness included multiple interactivity. The higher level of gap closure in experimental group than control group is due to the discussion in addition to implementation of Video Conferencing.

Table 4: Profile of Control Group and Experimental Group

Units	Control Group		Experimental Group	
	Mean	Stanine	Mean	Stanine
Taxonomy of educational objectives	15.91	2	26.96	5
Methods of teaching	15.84	3	27.00	5

The table 4 shows that the mean scores and corresponding stanine values for the control group and experimental group in the post test performance. The profile 1 shows that there is a gap of one or more stanine between control group and experimental group in two units. A stanine of 5 and above indicates higher level of Acheivement in physical science education and a stanine of below 5 indicates lower level of Acheivement in physical science education.

The inferences drawn from the profile show that the Experimental group I student teachers have higher level of Acheivement in "Taxonomy of Educational Objectives and Methods of Teaching. it is due to the effectiveness of Video conference teaching . It is an instruction and practice alternative when real – world experience is hazardous to learners and instructors. It provides an exciting instructional medium and a unique way to the effective learning.

Educational Implications

Future educational institutions must necessarily involve how they intend to become more open and flexible to the scheduling demands of their learners. The videoconferencing session Evans and the other students experienced is the type of communication that is becoming more common in education at all levels around the world, as the walls between classrooms disappear. Collaboration of Colleges of Education is an essential part of the K-20 education environment that enables cost savings, engages students and creates a more productive learning experience. It prepares students with the skills to thrive in a future workforce that will depend on institutional collaboration technologies.

Conclusion

The collaboration of educational institutions has removed the restrictions imposed by the clock and geography by enabling people to attend video conference teaching. The ability of videoconference communications to reach large number of student teachers with the same high quality of instruction has raised hopes for economies of scale never possible in the very labor intensive traditional forms of instruction. Video conferencing group student teachers has done better than those who learned by the traditional method of instruction. It has explored real world environments. It has provided immediate response from both instructor and student teacher. Video conference teaching provided three types of interaction namely learner – instructor interaction, learner–content interaction, learner-learner interaction within the college and from other colleges simultaneously. It has been realized as the highest level of learning by the student teachers.

References

- Aggarwal, Y.P., (1990). *Statistical Methods – Concepts, Application and computation.* New Delhi: Sterling Publishers Pvt .Ltd.
- Bloom.B.S. (1974), Technology of Educational Objectives, Cognitive Domain. London: Longman
- Davis J.R.(1976)*Teaching Strategies for the College Classroom.* Colorado: West View Press.
- Gallagher.J.D.(1998), *Classroom Assessment for Teachers.* Upper Saddle River, NJ: Prentice – Hall Inc.

❐

19.

Attitude of B.Ed. Trainees towards Teaching with Reference to Social Maturity

The destiny of India is being shaped in the class room in which a teacher plays a significant role as per the Kothari commission report on Education (1964-66). The basic personality pattern of the teacher's behavior and attitudes are important factors in building an emotionally balanced classroom climate that promotes the mental health of school children. Schools are social systems, if one wishes to work in them or manage them then it is necessary to understand how the operate, combine education and people. As the school is a web of interactions among people who live and work together under the management such type of interactive environment of the school controls teachers adjustment and attitude and also the basic personality pattern.

Attitude - Meaning

According to modern psychological literature, an attitude represents individual feelings for against something. We may also define an attitude as the degree of acceptance given by an individual for something. Edwards (1969) "An attitude may be defined as a learned emotional response set for or against something."

Importance of Attitude towards Teaching

Attitude is a tendency to react favourably or unfavourably towards a designated class of stimuli such as a national or racial group a custom or an institution (Anastasi, 1982). Attitude is an underlying disposition the enters, along with many other influences, into the determination of the variety of behaviours towards the attitude object or class of objects, including statements of beliefs and feelings about the attitudes object and approach-avoidance actions with respect to it, Cook and Selltiz (1964).

Definition of Social Maturity

Nazareth RJM, N.Pai and Marie.E.Wapels (1978) defines that maturity is the blossoming of man's character in to a unified totality. It discerns the process that contributes to the psychological and physical growth and well begins of man.

Abraham Sperling (1967) defines that an adolescent who gets along with and work well with others, he ought to develop self reliance in manners of taste and they ought to develop tolerance of human differences.

Importance of Social Maturity

Maturity assures accountability, constantly asset, judge and takes appropriative decisions. Maturity develops a balanced emotional outlook, helping the individual to accept himself his talents and limitations and accept others as they are. It helps towards progressive advancement in spiritual growth, impelling the individual to adapt himself to change life without emotional crisis.

Need for the Study

Man is basically a social animal. His existence without social set up can hardly be imagined. He is born in a society, develops in a society works, and progresses in a society. There are various factors behind the social maturity of an individual. Parents, family members, neighbours, peer group, society, etc. expect him to behave in the way acceptable to the society. Adolescents are expected more by the society in which they live. Social maturity increases as age increases for normal human beings. They learn to be in a group, share and care for others, respect the norms and values of the society.

The word social maturity is comprised of two words social and maturity. Social means 'Living in Communities' and Maturity means 'Adjust himself to the social world around him. Thus social maturity refers to attaining maturity in social relationships i.e. to establish good relations with family, friends, neighbours and all other persons living in our society. Parents and teachers must be very particular in maintaining interpersonal relationship with the young students in order to channelize their energy in right direction.

Teaching includes all the activities of providing education to other. The person who provides education is called teacher. The teacher uses different method for giving best knowledge to his students. He tries his best to make understand students. His duty is to encourage students to learn the subjects.

Many great teachers of world define teaching in different way and we can say that teaching is just to train the students so that they can stand on their own foot in society. Teacher alone can develop the social maturity to students in proper way. Teacher Education Colleges play significant role in developing not only intellectual but also social maturity. Therefore, the B.Ed. trainees have social maturity as a part of their training. Hence, the present study is under taken.

Statement of the Problem

The problem stated for the present study has been given as ***"Attitude of B.Ed. Trainees towards Teaching with reference to Social Maturity".***

Objectives of the Study

The researcher has framed the following objectives for the present study,

- To find out the significance of mean difference in their attitude towards teaching and social maturity with reference to gender.
- To find out the significance of mean difference in their attitude towards teaching and social maturity with reference to locality.
- To find out the significance of mean difference in their attitude towards teaching and social maturity with reference to parents educational qualification.
- To find out the relationship between the attitude towards teaching and social maturity of B.Ed. Trainees.

Hypotheses of the Study

For the present study, the researcher has framed the following hypotheses.

- There is no significant difference in their attitude towards teaching and social maturity with reference to gender.
- There is no significant difference in their attitude towards teaching and social maturity with reference to locality.
- There is no significant difference in their attitude towards teaching and social maturity with reference to parents' educational qualification.
- There is no relationship between the attitude towards teaching and social maturity of B.Ed. Trainees.

Method used in the study

Normative survey method has been used in the present study to collect the data from the B.Ed. trainees in the selected colleges of Education of Ariyalur District in Tamilnadu. Using Random Sampling 200 samples has been collected from the Colleges of Ariyalur District in Tamilnadu for the present study.

Tools used in the study

The following tools are used in the present study.

Scale of Attitude towards Teaching - constructed and standardized by the researcher and R. Muthaiyan.

Testing of the Hypothesis

Hypothesis - 1: There is no significant difference in their attitude towards teaching and social maturity with reference to gender. The hypothesis was tested using 't' test

Attitude towards teaching					
Gender	N	Mean	Standard Deviation	't' value	Level of Significance
Male	100	159.5347	18.6524	0.4487	NS
Female	100	158.4343	15.8114		
Social maturity					
Male	100	257.8020	29.0852	3.431*	0.01
Female	100	263.3737	27.1546		

The above table shows that the computed value of 't' 0.4487 is less than the critical values of 2.58 and 1.96 at 0.01 and 0.05 levels respectively and hence it is not significant. Consequently, the null hypothesis is not to be rejected and it can be said that there is no significant difference between B.Ed. trainees in their attitude towards Teaching with reference to gender.

The second part of the table shows that the computed value of 't' 3.431 is greater than the critical value of 2.58 at 0.01 level and hence it is significant. Consequently, the null hypothesis is to be rejected and it can be said that there is a significant difference between B.Ed. trainees in their Social Maturity with reference to gender. It is also inferred from the above table that the female trainees are socially matured than the male trainees.

Hypothesis - 2: To find out the significance of mean difference in their attitude towards teaching and social maturity with reference to locality. The hypothesis was tested using 't' test.

Attitude towards teaching					
Locality	N	Mean	Standard Deviation	't' value	Level of Significance
Rural	136	158.4426	17.0010	0.5286	NS
Urban	64	159.8462	17.7572		
Social maturity					
Rural	136	262.4590	28.7225	2.951*	0.01
Urban	64	257.5897	27.3194		

The above table shows that the computed value of 't' 0.5286 is less than the critical values of 2.58 and 1.96 at 0.01 and 0.05 levels respectively and hence it is not significant. Consequently, the null hypothesis is not to be rejected and it can be said that there is no significant difference between B.Ed. trainees in their attitude towards Teaching with reference to locality.

The second part of the table shows that the computed value of 't' 2.951 is greater than the critical value of 2.58 at 0.01 level and hence it is significant. Consequently, the null hypothesis is to be rejected and it can be said that there is a significant difference between B.Ed. trainees in their Social Maturity with reference to locality. It is also inferred from the above table that the rural trainees are socially matured than the urban trainees.

Hypothesis -3: There is no significant difference in their attitude towards teaching and social maturity with reference to parents' educational qualification. The hypothesis was tested using 'F' test

Attitude towards teaching					
Source of Variation	Sum of Squares	df	Mean Variance of Squares	'F' value	Level of Significance
Between groups	2793.131	3	931.044	3.125**	0.05
Within groups	58391.34	196	297.915		
Social maturity					
Between groups	21036.600	3	7012.200	8.947*	0.01
Within groups	153610.688	196	783.728		

The above table shows that the computed value of 'F' 3.125 is less than the critical value of 3.78 at 0.01 level and greater than the critical value of 2.60 at 0.05 level and hence it is significant at 0.05 level. Consequently, the null hypothesis is to be rejected and it can be said that there is a significant difference between B.Ed. trainees in their attitude towards Teaching with reference to parent's educational qualification.

The second part of the table shows that the computed value of 'F' 8.947 is greater than the critical value of 3.78 at 0.01 level and hence it is significant at 0.01 level. Consequently, the null hypothesis is to be rejected and it can be said that there is a significant difference between B.Ed. trainees in their social maturity with reference to parent's educational qualification.

Hypothesis -4: There is no relationship between the attitude towards Teaching and Social Maturity of B.Ed. Trainees. The hypothesis was tested using Karl Pearson's Product Moment Coefficient of Correlation.

Correlations			
		Attitude towards Teaching	Social Maturity
Attitude towards Teaching	Pearson Correlation	1	0.137*
Social Maturity	Pearson Correlation	0.137*	1

The above table shows that the computed value of 'r'(0.137) is greater than the critical values of 0.081 at 0.01 level and hence, it is significant. Consequently, the null hypothesis is to be rejected and it can be said that, there is a relationship between the attitude towards Teaching and Social Maturity of B.Ed. Trainees. Even though the value of 'r' is positive, the relationship is negligible.

Summary of findings

The following are the findings of the present study.

- There is no significant difference between B.Ed. Trainees in their attitude towards Teaching with reference to gender.
- There is no significant difference between B.Ed. Trainees in their attitude towards Teaching with reference to locality.
- There is a significant difference between B.Ed. Trainees in their attitude towards Teaching with reference to parent's educational qualification. It is also inferred that trainees whose parents' educational qualification is 1st Standard to 10th Standard (161.4231) have high level of attitude than the trainees whose parents' educational qualification is 11th Standard to 12th Standard (158.1832), the trainees whose parents' educational qualification is Under Graduate Degree (160.8108) and trainees whose parents' educational qualification is Post Graduate Degree and above (154.8333).
- There is a significant difference between B.Ed. Trainees in their Social Maturity with reference to gender. It is also inferred that the Female trainees are socially matured than the male trainees.
- There is a significant difference between B.Ed. Trainees in their Social Maturity with reference to locality. It is also inferred that the rural trainees are socially matured than the urban trainees.
- There is a significant difference between B.Ed. Trainees in their social maturity with reference to parent's educational qualification. It is also inferred that the trainees whose parents' educational qualification is Post Graduate Degree and above (276.3333) are socially matured than the trainees whose parents' educational qualification is 1st Standard to 10th Standard (257.6923), trainees whose parents' educational qualification is 11th Standard to 12th Standard (258.7023) and the trainees whose parents' educational qualification is Under Graduate Degree (266.5946).
- There is a relationship between the attitude towards Teaching and Social Maturity of B.Ed. Trainees. Even though the value of 'r' is positive, the relationship is negligible.

Conclusion

The present study has investigated the Attitude of B.Ed. Trainees towards Teaching with reference to Social Maturity. From the findings of the study, it is concluded that the B.Ed. trainees attitude towards teaching do not differ significantly with reference to gender and locality. But, the B.Ed. trainees attitude towards teaching differs significantly with reference to Parent's Educational Qualification. It is also concluded that the B.Ed. trainees Social Maturity differs significantly with reference to gender, locality and Parent's Educational Qualification.

References

- Affizal Ahmad & Rafidah Sahak (2009). Teacher-Student Attachment and Teachers' Attitudes Towards Work. *Jurnal Pendidik dan Pendidikan, Jil. 24,* 55–72.
- Allport, G.W. (1935). "Attitudes" in C. Murchison (Ed.), Handbook of Social Psychology, Worcester, Mass: Clark University Press, 810.
- Arthur Regnolds, Erin cowell & Kristy Kohler (2005). Social emotion mediators: A longitudinal study, Chicago project.
- Bhalla, A., Jajoo, U.N. & Kalantri, S.P. (2002). Attitude of teachers towards teaching. Journal Association Physicians India, 50:1405-8.
- Buch, M.B. (ed). (1991). Fourth Survey of research in Education. New Delhi: National Council of Educational Research and Training
- Keisham Shitaljit Singh (2012). Teachers' Attitude towards Information and Communication Technology (ICT). *Shodh Sanchayan, 3(2),* 1-4.
- Nalini Rao (1986). Manual for Rao's Social Maturity Scale. Agra: National Psychological Corporation.
- Thurstone, L.L. (1932). The Measurement of Social Attitude. Journal of Abnormal Social Psychology, Vol. 26.

❐

20.

The Effect of CCE on Total Academic Achievement among High School Students

Introduction

Various studies had showed that scholastic achievement is positively related to intelligence. Some of the pioneers in the improvement of the academic testing include the superiority of the written over the oral exam, Thorndike, who championed the early cause of measurement. Also so many educators and psychologists have given the principles of educational measurement and principles of classroom test measurement. There is greater tendency to interpret academic achievement in relation to other phases of development. The NPE (1986) made a strong plea for evaluation reform and indicated the need for development of an evaluation framework. It de-emphasized rote learning, focused on continuous and comprehensive evaluation (CCE) and introduction of semester system, including grading etc. These provisions have been incorporated into a law, the RTE Act, 2009 vide section 29(2) of this Act. This obviously calls for a greater amount of responsibility and accountability on the part of the teacher. Perhaps this has the germ of improving the inter-school quality to be judged in the performance of the students in entrance examinations for admission to higher and professional education. Thus the investigator and Dr. R. Muthuvel M.A., Ph.D. focused on "the effect of CCE on total academic achievement among high school students".

Objectives

The study has the following objectives

- To study the effect of CCE on total academic achievement among high school students.
- To study the significant improvement in the total academic achievement before introducing CCE and after introducing CCE.
- To study the significant improvement in the total academic achievement before introducing CCE and after introducing CCE with trimester
- To study the significant improvement in the total academic achievement after introducing CCE and after introducing CCE with trimester.
- To study the relationship between total academic achievement before introducing CCE and after introducing CCE; before introducing CCE and after introducing CCE with trimester; and after introducing CCE and after introducing CCE with trimester.

Variable

The Dependent variable is the total Achievement. It is studied with following criteria

- Total Academic Achievement before introducing CCE
- Total Academic Achievement after introducing CCE
- Total Academic Achievement after introducing CCE with trimester

Hypotheses of the Study

Based on the objectives and variables the following hypotheses were framed

- There will be a significant improvement in the total academic achievement after introducing the CCE than before introducing the CCE.
- There will be a significant improvement in the total academic achievement after introducing the CCE with trimester than before introducing the CCE.
- There will be a significant improvement in the total academic achievement after introducing the CCE with trimester than after introducing the CCE.
- There will be significant relationship between total academic achievement before introducing the CCE and after introducing the CCE .
- There will be significant relationship between total academic achievement before introducing the CCE and after introducing the CCE with trimester.
- There will be significant relationship between total academic achievement after introducing the CCE and after introducing the CCE with trimester.

Methodology

Method: To study the effect of CCE on total academic achievement of high school students, Ex-Post Facto design was adopted in the study.

Sample: The students studying 9th std. from Little Flower Girls Higher Secondary School, Manaparai; the students studying 9th std. from St. Montfort

Matriculation Higher Secondary school, Manjampatti, Manaparai; and the students studying 9th std. from Servite Matriculation Higher Secondary School, Thogaimalai were selected through purposive Sampling technique. The distribution of the sample is shown in Table-1

Table-1 showing the distribution of the sample

S. No.	Name of the School	N
1.	Little Flower Girls Hr. Sec. School, Manaparai.	124
2.	St. Montfort Matriculation Hr. Sec. School, Manjampatti.	90
3.	Servite Matriculation Hr. Sec. School, Thogaimalai.	40
	Total	254

Statistical Techniques Applied in the Study

The following statistical techniques were used to analyze the data
Differential analysis-'t'-test
Correlation analysis-product moment method 'r'
Testing the Hypotheses

Hypothesis: 1: There will be a significant improvement in the total academic achievement after introducing the CCE than before introducing the CCE. The above hypothesis was tested by using the't'-test. The significance of improvement between the means of High school students in their Total Academic Achievement after introducing the CCE and before introducing the CCE is shown in Table-2.

Table-2

Variable	N	M	S.D	't'	p-value
Tot. Aca. Achievement before introducing the CCE	254	48.79	15.16	10.566**	0.000
Tot. Aca. Achievement after introducing the CCE	254	54.21	16.79		

**- significant at 0.01 level.

The calculated value of't' is significant at 0.01 level of significance. It is concluded that there is significant improvement in the total academic achievement after introducing the CCE than before introducing the CCE. Thus the total academic achievement after introducing the CCE is higher than before introducing the CCE.

Hypothesis: 2: There will be a significant improvement in the total academic achievement after introducing the CCE with trimester than before introducing the CCE. The above hypothesis was tested by using the't'-test. The significance of improvement between the means of High school students in their Total Academic

Achievement after introducing the CCE with trimester than before introducing the CCE is shown in Table-3

Table-3

Variable	N	M	S.D	't'	p-value
Tot. Aca. Achievement before introducing the CCE	164	48.40	14.80		
Tot. Aca. Achievement after introducing the CCE with trimester	164	77.74	13.02	27.008**	0.000

**- significant at 0.01 level.

The calculated value of 't' is significant at 0.01 level of significance. It is concluded that there is significant improvement in the total academic achievement after introducing the CCE with trimester than before introducing the CCE. Thus the total academic achievement after introducing the CCE with trimester is higher than before introducing the CCE.

Hypothesis: 3: There will be a significant improvement in the total academic achievement after introducing the CCE with trimester than after introducing the CCE. The above hypothesis was tested by using the't'-test. The significance of improvement between the means of High school students in their Total Academic Achievement after introducing the CCE with trimester than after introducing the CCE is shown in Table-4

Table-4

Variable	N	M	S.D	't'	p-value
Tot. Aca. Achievement after introducing the CCE	164	54.19	16.19	22.780**	0.000
Tot. Aca. Achievement after introducing CCE with trimester	164	77.74	13.02		

The calculated value of 't' is significant at 0.01 level of significance. It is concluded that there is significant improvement in the total academic achievement after introducing the CCE with trimester than after introducing the CCE. The total academic achievement after introducing the CCE with trimester is higher than after introducing the CCE.

Hypothesis: 4: There is significant relationship between total academic achievement before introducing the CCE and achievement after introducing the CCE of High school students. The above hypothesis was tested by using the Product moment method.The significance of relationship between total academic achievement before introducing the CCE and total academic achievement after introducing the CCE of High school students is shown in Table-5

Table-5

Variable	N	'r'	p-value
Tot. Aca. Achievement before introducing the CCE	254	0.874**	0.000
Tot. Aca. Achievement after introducing the CCE	254		

The calculated value of 'r' is significant at 0.01 level of significance. It is concluded that there is significant positive relationship between total academic achievement before introducing the CCE and total academic achievement after introducing the CCE of High school students.

Hypothesis 5: There is significant relationship between total academic achievement before introducing the CCE and total academic achievement after introducing the CCE with trimester of High school students. The above hypothesis was tested by using the Product moment method.

The significance of relationship between total academic achievement before introducing the CCE and total academic achievement after introducing the CCE with trimester of High school students is shown in Table-6

Table-6

Variable	N	'r'	p-value
Tot. Aca. Achievement before introducing the CCE	164	0.506**	0.000
Tot. Aca. Achievement after introducing the CCE with trimester	164		

The calculated value of 'r' is significant at 0.01 level of significance. It is concluded that there is significant positive relationship between total academic achievement before introducing the CCE and achievement after introducing the CCE with trimester of High school students.

Hypothesis 6: There is significant relationship between total academic achievement after introducing the CCE and total academic achievement after introducing the CCE with trimester of High school students. The above hypothesis was tested by using the Product moment method.The significance of relationship between total academic achievement after introducing the CCE and achievement after introducing the CCE with trimester of High school students is shown in Table-7

Table-7

Variable	N	'r'	p-value
Tot. Aca. Achievement after introducing the CCE	164	0.608**	0.000
Tot. Aca. Achievement after introducing the CCE with trimester	164		

The calculated value of 'r' is significant at 0.01 level of significance. It is concluded that there is significant positive relationship between total academic achievement after introducing the CCE and total academic achievement after introducing the CCE with trimester of High school students.

Result: Total academic achievement of high school students after introducing CCE with trimester seems to be effective than the previous evaluations.

Conclusion and Educational Implications

Research and anecdotal evidence overwhelmingly support the claim that students learn best when they engage with course material and actively participative in their learning. This research too proclaims the truth that the implementation of CCE with trimester brought the tremendous change among high school students. This can give much fruit if it is done by educationists with more enthusiasm.

References

- Aggarwal, J. C. (2006). *Modern Indian Education History, Development and Problems-4th revised edition.* Shipra Publication. (ISBN: 978-81-7541-332-0).
- Amutharanjini, G., & Mohanasundaram, K. (2012). A Study on Teacher's Competencies and Academic Achievement of Secondary Teacher Trainees. *New Horizons in Educational Research*, IV (1), 50-58. (ISSN: 0975-4008).
- Best, J. W., & Khan, J. V. (2005). *Research in Education -9th edition.* New Delhi: Prentice Hall of India Private Ltd.
- Henry, E.,&Garrett. (2006). *Statistics in Psychology and Education.* India: Surjeet Publications.
- Mohanasundaram, K. (2005). *New Teachnologies in Physical Science Teaching.* Mannargudi: Mohan Publishers.
- Poorana Sheela, P. (2014). *Study on the impact of mind map teaching strategy on achievement in mathematics and certain select variables of high school Students.* Unpublished doctoral dissertation, Manonmaniam Sundaranar University, Tirunelveli.
- *Field visit to sarva shiksha abhiyan in Tamil Nadu*, Back to office report. (2008). Retrieved , February 9, 2015, from http://www.ssa.tn.nic.inDocuWorld_BankTeam%20_Report.pdf.

❐

21. Scientific Aptitude among the Arts and Science Students in Puducherry Region

Introduction

The modern world of ours is certainly different from the ancient world or the middle ages. This breakthrough is largely due to science and its advancements. Science is the investigation and interpretation of events in the natural and physical environment of man. Science as a core subject develops the personal and social responsibility and competency needed by all youth to serve the needs of democratic society. Perceiving the problem, relating the problem to previous experience, formulating hypothesis after testing, deriving conclusions and arriving at generalizations are the scientific aptitudes. The study of scientific aptitude among the college students is a mandatory work to estimate scientific knowledge, problem solving skills and scientific attitude of college students in order to improve scientific aptitude of students to serve in this technological world.

Purpose of the Study

Since the students are not opting the subjects only because of their interest in it, and there are various external forces that are driving the students to opt a subject in which they are not interested, it is realized that a study to find out whether the students really get the necessary aptitude towards the subjects they are studying. The main purpose of this study is to determine whether the science students have scientific aptitude or not. It also determines the scientific aptitude of arts students. The arts students may be selected their study for various reasons. This study is used to find the scientific aptitude of interested arts students in colleges. This research will enable to find out the scientific aptitude among the college students in Puducherry region.

Objectives of the Study

The present investigation has been undertaken in order to find out the following

- To study the levels of scientific aptitude among the arts and science students in Puducherry region.
- To study the difference between male and female college students in respect of their scientific aptitudes.
- To study the difference between urban and rural college students in respect of their scientific aptitudes.
- To study the difference between government and private college students in respect of their scientific aptitudes.
- To study the difference between students of English and Tamil medium of instruction at school level in respect of their scientific aptitudes.

Hypothesis of the Study

- There is no significant difference between arts and science students towards scientific aptitude.
- There is no significant difference between male and female students towards scientific aptitude.
- There is no significant difference between urban and rural students towards scientific aptitude.
- There is no significant difference between government and private college students towards scientific aptitude.
- There is no significant difference between Tamil and English medium students towards scientific aptitude.

Method of Study

In the present investigation, the investigation is forms using Descriptive Survey Method.

Sample of the Study

Sampling is the process by which a relatively small number of individuals or measure of individuals objects or events selected and analyzed in order to find out something about entire population from which it was selected. The sample for the study consists of college students of Puducherry region. 400 samples taken for this present research study. The selection of the sample is made by simple Random sampling technique and the method is adopted to achieve the objectives of the study is Normative Survey Method.

Tool

For the purpose of data collection, the investigator adopted scientific aptitude test for college students' constructed by A.K.P.Sinha & L.N.K.Sinha (2000). This test aim to measure the scientific aptitude among the college students. There are 34 items in seven areas. There is no time limit for the test, but usually it takes

30 minutes to conduct the test. The areas of scientific aptitude are as follows. Experiment Bent, Detection of inconsistencies or illogical conclusions, Ability to deduce conclusion from the data provided, Accuracy of interpretation, Ability to reason and solve problems, Caution and thoroughness and Accuracy of observation.

Reliability and Validity of the Tool

Reliability is the degree of consistency that the instrument or procedure demonstrate whatever it is measuring it does so consistently. Since reliability is the most essential and significant feature of the test, the split half test have been calculated for this test .The test-retest reliability for the sample of 58 is found 0.81. Total scores of the test were used for accessing temporal stability; the retest period was 3 weeks approximately.

Validity is that quality of the data gathering instrument on procedure that enables it to measure what it is supposed to measure. Reliability is a necessary but not sufficient condition for validity.

Data Collection

The scores of the scientific aptitude for college students have been calculated from 400 college students studied English or Tamil medium in their higher secondary level. Clear instructions have been given to the respondents and their earnest co-operation was sought. Sufficient time was given to all the respondents and they were asked to freely register their responses for all the items without omitting any, under the direct supervision of investigation.

Statistical Technique Used

Analysis of the data in the present study is done in such a way as to give focus on the comparison among given objectives. The data is descriptively analyzed by computing mean, median, standard deviation and t-test

Analysis of the Data

Objective Test : To study the levels of scientific aptitude among the arts and science students in Puducherry region.

Level of Scientific Aptitude among Arts and Science Students

Variable	Low		Moderate		High	
	F	%	F	%	F	%
Scientific Aptitude	75	18.75	265	66.25	60	15

Hypothesis Test

Null Hypothesis.1: There is significant difference between arts and science students towards scientific aptitude.

The significance of the difference between the means of Arts and Science students

Course	N	Mean	SD	t - value	DF	
Arts	155	67.72	9.38	2.21	398	
Science	245	87.41	13.71			

The t value is found to be 2.21 and it is significant at 0.05 levels. Therefore the Null hypothesis is rejected and it is concluded that there is significant difference between arts and science towards scientific aptitude.

Null Hypothesis.2: There is no significant difference between Male and Female students towards scientific aptitude.

The significance of the difference between the means of Male and Female Science students

Gender	N	Mean	SD	t - value	DF	Remarks
Male	185	79.84	15.38	0.06	398	Not Significant
Female	215	79.73	15.69			

The t value is found to be 0.069 and it is not significant at 0.05 levels. Therefore the Null hypothesis is retained and it is concluded that there is significant difference between Male and Female students towards scientific aptitude.

Null Hypothesis.3: There is no significant difference between Urban and Rural students towards scientific aptitude.

The significance of the difference between the means of Urban and Rural Science students

Residence	N	Mean	SD	t - value	DF	Remarks
Urban	261	80.87	15.59	0.06	1.97	Significant
Rural	139	77.73	15.25			

The t value is found to be 1.967 and it is significant at 0.05 levels. Therefore the Null hypothesis is rejected and it is concluded that there is significant difference between the Urban and Rural students towards scientific aptitude.

NULL HYPOTHESIS.16: There is no significant difference between Government and Private college students towards scientific aptitude.

The significance of the difference between the means of Government and Private students

College	N	Mean	SD	t - value	DF	Remarks
Government	146	78.14	16.28	0.06	1.98	Significant
Private	254	80.72	15.03			

The t value is found to be 1.98 and it is significant at 0.05 levels. Therefore the Null hypothesis is rejected and it is concluded that there is significant difference between the Government and Private college students towards scientific aptitude.

Null Hypothesis.17: There is no significant difference between Tamil and English medium students towards scientific aptitude.

The significance of the difference between the means of Tamil and English medium students

College	N	Mean	SD	t - value	DF	Remarks
Tamil	117	73062	14.22	5.27	398	Significant
English	283	82.33	15.35			

The t value is found to be 5.275 and it is significant at 0.05 levels. Therefore the Null hypothesis is rejected and it is concluded that there is significant difference between the Tamil and English medium students towards scientific aptitude.

Suggestions for Further Research

A research study can be undertaken to study the scientific aptitude among the college students in Puducherry in order to suggest the suitable measures to improve their scientific aptitude.

A similar may be undertaken on a large sample covering all the colleges in Puducherry and colleges in other areas also.

The present study is limited to only arts and science students of 400 numbers. Further it has been observed that in this study only few variables are considered to make the suggestions.

Conclusion

Based upon research conduct, we conclude that the boys and girls have the same scientific aptitude. Here the sex has no play role in describing the level of aptitude.

References

- Bhaskera Rao, Digumarti ti, Editor (1961). “Scientific attitude and Scientific aptitude”, New Delhi, Discovery Publication House, ISBN 81-7141-308-O.
- BABBIE .E.R, (1973). “Survey Research Methods” Belmont, CA; Woodsworth

❐

22.

A study of Attitude of college and University Students towards Teaching Methods of their Teachers in relation their Academic Achievement

Introduction

Educational technology existed in the form of educational toys and other learning facileness. But frequent use came to light in 1926. In Ohio state university it was used in the form of a teaching machine. Then around 1930-40, landsman and Glaser tried to make education as mechanical by presenting some special types of scrambled books, cards and boards. 1950 – B.F. Skinner developed programmed learning while carrying on experiments with animals. In 1950 Brynmor, in England, used educational technological steps for the first time. It is to be cared that in 1960 as a result of industrial revolution in America and Russia. In this way, the beginning of Educational technology took place in 1950 from America and Russia and now it has reached England, Europe and India.

Teaching constitutes one of the major tasks of a teacher. Competency over this task of teaching is the essence of a successful educational system. The development of teaching competency among teachers necessitates a clear understanding of the term as well as the method for its assessment. With more than half a century of research in this area, there has been no consensus regarding the meanings of the term “teaching”, ‘Competency’ and hence ‘teaching competency’ itself. As regards the term teaching although defined in different ways (Bhattacharaya, 1974) there has been a trend in perceiving the process analytically as constituting a host of activities (Brown, 1975, Gage, 1972). This analytical approach to perceive teaching has given a basis for innovations in teacher education like microteaching (Allen & Ryan, 1969). The term competency refers to the criteria that determine teacher effectiveness. Although the reviews of research on teacher effectiveness (Ebel, 1969) point out the futility of efforts in indentifying teacher effectiveness criteria, the recent upsurge in research provides a cautious optimism (Rosen shine, 1971). It can now be stated with fairly high confidence that pupil achievement student liking may be taken as the criteria of teacher effectiveness (Flanders and Simon, 1969). But the ‘Teaching Competency’ as defined by various authors includes more than mere teacher effects or pupil outcomes. Rama (1979) defines teacher competency as the ability of a teacher manifested through a set of overt teacher class room behaviors which is a resultant of the interaction between the presage and the product variables of teaching within a social setting. This lack of consensus of the term ‘teaching competency’ highlights the difficulty of its measurement. If measurement of teaching competency has to be valid, objective and reliable one has to delimit to such variables that can be subjected to scientific study. While arrive at definition of the term it may be pointed out that teaching process is determined by knowledge, a set of abilities, attitudes and skills (presage variables) which in turn determine pupil outcomes. Thus the term ‘teaching’ can be defined as a set of observable teacher behaviours that facilitate or bring about pupil learning and ‘teaching competency’ means an effective performance of all the observable teacher behaviour that bring about desired pupil outcomes. Based on the micro-criteria approach of study ‘teaching’ (Gage, 1963), teaching is perceived as a set of teaching skills where in a teaching skill is a set of teaching behaviours that facilitate or bring about a specific instructional objective. In other words, teaching competence involves effective use of these various teaching skills.

As cited earlier, the lack of clarity and agreement about the concept of teaching competence has made its measurement difficult. The definition of ‘teaching competence’ cited above provides guidelines for objective and reliable measurement of the concept. Its measurement involves identifying all the teaching skills constituting the entire teaching task and making observations regarding the effectiveness of performance of each of those teaching skills. In the light the above observations, in the present investigation, an attempt has been madeto study of Attitude of University and college of Students towards Teaching Methods of their Teachers in relation their Academic Achievement in the Bijapur city of Karnataka state.

STATEMENT OF THE PROBLEM

A study of Attitude of college and University of Students towards Teaching Methods of their Teachers in relation their Academic Achievement

Materials

Attitude Scale of college and University of Students towards Teaching Methods of their Teachers, Answer sheet and manual.

Description of the material

The Scale consists of 51 statements with five responses from strongly agree to strongly disagree.

The items are related to 10 constructs namely health and vigour, abilities, self-confidence, self-acceptance, worthiness, present, past and future, beliefs and convictions, feelings of shame and guilt, sociability, and emotional maturity.

Procedure

The subject was seated comfortably.Attitude Scale of college and University of Students towards Teaching Methods of their Teachers was given to the subject and the following instructions were given, here are given 51 statements. Below each statement are given five responses (strongly agree, agree, undecided, disagree and strongly disagree). Please read each statement carefully and respond to it by marking a tick on any one of the five responses given in the answer sheet. If you strongly agree with the statement mark (√) on strongly agree, if you only agree with the statement mark (√) on "agree" and so on. There is no right or wrong response. Try to give your response according to what you feel about yourself in reference to that statement. Your answers will be kept confidential. There is no time limit. However, most people complete in fifteen minute.

ANALYSIS OF DATA

The means and standard deviations were completed for the selected sample. To find out the significant difference between sub-groups"-test was employed.And to find out the positive therelationship between Attitude of University and college of Students towards Teaching Methods of their teachersand academic of students and academic achievement, Karl Pearson's 'r' was employed.

Null hypothesis 1: There is no high of Attitude of University and college of Students towards Teaching Methods of their Teachersamong the college and university students.

Table-1: Mean score of Attitude of University and college of Students towards Teaching Methods of their Teachers

Group	N	Mean	SD
All UG and PG students	320	174.28	32.7

The above table reveals that the mean score of graduate and post-graduate students is very high. Hence, the students both graduate and post-graduate are havingAttitude of University and college of Students towards Teaching Methods of the Teachers.

Null hypothesis 2: There is no significant difference between the respective sub-groups in their Attitude of University and college of Students towards Teaching Methods of the Teachers.

Table 2: Significant difference between the different sub-groups in their Attitude of University and college of Students towards Teaching Methods of their Teachers.

Variable	Sub-group	n	Mean	SD	Obtained 't'-value	Level of significance
level of education	Under-graduate	120	115.14	24.2	4.43	Significant at 0.05 level
	Post-Graduate	120	203.51	33.0		
Institution	Government	100	189.65	23.12	1.74	Significant at 0.05 level
	Private	100	188.21	21.42		
gender	men	60	205.5	28.2	1.47	Not Significant at 0.05 level
	women	60	213.96	22.2		
Faculty	Arts	100	220.5	23.96	3.00	Significant at 0.05 level
	Science	100	198.5	24.9		
Faculty	Kswub-Arts	20	199.44	24	2.59	Significant at 0.05 level
	Kswub-Social Science	20	217.31	21		
Faculty	Kswub-Arts	20	199.44	24	1.16	Not Significant at 0.05 level
	Kswub-Commerce	20	204.44	39		
Faculty	Kswub-Arts	20	199.44	24	0.30	Not Significant at 0.05 level
	Kswub-Education	20	204.44	16.5		

Faculty	Kswub-Education	20	204.44	24	2.25	Significant at 0.05 level
	Kswub-Commerce	20	209.4	25.5		
Faculty	Govt.Arts	20	226.30	28.5	1.83	Not Significant at 0.05 level
	Govt. Science	20	206.44	48.5		
Faculty	Govt.Arts	20	214.91	28.5	0.14	Not Significant at 0.05 level
	Govt. Commerce	20	71.17	21.23		
Faculty	Govt. Science	20	206.44	21.4	0.67	Not Significant at 0.05 level
	Govt. Commerce	20	128.23	18.12		
Faculty	Private-Arts	20	256.9	23.8	1.12	Not Significant at 0.05 level
	Private-Science	20	206.44	21.6		
Faculty	Private-Arts	20	123.34	13.6	0.56	Not Significant at 0.05 level
	Private-Commerce	20	127.5	17.5		
Faculty	Private-Science	20	106.44	14.8	0.78	Not Significant at 0.05 level
	Private-Commerce	20	167.4	14.6		

Null hypothesis 3 : There is no relationship between Attitude of University and college of Students towards Teaching Methods of their teachersand academic of students.

Table-3 : relationship between Attitude of University and college of Students towards Teaching Methods of their teachersand academic ofstudents.

Sub-Group	Variable	N	Mean	SD	r-value 0.05	Obtained r-Value	Level of significance
All students	Attitude	320	120.87	38.1	0.139	0.683	Significant at 0.05 level
	Academic achievement		45.5	13.4			
Graduate	Attitude	120	121.5	20.00	0.196	0.363	Significant at 0.05 level
	Academic achievement		45.1	12.6			
Post Graduate	Attitude	120	120.25	16.1	0.196	0.246	Significant at 0.05 level
	Academic achievement		46.68	14.1			
Govt.	Attitude	30	122.33	20.32	0.361	0.683	Significant at 0.05 level
	Academic achievement		36.33	22.22			
Private	Attitude	15	121.66	25.61	0.514	0.640	Significant at 0.05 level
	Academic achievement		29.66	15.06			
men	Attitude	15	123.00	24.5	0.514	0.930	Significant at 0.05 level
	Academic achievement		43.00	13.3			
women	Attitude	30	116.00	15.55	0.361	0.834	Significant at 0.05 level
	Academic achievement		18.60	8.5			
ARTS	Attitude	15	114.00	17.5	0.514	0.891	Significant at 0.05 level
	Academic achievement		18.68	8.5			
SCIENCE	Attitude	15	117.00	18.68	0.514	0.697	Significant at 0.05 level
	Academic achievement		47.66	8.5			
KSWUB-ARTS	Attitude	30	114.33	22.36	0.361	0.816	Significant at 0.05 level
	Academic achievement		47.33	7.81			
KSWUB-SOCIAL SCIENCE	Attitude	15	111.66	29.59	0.514	0.689	Significant at 0.05 level
	Academic achievement	15	47.00	18.16			
KSWUB-ARTS	Attitude	15	116.33	18.57	0.514	0.802	Significant at 0.05 level
	Attitude		47.66	7.4			
KSWUB-COMMERCE	Attitude	30	133.00	20.46	0.361	0.508	Significant at 0.05 level
	Academic achievement		47.33	13.8			
GOVT.ARTS	Attitude	15	143.66	16.47	0.514	0.617	Significant at 0.05 level
	Academic achievement		49.66	10.24			

GOVT. SCIENCE	Attitude	15	123.00	9.05	0.514	0.905	Significant at 0.05 level
	Academic achievement		45.00	16.30			
GOVT. COMMERCE	Attitude	60	116.5	10.35	0.254	0.380	Significant at 0.05 level
	Academic achievement		42.66	19.02			
PRIVATE-ARTS	Attitude	30	118.83	11.04	0.361	0.603	Significant at 0.05 level
	Academic achievement		38.33	14.73			
PRIVATE-SCIENCE	Attitude	30	119.33	9.69	0.361	0.966	Significant at 0.05 level
	Academic achievement		46.05	16.00			
PRIVATE-COMMERCE	Attitude	60	123.00	17.3	0.254	0.815	Significant at 0.05 level
	Academic achievement		40.5	13.4			
kannada	Attitude	30	118.66	14.73	0.361	0.683	Significant at 0.05 level
	Academic achievement		45.00	129.3			
English	Attitude	30	127.33	19.0	0.361	0.619	Significant at 0.05 level
	Academic achievement		52.66	9.4			

The above reveals that the obtained 'r'-valuesshows that there is a significant positive relationship between Attitude of University and college of Students towards Teaching Methods of their teachersand academic achievement of students. Hence, the framed null hypothesis is rejected in favor alternative hypothesis.

Findings and Conclusion

The students of both graduate and post-graduate are expressed favorable Attitude of University and college of Students towards Teaching Methods of their teachers.

There is a significant difference between graduate and post-graduate students in theirAttitude of University and college of Students towards Teaching Methods of their teachers.

There is no significant difference between students of men and women,KSWUB Arts and Commerce,KSWUB Arts and Education,KSWUB Education and commerce,Govt.Arts and science, Govt.Arts and Commerce, Govt. commerce and science, private Arts and science, private Arts and Commerce, private commerce and science, in their Attitude of University and college of Students towards Teaching Methods of their teachers.

There is a significant difference between students, post graduates and under graduates, Government and Private college students in their Attitude of University and college of Students towards Teaching Methods of their teachers.

There is a significant positive correlation betweenAttitude of University and college of Students towards Teaching Methods of their teachersand academic achievement of all respective groups' students.

References

- Aggarwal J.C. (1975). *Education Research*, Arya Book Depot, New Delhi.
- Anderson Alwin (1966). *A comparatively study of value scores of secondary and college teachers*, Journal of educational research vol.60(2)
- Best J.W. (2004). *Research in Education*, Prentice Hall of India Pvt Ltd, New Delhi
- Baron, A R and Byrne, D Social psychology, new Delhi, prentice- Hall of India 1988.
- Brehm S.S and Kassin M.S social psychology, Boston: Houghton Mifflin co 1990.
- Friedman M and Rosenman, R.H type A behavior and your heart, NY: Knopf, 1974.

❐

23.

Moral Values and Student-Teacher Relationship of High School Students in Relation to their Achievement in Mathematics

Introduction

Values are not absolute and they change from time to time. Moral values help every individual to form character with good habits. On his being a good habit is a good and useful member of the society and on his understanding the final purpose for which he courts is doing all activities with reason dictates, in order to achieve this purpose.

Moral values refer to the genuine life principles in a person that make him a wholesome person. It focuses on values that motivate a person to pursue higher needs, the for self actualization. Teacher student relationship is a positive activity of "building a coalition among the multiple, shifting, intersecting and sometimes contradicting groups" for the all round development of the individual (**Nicholas Burbules**). **Chaplin** (1968) achievement defined as a specified level of attainment or proficiency in academic work as evaluated by the teachers or standard test or combination of both"

Need For The Study

Academic achievement is an important aim in the field of education. A student's ambition can be fulfilled only if his achievement in school is high which is the basic attainment in judging the educational capacity of an individual. It is essential to raise the standard of achievement in education. Hence it is imperative to undertake research in this area.

The students who are capable of learning well but do not perform well in mathematics need a little more individual attention. A proper study habit of the various factors which affect their performance will help the teacher to understand the students and give proper guidance. If this is not done in schools the world may have to lose huge amount human resources.

To reduce a large number of failures in mathematics at the high school level, high Student-Teacher relationship is necessary. If the pupils have good relationship with their teacher they can whine in their studies. So, here researcher made an attempt to know the importance and influence of these variables.

'Value Education' has become the latest trend in high school education. Today pupils are much worried about their behavior, attitude towards optimistic ideas. This study is conducted to analyze the students attitude towards 'moral values' students from different schools in cuddalore district were taken into consideration for their study and two different categories of schools were selected to conduct the study and they are of Government schools, Government aided schools. In these different schools inculcation of moral values differ according to the school in which they study.

Objectives of The Study

The following objectives have been set in the present study.

- To find out the level of Moral values of 9th standard students.
- To find out the level of student-teacher relationship of 9th standard students
- To find out the level of achievement in Mathematics of 9th standard students.
- To find whether there is any significant difference between the mean scores of Moral values of students studying in 9th standard with regard to
  - (a) Gender (Male/Female)
  - (b) Type of family (Joint/Nuclear)

To find whether there is any significant difference between the mean scores of personal values of students studying in 9th standard with regard to

(a) Gender

(b) Type of family

Hypotheses Of The Study

The following hypotheses have been set in the present study.

- The category of moral values of IX standard students is personal value in nature
- The level of student – teacher relationship of IX standard students is

average in nature.

- The level of achievement in mathematics of IX standard students is average in nature.
- There is no significant difference between the mean score of moral values of IX standard students with regard to Gender (Male/Female)
- Type of family (Joint/Nuclear)
- There is no significant difference between the mean scores of personal values of students studying in IX standard with regard to Gender
- Type of family

STATEMENT OF THE PROBLEM

The problem is stated as follows: **Moral values and student-teacher relationship among high school students in relation to their achievement in Mathematics**.

TOOLS USED FOR THE PRESENT STUDY

The following are the tools selected for the present study.

Moral judgement scale constructed by the **investigator**.

Student-Teacher relationship inventory by the **investigator.**

Marks scored by the students in mathematics paper in their quarterly examination held in September 2009.

LIMITATIONS OF THE STUDY

The present investigation has the following limitations.

The investigation is limited to 9th standard students only.

The study is restricted to few schools in cuddalore district.

The sample size is restricted to 297 students due to lack of time.

Student-teacher relationship with respect to teaching of mathematics alone has been considered in the present study.

SAMPLE OF THE STUDY

The present study is mainly concerned with the IX standard students studying in schools following the syllabus of Tamilnadu boards of high school education.

For the present study, the sample of 297 IX standard students studying in different management of the schools at cuddalore district during the academic year 2009-2010 were chosen, using stratified random sampling technique.

Out of the 10 schools in the sample six are government schools and four government aided schools. Among the 297 students in the samples 140 are boys and 157 are girls

The details of the sample composition with respect to the different characteristics are presented below

Table 1: Showing the criteria of classifying the sample into four categories based on their values.

Categories	No. of Students	Percentage
Personal	70	23.57
Family	62	20.88
Social	94	31.65
Spiritual	71	23.90
Total	**297**	**100.00**

From the table, it is seen that the category of moral values of IX standard students is social values in nature.

Hence hypothesis I stating that " The category of moral values of IX standard students is personal values in nature" is rejected

Student – teacher relationship

Based on the information obtained from the IX standard students regarding their student-teacher relationship, the students are divided into three groups namely low, moderate and high level of students – teacher relationship the details of which are presented below.

Table 2: Showing the criteria of classifying the sample into three groups of student – teacher relationship

Groups	Student – teacher relationship score range	No. of students	Percentage
Low	0 to 58	15	5.1
Moderate	59 to 79	57	19.2
High	80 to 100	225	75.8
Total		297	100.0

From the table, it is seen that the level of student – teacher relationship of IX standard students is high in nature.

Hence hypotheses II stating that " The level of student – teacher relationship of IX standard students is average in nature is rejected.

Achievement in mathematics

Based on the information obtained from the IX standard students regarding their achievement in mathematics, the students are divided into three groups namely low, moderate and high level of achievement in mathematics the detail of which are presented below.

Table 3: Showing the criteria of classifying the sample into three groups of achievement in mathematics

Groups	Achievement in Mathematics score range	No. of students	Percentage
Low	2 to 34	98	33.0
Moderate	35 to 67	151	50.8
High	68 to 100	48	16.2
Total		297	100.0

From the table, it is seen that the level of achievement in mathematics of IX standard student is moderate in nature

Hence hypotheses III stating that "The level of achievement in mathematics of IX standard students is average in nature" is accepted.

INFLUENCE OF GENDER ON MORAL VALUES

The scores of moral values of boys and girls have been analyzed as shown below

Table 4: Showing the significant difference between the mean scores of moral values of boys and girls

Group comparison	N	Mean	SD	SE	't' Value	Level of significance
Boys	140	181.242357	12.713	1.074	2.92	0.01
Girls	157	185.161592	10.1546	0.810		

From the above, table it is clear that girls are significantly higher than their counterparts with regard to moral values.

Hence the hypothesis IV(a) stating that " There is no significant difference between the mean scores of moral values of IX standard students with regard to gender" is rejected.

INFLUENCE OF TYPE OF FAMILY ON MORAL VALUES

The scores of moral values of students hailing from joint/nuclear families have been analyzed and the obtained results is presented below

Table 5: Showing the significant difference between the mean scores of moral values of students hailing from joint and nuclear families

Group comparison	N	Mean	SD	SE	't' Value	Level of significance
Joint	233	183.6009	11.3218	0.741	0.78	NS
Nuclear	64	182.2500	12.505	1.563		

The above table reveals that students from joint family do not differ much from that of nuclear ones in the case of moral values

Hence the hypothesis IV(b) stating that " There is no significant difference between the mean scores of moral values of IX standard students with regard to the type of family of the students" is accepted.

MAJOR FINDINGS

A careful analysis of the data had resulted in the following findings:

The category of moral values of IXth standard students is social values in nature.

The level of Student-Teacher relationship of IXth standard students is high in nature

The level of achievement in Mathematics of IXth standard students is moderate in nature

Girls are significantly higher than their counter parts with regard to moral values.

Students from Joint family do not differ much from that of Nuclear ones in the case of moral values.

EDUCATIONAL IMPLICATIONS

Education plays a vital role in understanding the importance of moral values in life. Proper education attempts to balance the frustration level and gradually inculcate the moral values in the life of an individual

The aim of education is to develop broadmindedness and universal outlook in the individuals with right wisdom. The Educational system must impart values in students such as tolerance, patience, understanding, truthfulness, gratitude, faith in God, self respect and also in the light of perspective, education should raise humanity and values such as brother hood, mercy, love etc.

If a student becomes a good social citizen, it means he is morally well sound. Absence of this education results in disorder, distraction, exploitation, selfishness, aggression, hatred and frustration in the world. The objective of education should be for shaping and bringing out useful and self-dependent citizens with all good qualities.

CONCLUSION

The purpose of the present investigation is to investigate the relationships among the variables of moral values, student-teacher relationship and achievement in mathematics. The investigation is sure to find some usefulness in the field of education and findings of the investigation can serve as a database for further research.

BIBLIOGRAPHY

- Burbules and Rice (1991), Difference, Authority and the Teacher Student Relationship by Clive Bieck, P.2
- Clive Bieck, "Difference, Authority and the Teacher Student Relationship",

Ontario Institute for studies in Education, P.1

- Daniel, J.K and SelvamonyNirmal, "Value Education Today: Explorations in Social Ethics", All India Association for Christian Higher Education, New Delhi, 1990
- Downie,R.S, "Roles and Values: An Introduction to Social Ethics", Methuen and Co, Ltd, London, 1971
- Ignacimuth,S, "Values for Life", Better Yourself Books, Bombay, 1994
- Kalra,M.Rajinder, "Value – Oriented Education in Schools: Theory and practices, "Shirpa Publications, Delhi, 2003

❐

24.

Technology Skill and Cognitive Skill of Teachers at High School Level

Introduction

Technological advancement has contributed greatly to the acceleration of human progress in the past several centuries. The information and communication technology has been a tremendous force for human development by providing information rich environment and raising standards of living. Technology globalizes communication. Globalization and its new rules are also shaping the path for new technologies. The demand for more open and accessible learning has started increasing since the early 1950s. Many factors are contributing to this changing educational culture. The most important of which are economic, social and technological forces. Education and training are not limited to only the fortunate few now. It has spread far and wide. It has reached all levels of society due to technological advancements.

Cognitive skill

Cognitive functioning is a term referring to a human's ability to process to that should not deplete on a large scale in healthy individuals. Cognition mainly refers to things like memory, the ability to learn new information, speech, and understanding of written material. The brain is usually capable of learning new skills in the aforementioned areas, typically in early childhood, and of developing personal thoughts and beliefs about the world.

Statement of the Problem

The investigator has selected the present study with the aim of knowing the technological skill and cognitive skill of teachers at high school level. Therefore it has been entitled as "Technology Skill and Cognitive Skill of Teachers at High School Level".

Definition of the Terms

Technology Skill: It refers to technological proficiency of teachers in handling hardware and software of educational technology.

Cognitive Skill: It refers to things like memory, the ability to learn new information, speech, and understanding of written material.

High School Level

The 9th and 10th STD level in 10+2+3 system of education.

Objectives

To find out the level of technology skill of teachers at high school level.

To find out the difference in technology skill among teacher in terms of sex.

To find out the difference in technology skill among teacher in terms of experience.

To find out the relationship between technology skill and cognitive skill of teachers at high school level.

Hypotheses

The level of technology skill of high school teachers is average.

There is no significant difference in technology skill among teachers at high school level in terms of sex.

There is no significant difference in technology skill among teachers at high school level in terms of experience.

There is no relationship between technology skill and cognitive skill among teachers at high school level.

Methodology

Construction of tool is an essential part in any research work. A valid tool will give the needed findings more specifically. Hence, designing a tool is very important. The researcher has collected 38 items on awareness and knowledge on educational technology was prepared by the investigator. The investigator based on his experience and after a thorough review of literature on technology skill prepared the questionnaire. There were 30 items on cognitive skills developed and validated by the investigator. The investigator had discussion personally with the teacher educators and the persons knowledgeable in the field of educational technology.

Establishment of reliability and validity of the tool

The questionnaires were administered among the 50 high school teachers and re-administered among the same 50 high school teachers after a gap of 15 days. The correlation found between the two tests was 0.86. It is a high level of correlation. Thus the reliability was ensured. The investigator has consulted experts for the preliminary form of the questionnaire on Technology skill and cognitive skill of Teachers. The consultation had with subject experts ensures face and content validity of the tool. According to Garret, H.E (1967, P.365) the index of reliability is sometimes taken as a measure of validity. The test is found to be having reliability, hence it may be considered as having validity.

Scoring

For the purpose of scoring, the response given by the high school teachers were calculated. The correct response was given 1 mark. Thus the maximum score in the questionnaire on educational technology would be 38 and the maximum score in the cognitive skill would be 30.

Sample Design

The investigator has followed simple random sampling method for the present study. The investigator has collected a sample of 303 high school teachers in Madurai district for the present study.

Analysis and Interpretation of Data

The investigator has tested the hypothesis one by one.

Hypothesis1: The level of technology skill of high school teachers is average.

Score	Technology skill of high school teachers	No. Of students	**Percentage**
81-100	V.Good	0	0
61-80	Good	2	0.66
41-60	Average	65	21.45
21-40	Poor	186	61.38
0-20	V.Poor	50	16.5
	Total	303	100

It is evident from the table 1 that 61.38 % of high school teachers are having poor technology skill. 21.45 % of teachers are having average level of technology skill. 16.5% of teachers are having very poor technology skill. 0.66% of teachers are having good technology skill. However, there is no one in the sample selected have Very good level of technology skill. Hence the hypothesis stated is rejected.

Hypothesis 2: There is no significant difference in technology skill among teachers at high school level in terms of sex.

Table 2. Mean, S.D and 't' value for the significant difference in technology skill among high school teachers in terms of sex.

Gender	N	Mean	S.D.	't'	Critical value	Level of significance
Male	84	12.09	4.83	0.062	1.986 for df of 301 at 0.05 level	N.S.
Female	219	13.23	4.39			

It is evident from table 2 that the obtained 't' value is 0.062. It is lesser than the critical value of 1.986 for degrees of freedom at 0.05 level. It is not significant. Hence the hypothesis stated is rejected. It can be concluded from the above finding that there is no significant difference in technology skill among high school teachers in terms of sex.

Hypothesis 3: There is no significant difference in technology skill among teachers at high school level in terms of experience.

Table 3. Mean, S.D and 't' value for the significant difference in technology skill among high school teachers in terms of experience.

Teaching Experience	N	Mean	S.D.	't'	Critical value	Level of significance
Below 5 years	31	11.19	5.24	0.079	1.986 for df of 232 at 0.05 level	N.S.
5 years to 10 years	203	12.98	4.37			
Below 5 years	31	11.19	5.24	0.038	1.986 for df of 98 at 0.05 level	N.S.
10 years and above	69	13.50	4.54			
5 years to 10 years	203	12.98	4.37	0.403	1.986 for df of 270 at 0.05 level	N.S.
10 years and above	69	13.5	4.54			

It is evident from table 3 that the obtained 't' value is 0.079. It is lesser than the critical value of 1.986 for degrees of freedom at 0.05 level. It is not significant. Hence the hypothesis stated is rejected. It is evident from table 3 that the obtained 't' value is 0.038. It is lesser than the critical value of 1.986 for degrees of freedom at 0.05 level. It is not significant. Hence the hypothesis stated is rejected. It is evident from table 3 that the obtained 't' value is 0.403. It is lesser than the critical value of 1.986 for degrees of freedom at 0.05 level. It is not significant. Hence the hypothesis stated is rejected. It is concluded from the above finding that there is no significant difference in technology skill among high school teachers in terms of experience.

Hypothesis 4: There is no correlation between technology skill and cognitive skill among teachers at high school level.

Table 4. Correlation between technology skill and cogntive skill among teachers at high school level

S.No.	Variable	N	Df	"r"	Significance level 0.05
1	Technology Skill Cognitive Skill	303	301	0.17951	.088

It is evident from Table 4 that 'r' value is 0.179. It exceeds the critical value of .088 at 0.05 levels. Hence it can be interpreted that there exists significant positive correlation between technology skill and cognitive skill among teachers at high school level. It can be surmised that the technology skill and cognitive skill are positively correlated. Hence the hypothesis stated as there is no correlation between technology skill and cognitive skill is rejected.

Findings of the Study

61.38 % of high school teachers are having poor technology skill. 21.45 % of teachers are having average level of technology skill. 16.5% of teachers are having very poor technology skill. 0.66% of teachers are having good technology skill. However, there is no one in the sample selected have Very good level of technology skill.

There is no significant difference in technology skill among high school teachers in terms of sex.

There is no significant difference in technology skill among high school teachers in terms of experience.

There is a positive correlation between technology skill and cognitive skill among teachers at high school level.

Reference

- Arul Sekar, J.M and Thiyagu.K (2007). 'Information and Communication Technology', Prophet publishers, Trichi.
- Alexis Leon and Mathews Leon (1999). "The Fundamentals of Information Technology, Leon Vikas publications, New Delhi.
- Bimal ghosh (1979). "Profiles of social change", oxford publication, New Delhi.

❒

25.

Effectiveness of Computer Based Multimedia Learning

INTRODUCTION

Multimedia refers to any computer-mediated software or interactive application that integrates text, color, graphical images, animation, audio sound, and full motion video in a single application. Multimedia learning systems consist of animation and narration, which offer a potential venue for improving student understanding. Multimedia programme is an integral part of the educational technology. As a technique, it offers a high potential in application at different stages of education for the purpose of enhancing the teaching and learning processes, as is evident from the experience of developed countries.

The integration of multimedia technology into the communication environment has the potential to transform the students from passive recipients of information to active participants in a media-rich learning process. The introduction of multimedia or any other computer-based information technology is not intended to substitute a presenter. This new technology is intended to provide the presenter with a powerful tool that can greatly enhance communication by delivering a multisensory experience. With interactive multimedia technology, a teacher can communicate with the students by means of a presentation that becomes more than message-it becomes an active, exciting experience in a multisensory environment to create a multisensory experience. Multimedia reaches users in many different ways, enabling them to retain more knowledge and increase their understanding.

There are 4 steps in learning like attention, rehearsal, encoding and retrieval. A well designed multimedia application demands the simultaneous attention of several senses through dual encoding or the process of appealing to more than one sense simultaneously. Dual encoding facilitates and enhances the rehearsal process. Multimedia helps retrieval by associating sound, text and images with the concept being presented. Using text, images, animation and sound simultaneously greatly improves the students' retention of the knowledge and directs the students' attention to classroom (Louis, 2001).

Multimedia consists of the combination of video and movie clips and sound, text and graphic files all controlled by a piece of software and a computer which is equipped with a sound card, a video card, a CD-ROM drive and speakers or headphone. Sometimes, there is also a videodisk player, which is controlled by the software.

Computer based multimedia delivers information in a variety of ways but achieves its greatest effectiveness through interaction. In the first case, music and informative knowledge combine to convey the message. In the second case, technology provides a more effective presentation wherein information, images and sounds are technically and aesthetically integrated, focusing on a single specific purpose. The ability of students to work independently and to receive instruction suited to their needs and learning styles is inherently attractive.

REVIEW OF LITERATURE

Dalacosta et al. (2009) developed and studied the effectiveness of Multimedia **application with animated cartoons in teaching science in elementary education.** The results of the study provide evidence that the use of animated cartoons significantly increases the young students' knowledge and understanding of specific science concepts, which are normally difficult to comprehend and often cause misconceptions to them.

Jian Hu et al. (2009) investigated the effects of introducing a software program, named the Dental 3D Multimedia System (D3DM), into the education of a group of junior dental students in their preclinical practice. One group received their training program in the traditional way, unassisted by 3D technology. The second group received their training program in the traditional manner, but also used the D3DM to supplement their education. The results showed that the D3DM-assisted group achieved higher scores and also indicated that the usage of 3D multimedia PC software had a positive impact on several aspects of subjects' performance.

Kanmani and Radha (2009) studied the Effectiveness of CAI package in basic electronics teaching. There was a significant difference between the control and the experimental group students in attainment of knowledge level, understanding level, and application level objective in the gain scores. Hence, the experimental group students were better than the control group students in attainment of knowledge level, understanding level, and application level objective in the gain scores. It was inferred from the finding that the experimental treatment is effective to the students.

Korakakis et al. (2009) made a study on the **"3D visualization types in multimedia applications for science learning for 8th grade students in Greece".** The aim of the study was to determine whether the use of specific types of visualization (3D illustration, 3D animation, and interactive 3D animation) combined with narration and text, contributes to the learning process in science courses. The results indicated that multimedia applications with interactive 3D animations as well as with 3D animations do in fact increase the interest of students and make the material more appealing to them.

She, Hsiao-Ching and Chen, Yi-Zen (2009) examined how middle school students constructed their understanding of the mitosis and meiosis processes at a molecular level through multimedia learning materials presented in different interaction and sensory modality modes. The dependent variables included subjects' pre-test, post-test, and retention-test scores, showing their understanding of mitosis and meiosis process at molecular level. The results of the study showed that the group which used multimedia learning material has a greater amount of visual attention and consistent with their long term retained learning than the group which did not use the same. This study adds empirical evidence of a direct correlation between the length of eye fixation behavior and the depth of learning. Moreover, it provides insight into the multimedia effect on students' cognitive process through the use of eye fixation behavior evidence.

Anboucarassy (2010) studied the effectiveness of Multimedia in Teaching Biological Science to IX Standard students. The results of the study revealed that experiment group performed better than the control group due to the exposure of multimedia based learning. Thus multimedia helps the students to sustain their interest and also their retention power compared to the traditional method of teaching. The constant use of multimedia will make students understand more and achieve more in their academic achievement. Hence it was concluded that the multimedia approach is considered to be one of the best techniques for biology teaching at IX standard level.

Ponraj and Sivakumar (2010) studied the effectiveness of Computer-Assisted Instruction in Teaching Zoology in Relation to Learners' Personality. The major findings of the study indicated that achievement scores of experimental group students were higher than the control group students after the treatment.

Yusuf, Mudasiru and Afolabi, Adedeji (2010) investigated the effects of computer assisted instruction (CAI) on secondary school students' performance in biology. The findings of the study showed that the performance of students exposed to CAI either individually or cooperatively were better than their counterparts exposed to the conventional classroom instruction. Based on the research findings recommendations were made on the need to develop relevant CAI packages for teaching biology in Nigerian secondary schools.

OBJECTIVES

- To measure behaviour and performance of high school student.
- To assess effectiveness in performance of high school student
- To assess effective in behaviuoral outcome of the high school student.
- To assess effectiveness in traditional and multimedia method of teaching.
- To find out relevant effectiveness of computer based multimedia learning material on performance and behaviour outcome.

HYPOTHESIS OF THE STUDY

High school students do not differ in their average level of relevant effectiveness of computer based on multimedia learning material on performance and behaviour outcome in traditional method and multimedia teaching of entire samples.

Respondents do not differ in their relevant effectiveness of computer based multimedia learning material on performance and behaviour outcome in pre test on the basis of groups.

Respondents do not differ in their relevant effectiveness of computer based multimedia learning material on performance and behaviour outcome in pre test on the basis of type of school.

Respondents do not differ in their relevant effectiveness of computer based multimedia learning material on performance and behaviour outcome in pre test on the basis of parents education.

Respondents do not differ in their relevant effectiveness of computer based multimedia learning material on performance and behaviour outcome in pre test on the basis of parents income.

Respondents do not differ in their relevant effectiveness of computer based multimedia learning material on performance and behaviour outcome in post test on the basis of type of school.

Respondents do not differ in their relevant effectiveness of computer based multimedia learning material on performance and behaviour outcome in post test on the basis of parents education.

Respondents do not differ in their relevant effectiveness of computer based multimedia learning material on performance and behaviour outcome in post test on the basis of parents income.

METHODOLOGY

The methodology adopted for the study is explained in detail. The sampling technique, size of the sample, variables of the study, description of the tool used and administration of tool are elaborated.

SAMPLING TECHNIQUE

The random sampling techniques used in the present study. The survey should cover all the aspects of the subject selected of the study others are inferred from a study of a sample group carefully selected to be representative of the total population. At time, the survey describes a limited population which is the only group under consideration. It involves a clearly defined problem and defined objectives. It requires expert and imaginative planning. Careful analysis and interpretation of the data gathered and logical and skillful reporting of the findings. There are different findings such as social surveys, market surveys. The survey method is applied to the analysis of existing social conditions including educational conditions and to the analysis of public opinion. So in this present study, the investigator has used stratified disposition random sampling method.

Sample : Samples of 100 high school students selected randomly were studied in Tindivanam Town. Out of these high schools as many as 5 higher secondary schools have been chosen by appropriate method. All the available high school students studying in each of this selected high school were chosen as sample. Stratified disposition random sampling technique has been used in the selection of the sample.

Data Collection

Primary data, required for the present research work were collected by conducting direct interviews using questionnaire. All the respondents were given sufficient information about the study. These respondents were provided with the same questionnaires. They were also informed that they have to answer in the same fashion.

Tools used for the study

Development of effectiveness of multimedia programme and Scale by the investigator. The scale for measuring the high school student's effectiveness of multimedia towards science in the study. This scale has as many as 25 statements of which 3 point scale method.

ANALYSIS AND INTERPRETATION

Table 1: Showing the Mean, Standard deviation of relevant effectiveness of computer based multimedia learning material on performance and behaviour outcome in pre and post test of entire samples

Groups	N	Mean	SD	r value
Pre test	100	14.79	2.69	0.346**
Post test	100	19.30	2.86	

Hypothesis: High school students do not differ in their average level of relevant effectiveness of computer based on multimedia learning material on performance and behaviour outcome in traditional method and multimedia teaching of entire samples.

The mean and standard deviation of relevant effectiveness of computer based multimedia learning material on performance and behaviour outcome scores of entire samples are 14.79 and 2.69 in pre test and 19.30 and 2.86 in post test. The mean score of all categories are lay in between (M ± 1σ) value. So it is concluded that average level of relevant effectiveness of computer based multimedia learning material on performance and behaviour outcome of entire samples.

Table 2: Showing the Mean, Standard deviation and t-test for relevant effectiveness of computer based multimedia learning material on performance and behaviour outcome on the basis of groups

Groups	Sample size	Mean	Standard Deviation	t-value	Level of Significance
Pre test	100	14.79	2.69	12.86	0.01 (Significant)
Post test	100	19.30	2.86		

Hypothesis: Respondents do not differ in their relevant effectiveness of computer based multimedia learning material on performance and behaviour outcome in pre test on the basis of groups.

The calculated t-value (12.86), which is significant at 0.01 level, confirms that there is a significant difference between relevant effectiveness of computer based multimedia learning material on performance and behaviour outcome on the basis of groups. So the null hypothesis is rejected and alternate hypothesis is accepted. Therefore it is concluded that pre test and post test groups differ in their effectiveness of computer based multimedia learning material on performance and behaviour outcome.

Table 3: Showing mean, standard deviation and t-value for traditional method among the high school student on the basis of type of school

Sl. No	Type of school	Sample size	Mean	Standard Deviation	t-value	Level of Significance
1	Government	75	14.73	2.71	0.37	0.716 (Not Significant)
2	Aided	25	14.96	2.67		

Hypothesis: Respondents do not differ in their relevant effectiveness of computer based multimedia learning material on performance and behaviour outcome in pre test on the basis of type of school.

The calculated t-value (0.37), which is not significant, confirms that there is a no significant difference between relevant effectiveness of computer based multimedia learning material on performance and behaviour outcome in pre test on the basis of type of school. So the null hypothesis is accepted and alternate hypothesis is rejected. Therefore it is concluded that government and aided school groups do not differ in their pre test score.

Table 4: Showing mean, standard deviation and t-value for traditional method among the high school student on the basis of parents education

Sl No	Parents education	Sample size	Mean	Standard Deviation	F-value	Level of Significance
1	School	86	14.82	2.75	0.58	0.560 (Not Significant)
2	Under graduate	8	14.13	2.03		
3	Post graduate	6	14.21	2.44		
	Total	100	14.79	2.69		

Hypothesis: Respondents do not differ in their relevant effectiveness of computer based multimedia learning material on performance and behaviour outcome in pre test on the basis of parents education.

The calculated F-value (0.58), which is not significant, confirms that there is a no significant difference between relevant effectiveness of computer based multimedia learning material on performance and behaviour outcome in pre test on the basis of parents education. So the null hypothesis is accepted and alternate hypothesis is rejected. Therefore it is concluded that different parents education students groups do not differ in their pre test score.

Table 5: Showing mean, standard deviation and t-value for traditional method among the high school student on the basis of parents income

Sl. No	Parents income	Sample size	Mean	Standard Deviation	F-value	Level of Significance
1	Below Rs.50,000	70	14.51	2.53	1.56	0.215 (Not Significant)
2	Rs.50,000 – 2,00,000	24	15.50	3.09		
3	Above Rs.2,00,000	6	16.00	2.65		
	Total	100	14.79	2.69		

Hypothesis: Respondents do not differ in their relevant effectiveness of computer based multimedia learning material on performance and behaviour outcome in pre test on the basis of parents income.

The calculated F-value (1.56), which is not significant, confirms that there is a no significant difference between relevant effectiveness of computer based multimedia learning material on performance and behaviour outcome in pre test on the basis of parents income. So the null hypothesis is accepted and alternate hypothesis is rejected. Therefore it is concluded that different parents income students groups do not differ in their pre test score.

Table 6: Showing mean, standard deviation and t-value for multimedia method among the high school student on the basis of type of school

Sl. No	Type of school	Sample size	Mean	Standard Deviation	t-value	Level of Significance
1	Government	75	18.75	2.91	4.33	0.01 (Significant)
2	Aided	25	20.96	1.93		

Hypothesis: Respondents do not differ in their relevant effectiveness of computer based multimedia learning material on performance and behaviour outcome in post test on the basis of type of school.

The calculated t-value (4.33), which is significant at 0.01 level, confirms that there is a significant difference between relevant effectiveness of computer based multimedia learning material on performance and behaviour outcome in post test on the basis of type of school. So the null hypothesis is rejected and alternate hypothesis is accepted. Therefore it is concluded that aided school students (20.96) scored higher mean value than government school students (18.75).

Table 7: Showing mean, standard deviation and t-value for multimedia method among the high school student on the basis of parents education

Sl. No	Parents education	Sample size	Mean	Standard Deviation	F-value	Level of Significance
1	School	86	19.34	2.87	3.19	0.01 (Significant)
2	Under graduate	8	16.75	3.01		
3	Post graduate	6	20.12	2.63		
	Total	100	19.30	2.86		

Hypothesis: Respondents do not differ in their relevant effectiveness of computer based multimedia learning material on performance and behaviour outcome in post test on the basis of parents education.

The calculated F-value (3.19), which is significant at 0.01 level, confirms that there is a significant difference between relevant effectiveness of computer based multimedia learning material on performance and behaviour outcome in post test on the basis of parents education. So the null hypothesis is rejected and alternate hypothesis is accepted. Therefore it is concluded that different parents education students groups differ in their post test score.

Table 8: Showing mean, standard deviation and t-value for multimedia method among the high school student on the basis of parents income

Sl. No	Parents income	Sample size	Mean	Standard Deviation	F-value	Level of Significance
1	Below Rs.50,000	70	19.11	2.64	3.29	0.01 (Significant)
2	Rs.50,000 – 2,00,000	24	20.04	3.24		
3	Above Rs.2,00,000	6	16.00	4.58		
	Total	100	19.30	2.86		

Hypothesis: Respondents do not differ in their relevant effectiveness of computer based multimedia learning material on performance and behaviour outcome in post test on the basis of parents income.

The calculated F-value (3.29), which is significant at 0.01 level, confirms that there is a significant difference between relevant effectiveness of computer based multimedia learning material on performance and behaviour outcome in post test on the basis of parents income. So the null hypothesis is rejected and alternate hypothesis is accepted. Therefore it is concluded that different parents income students groups differ in their post test score.

Findings

- High school students differ in their average level of relevant effectiveness of computer based on multimedia learning material on performance and behaviour outcome in traditional method and multimedia teaching of entire samples.
- Respondents differ in their relevant effectiveness of computer based multimedia learning material on performance and behaviour outcome in pre test on the basis of groups.
- Respondents do not differ in their relevant effectiveness of computer based multimedia learning material on performance and behaviour outcome in pre test on the basis of type of school.
- Respondents do not differ in their relevant effectiveness of computer based multimedia learning material on performance and behaviour outcome in pre test on the basis of parents education.
- Respondents do not differ in their relevant effectiveness of computer based multimedia learning material on performance and behaviour outcome in pre test on the basis of parents income.
- Respondents differ in their relevant effectiveness of computer based multimedia learning material on performance and behaviour outcome in post test on the basis of type of school.
- Respondents differ in their relevant effectiveness of computer based multimedia learning material on performance and behaviour outcome in post test on the basis of parents education.

- Respondents differ in their relevant effectiveness of computer based multimedia learning material on performance and behaviour outcome in post test on the basis of parents income.

CONCLUSION

In the present study, the researcher arrive the following conclusion based on the findings. In the present study, science students have relevant effectiveness of computer based multimedia learning material on performance and behaviour outcome of high school students in Tindivanam Town when compared with other students. The researcher framed objectives and hypotheses on the basis of the above context. 100 samples were selected randomly. A standard questionnaire was used to collect the relevant data. After collecting the data they were analyzed using statistical tools such as t-test and ANOVA in the both groups (pre and post test). The result concluded that the all the science students of average level of relevant effectiveness of computer based multimedia learning material on performance and behaviour outcome.

REFERENCES

- Anboucarassy, B. (2010). Effectiveness of Multimedia in Teaching Biological Science to IX Standard students. *EDUTRACKS, 9(5): 37-38.*
- Annaraja, P., & Jenitha Rani, J. R. (2003). Development of Visual Basic based CAI package in Commerce and its effectiveness on Achievement in Commerce. *Research and Reflections on Education.*
- Balasubramanian, N., & Jayaraman (2001). Relative Effectiveness among Different Modes of Computer Based Instruction. *Experiments in Education, 29(2): 9-13.*
- Chang, Chun-Yen (2002). The impact of different forms of multimedia CAI on students' science achievement. *Innovations in Education and Teaching International, 39 (4): 280-88.* Retrieved March 20, 2010
- Dawson, M. E., Skinner, S., & Zeitlin, A. (2003). Rules of Engagement: Proceed with Caution when Integrating Multimedia learning Tools into Existing Course Formats. *Electronic Journal of Science Education, 7(4).* Retrieved March 21, 2010
- Garnett, P., Hackling, M., & Oliver, R. (1997). An Interactive Multimedia Package Designed to Improve Beginning Students' Understanding of Chemical Equations. *UniServe Science News, Vol. 8, pp. 18-21.* Retrieved March 21, 2010
- Kadhiravan, S., & Suresh, V. (2001). Effect of Computer-assisted Instruction on Self-regulated Learning. *Perspective in Education, 18(3): 161-169.*
- Kanmani, M., & Radha, M. (2009). "Effectiveness of CAI package in basic electronics teaching", *Journal of All India Association for Educational*

Research, 21(1): 47-50.

- Korakakis, G., Pavlatou, E.A., Palyvos, J. A., & Spyrellis N. (2009). **3D visualization types in multimedia applications for science learning: A case study for 8th grade students in Greece.** *Computers & Education, 52(2): 390-401.* Retrieved March 21, 2010
- Liao, Yuen-kuang & Chen, Yu-wen (2007). The Effect of Computer Simulation Instruction on Student Learning: A Meta-analysis of Studies in Taiwan. *Journal of Information Technology and Applications, 2(2): 69-79.* Retrieved March 21, 2010
- O'Day, Danton H. (2007). The value of Animations in Biology Teaching: A Study of Long – Term Memory Retention. *Journal of CBE - Life Science Education, 6(3): 217-223.* Retrieved March 20, 2010
- O'Day, Danton H. (2007). The value of Animations in Biology Teaching: A Study of Long – Term Memory Retention. *Journal of CBE - Life Science Education, 6(3): 217-223.* Retrieved March 20, 2010
- Ponraj, P., & Sivakumar, R. (2010). Computer-Assisted Instruction in Zoology in Relation to Learners' Personality. *EDUTRACKS, 9(6): 34-37.*
- Pryor, Caroline R., & Bitter, Gary G. (2008). Using multimedia to teach in-service teachers: Impacts on learning, application, and retention. *Computers in Human Behavior, 24 (6): 2668-2681.* Retrieved March 20, 2010
- **Rotbain, Y., Marbach-Ad, G., & Stavy, R. (2008). Using a computer animation to teach high school molecular biology.** *Journal of Science Education and Technology*, **17(1): 49 – 58.** Retrieved March 21, 2010
- Segers, E., & Verhoeven, L. (2002). Multimedia support of early literacy learning. *Computers and Education, 39(3): 207-221.* Retrieved March 20, 2010
- She, Hsiao-Ching & Chen, Yi-Zen (2009). The impact of multimedia effect on science learning: Evidence from eye movements. *Computers & Education, 53(4): 1297-1307.* Retrieved March 20, 2010
- Thilaka Suresh (2000). Instructional strategy change on the achievement in biotechnology and attitude towards science among higher secondary school students. *Journal of All India Association for Educational Research, 12(3 & 7): 14-19.*
- Venkataraman, S. (2008). Relative effectiveness among selected modes of CAI in physics in relation to learner's personality. *Unpublished Doctoral Dissertation, Annamalai University. Chidambaram.*
- Vernadakis, N., Zetou, E., Tsitskari, E., Giannousi, M., & Kioumourtzoglou, E. (2008). Student attitude and learning outcomes of multimedia computer-assisted versus traditional instruction in basketball. *Education and Information Technologies, 13(3): 167-183.*
- Victor, Adeosun Olufemi (2008). Relative effects of three Multi-Media

Instructional Packages on Nigerian student's achievement in Social Studies. *Pakistan Journal of Social Sciences, 5 (5): 415 – 420.* Retrieved March 20, 2010

- Yusuf, Mudasiru O., & Afolabi, Adedeji O. (2010). Effects of Computer AssistedIinstruction (CAI) on Secondary School students' performance in biology. *TOJET: The Turkish Online Journal of Educational Technology, 9(1): 62-69.* Retrieved March 21, 2010.

❒

26.

Hyper Diversed Teacher and Digital Skills

INTRODUCTION

Social media have risen to prominence in recent years, beginning first with sites like Classmates in the mid-1990s, followed by Friendsterin 2003. The most significant growth of social media has occurred since 2004 when Facebook.com was introduced. Today there are over 550 million Facebook users alone, along with millions more using sites such as Twitter, MySpace, Plaxo, LinkedIn and others. While early adopters of these sites were digital natives (i.e., those born and/or raised in the internet era), all age groups are now embracing these sites. Teacher Educators and Student teachers always find it easier to use the already made teaching aids for teaching practice for preparation of lessons and in their theory learning and submission of assignments. In such situation the modern technology i.e. internet is challenging them to be more innovative, explorative and modern in their teaching and learning experiences. Teaching faculty is challenged by the digital world to be in pursuit of skills development. At present there is a gap between campus pedagogy and social media usage among students and faculty. Teaching community need to be skilled digitally. This paper works to examine that chasm, and to draw some conclusions as to why it may be time to incorporate this technology into our classrooms. The researcher used the self constructed tool HYPER ADOPTION SCALE (HAS) to achieve this motive. The samples were 100 teacher educators and 200 student teachers. In methodology the statistical used were MEAN, Standard Deviation and 't' test. The findings show that the level of hyper diversification among the samples is high, and there is no significant difference among the samples based on the variables Locality, Residence, Status(teacher educators/student teachers) and Educational qualification(UG/PG). However there exists a significant difference in term of Browsing habit. The educational implications suggest ways to diversify the teaching community and empower them digitally.

Social media have risen to prominence in recent years, beginning first with sites like Classmates in the mid-1990s, followed by Friendsterin 2003. The most significant growth of social media has occurred since 2004 when Facebook.com was introduced. Today there are over 550 million Facebook users alone, along with millions more using sites such as Twitter, MySpace, Plaxo, LinkedIn and others. While early adopters of these sites were digital natives (i.e., those born and/or raised in the internet era), all age groups are now embracing these sites. At present there is a gap between campus pedagogy and social media usage among students and faculty. Teaching community need to be skilled digitally. This paper works to examine that chasm, and to draw some conclusions as to why it may be time to incorporate this technology into our classrooms.

NEED FOR THE STUDY

Social media sites such as Face book and Twitter have come to dominate internet usage in recent years. Face book alone has over 550 million users as of fall 2010, while Twitter claims over 100 million users. While academia was fairly quick to adopt online education models in the 1990s, it has thus far not yet embraced social media portals as a way to deliver course content and engage students. This may be due to uncertainties regarding student perceptions about social media, its purposes, and its applications. Teacher Educators and Student teachers always find it easier to use the already made teaching aids for teaching practice for preparation of lessons and in their theory learning and submission of assignments. In such situation the modern technology i.e. internet is challenging them to be more innovative, explorative and modern in their teaching and learning experiences. Teaching faculty is challenged by the digital world to be in pursuit of skills development. Hence the need for the study.

BACKGROUND OF THE STUDY

The researcher is involved in the educational institution which is in the forefront to promote quality of pedagogy. The experience of the researcher has often been frustrating with lack of digital climate .Since the Tamil nadu Teachers Education University has created a platform for such pondering this study found its way out to reach out to the professional mob to leverage the educational system through virtualization of the academia. The HD (Hyper Diversified) Classroom is the need of the hour. Just as the digital divide vanished over time (males once dominated all computer and internet usage), it is possible that similar usage divides will also disappear. Online college courses, for example, have broad-based appeal, and even traditional campus-based courses often have high computer usage expectations. Given that social media are now part of the cultural fabric, it is necessary to explore if and how social media might find their place in academia. Therefore the researcher undertook this study.

SAMPLE FOR THE STUDY

300 Samples Comprising Teacher Educators and Student Teachers (100 teacher Educators and 200 Student Teachers)

OBJECTIVES OF THE STUDY

- To construct a tool to find out the level of hyper diversification among teacher educators and student teachers
- To realize the importance of hyper diversification and developing digital skills among teacher educators and student teachers.
- To find out whether any difference exists among teacher educators and student teachers in their hyper diversification and digital skills in terms of the following variables:
    - Locality
    - Residence
    - Status(teacher/student)
    - Educational qualification(UG/PG)
    - Browsing habit

HYPOTHESES OF THE STUDY

The level of hyper diversification among teacher educators and student teachers is high.

There is a significant difference among teacher educators and student teachers in their hyper diversification and digital skills in terms of the following variables:

- Locality
- Residence
- Status(teacher/student)
- Educational qualification(UG/PG)
- Browsing habit

METHODOLOGY

In order to carry out the study the researcher used the following statistical

Techniques

MEAN, STANDARD DEVIATION and 't' test

Mean

Mean was calculated by the formula

Where X = Score, N = Total Number of the scores.

Standard Deviation: Standard deviation was calculated by the following formula

$$t = \frac{M_1 - M_2}{\sqrt{\frac{\acute{o}_1^2}{N_1} + \frac{\acute{o}_2^2}{N_2}}}$$

Where = Mean

X = Individual score

N = Total Number of the scores

Test of significant difference ('t' test)

Since the groups were large independent samples, the 't' test was applied through the statistical package by using the following formula:

Where M_1 - denotes mean of group 1

M_2 - denotes mean of group 2

σ_1 - denotes standard deviation of group 1

σ_2 - denotes standard deviation of group 2

N_1 - denotes total number of respondents in group 1

N_2 - denotes total number of respondents in group 2

HYPOTHESIS 1

The level of hyper diversification and digital skills among teacher educators and student teachers is high.

Table 1 showing the analysis of hyper diversification and digital skills among teacher Educators and student teachers.

Entire Sample	N	Mean	S.D
Hyper Diversification	300	109.1	2.79
Digital Skills	300	24.21	3.40

The above table 1 shows that the mean and standard deviation on hyper diversification of the entire sample of teacher educators and student teachers' scores are 109.1 and 2.79 respectively. As 109.1 is higher than the mid-value of 64.1 (maximum score 129), it is concluded that the teacher educators and student teachers have a high level of hyper diversification. The mean and standard deviation on digital skills of the entire sample of teacher educators and student teachers' scores are 24.21 and 3.40 respectively. As 24.21 is higher than the mid-value of15 (maximum score 30), it is concluded that the teacher educators and student teachers have a high level of hyper diversification and digital skills.

HYPOTHESIS 2(a): There is a significant difference among teacher educators and student Teachers in their hyper diversification and digital skills in terms of Locality.

The details of the results of the't' test in the level of hyper diversification and digital skills among teacher educators and student teachers based on Locality is given in table no.2.

Table- 2 Difference in the level of hyper diversification and digital skills based on Locality

Variables	Sub variables	N	Mean	SD	't' value	Level of Significance	Result
Locality	Urban	160	21.31	3.12	1.13	0.05	NS
	Rural	140	23.52	2.86			

It is evident from table no.2 that the calculated't' value 1.13 is less than the table value 1.96 at 0.05 level. This shows that there is no significant difference among teacher educators and student teachers in their hyper diversification and digital skills in terms of Locality.

Hence, there is no significant difference between the samples (teacher educators and student teachers) that live in Urban and Rural areas in their hyper diversification and digital skills.

HYPOTHESIS 2(b): There is a significant difference among teacher educators and student teachers in their hyper diversification and digital skills in terms of Residence.

The details of the results of the 't' test in the level of hyper diversification and digital skills among teacher educators and student teachers based on Residence is given in table no.3.

Table- 3 Difference in the level of hyper diversification and digital skills based on Residence

Variables	**Sub variables**	**N**	**Mean**	**SD**	**' t' value**	**Level of Significance**	**Result**
Residence	Hostel	130	22.42	3.40	**1.049**	**0.05**	**NS**
	Home	170	25.63	4.60			

It is evident from table no.3 that the calculated 't' value 1.049 is less than the table value 1.96 at 0.05 levels. This shows that there is no significant difference among teacher educators and student teachers in their hyper diversification and digital skills in terms of Residence.

Hence, there is no significant difference between the samples (teacher educators and student teachers) who reside at hostel and at home in their hyper diversification and digital skills.

HYPOTHESIS (2C): There is a significant difference among teacher educators and student teachers in their hyper diversification and digital skills in terms of Status (teacher educator/student teacher).

The details of the results of the 't' test in the level of hyper diversification and digital skills among teacher educators and student teachers based on Status((teacher educator/student teacher) is given in table no.4.

Table- 4 Difference in the level of hyper diversification and digital skills based on Status (teacher educator/student teacher)

Variables	Sub variables	N	Mean	SD	't' value	Level of Significance	**Result**
STATUS	Teacher Educators	100	20.24	3.983	**1.61**	**0.05**	**NS**
	Student Teachers	200	22.57	3.793			

It is evident from table no.4 that the calculated 't' value 1.61 is less than the table value 1.96 at 0.05 levels. This shows that there is no significant difference among teacher educators and student teachers in their hyper diversification and digital skills in terms of Status.

Hence, there is no significant difference between the samples (teacher educators and student teachers) in Status in their hyper diversification and digital skills.

HYPOTHESIS 2(d): There is a significant difference among teacher educators and student teachers in their hyper diversification and digital skills in terms of Educational Qualification (UG/PG).

The details of the results of the 't' test in the level of hyper diversification and digital skills among teacher educators and student teachers based on Educational Qualification(UG/PG) is given in table no.5.

Table – 5 Difference in the level of hyper diversification and digital skills based on Educational Qualification(UG/PG)

Variables	Sub Variables	N	Mean	SD	't' value	Level of Significance	Result
Educational Qualification	UG	100	22.35	3.902	**1.21**	**0.05**	**NS**
	PG	200	21.50	3.340			

It is evident from table no.5 that the calculated 't' value 1.21 is less than the table value 1.96 at 0.05 levels. This shows that there is no significant difference among teacher educators and student teachers in their hyper diversification and digital skills in terms of Educational Qualification(UG/PG).

Hence, there is no significant difference among teacher educators and student teachers in their hyper diversification and digital skills in terms of Educational Qualification (UG/PG).

HYPOTHESIS 2(e): There is a significant difference among teacher educators and student teachers in their hyper diversification and digital skills in terms of Browsing habit. The details of the results of the 't' test in the level of hyper diversification and digital skills among teacher educators and student teachers based on browsing habit is given in table no.6.

Table – 6 Difference in the level of hyper diversification and digital skills based on Browsing Habit

Variable	Sub variables	N	Mean	SD	't' value	Level of Significance	Result
Browsing Habit	Frequently	120	17.73	3.679	**5.820**	**0.05**	S
	Rarely	180	19.28	3.431			

It is evident from table no.6 that the calculated 't' value 5.820 is higher than the table value 1.96 at 0.05 levels. This shows that there is a significant difference among teacher educators and student teachers in their hyper diversification and digital skills in terms of Browsing habit.

Hence, there is a significant difference among teacher educators and student teachers in their hyper diversification and digital skills in terms of Browsing habit.

HYPOTHESES VERIFICATION

The level of hyper diversification among teacher educators and student teachers is high-**Accepted**

There is a significant difference among teacher educators and student teachers in their hyper diversification and digital skills in terms of of Locality - **Rejected**

There is a significant difference among teacher educators and student teachers in their hyper diversification and digital skills in terms of Residence - **Rejected**

There is a significant difference among teacher educators and student teachers in their hyper diversification and digital skills in terms of Status(teacher/student) - **Rejected**

There is a significant difference among teacher educators and student teachers in their hyper diversification and digital skills in terms of educational qualification(UG/PG) - **Rejected**

There is a significant difference among teacher educators and student teachers in their hyper diversification and digital skills in terms of Browsing habit - **Accepted**

EDUCATIONAL IMPLICATIONS

- The result of the study leads to encourage Teacher Educators Student teachers to be hyper diversified and digitally skilled .
- The usage of virtual world can be enhanced in colleges to develop skills and build capacity as part of professional life.
- Therefore Teacher Educators and Student Teachers can:
- create and edit digital audios
- use Social bookmarking to share resources with and between learners
- use blogs and wikis to create online platforms for students
- Exploit digital images for classroom use

- Use video content to engage students
- Use infographics to visually stimulate students
- Use Social networking sites to connect with colleagues and grow professionally
- Create and deliver asynchronous presentations and training sessions
- Compile a digital e-portfolio for their own development
- Have a knowledge about online security
- be able to detect plagiarized works in students assignments
- Create screen capture videos and tutorials
- Curate web content for classroom learning
- Use and provide students with task management tools to organize their work and plan their learning
- Use polling software to create a real-time survey in class
- Understand issues related to copyright and fair use of online materials
- Exploit computer games for pedagogical purposes
- Use digital assessment tools to create quizzes
- Use of collaborative tools for text construction and editing
- Find and evaluate authentic web based content
- Identify online resources that are safe for students browsing
- Use digital tools for time management purposes
- Learn about the different ways to use YouTube in your classroom
- Use note taking tools to share interesting content with your students
- Annotate web pages and highlight parts of text to share with your class
- Use of online graphic organizers and printables
- Use of online sticky notes to capture interesting idea
- Use of screen casting tools to create and share tutorials
- Exploit group text messaging tools for collaborative project work
- Conduct an effective search query with the minimum time possible
- Conduct A Research Paper Using Digital Tools
- Use file sharing tools to share docs and files with students online
- Reduce Infrastructure Costs Through Consolidation
- Virtualize the Most Demanding Workloads
- Virtualize for High Availability
- Improve Security and Reliability with Microkernelized Hypervisor
- Protect Important Data Using Live Backup
- Minimize Downtime with Quick Migration
- Delegate Virtual Machine Management
- Reduce Support Time with Integrated Management
- Save Time and Money with a More Flexible Test Environment
- Take Advantage of Broad Compatibility
- Reduce Support Time with Integrated Management
- Save Time and Money with a More Flexible Test Environment

- Take Advantage of Broad Compatibility
- Exploit Facebook,Youtube,Flickr andSocial networking Sites(SNS) for sharing eduinformation
- Use Smartphones, iphones, tablets as educational resources.

Accomplish content delivery and student engagement by creating and maintaining a Fan Page, at no cost to anyone involved, and completely away from the limitations of course management systems such as Bloackboard, Angel and WebCT.

BIBLIOGRAPHY

- Baird, D., Fisher, M. (2005). Neomillennial user experience strategies: Utilizing social networking media to support "always on" learning styles. Journal of Educational Technology Systems. 34 (1) 5 - 32.
- Bimber, B. (2000). Measuring the gender gap on the Internet. Social Sciences Quarterly, 81 (3):25-32.
- Broos, A. (2005). Gender and information and communication technologies (ICT) anxiety: Male self-assurance and female hesitation. Cyber psychology & Behavior8(1):21-31.
- Dennis, A.R., Kinney, S.T., & Hung, Y.T.C. (1999) Gender differences in the effects of media richness.Small Group Research . 30 (4): 405-437.
- Diilon, D. (2001). E-books: The University of Texas Experience. Library Hi Tech. 19 (4) 350-62.
- Gefen, D. & Straub, D. W. (1997) Gender differences in the perception and use of email: an extension to the technology acceptance model. MIS Quarterly 4: 389-400.
- Horowitz, R. & Mohum, A. (1998). His and Hers: Gender Consumption & Technology. University of Virginia Press.
- Jackson L.A., Ervin, K.S., Gardner, P.D. & Schmitt,N. (2001). Gender and the internet: women communicating and men searching.
- Lenhart, M. (2010). Teens and Social Media, An Overview. Pew Internet and American Life Project.
- Summerfield, M., Mandel, C., Kantor, P. (1999). Online books at Columbia: Early findings on use, satisfaction, and effect. Technology and Scholarly Communication. Berkley; University of California Press 282-308.
- Wilska, A. (2003). Mobile use as part of young people's consumption styles.

27.

An Assessment of Edu Digital Skills of Teachers in Namakkal District

Introduction

Teacher is an ideal personality whose knowledge and skill play a major role in the development of the nation to the global standard education in general and tapping the potentialities of students to the maximum extent in particular. Teachers are expected to learn forever to withstand the innovations in teaching and updating the knowledge and widen the clarity of the conceptual framework of the subject of specialization too. Unless and until the teachers prepared to meet the requirements and challenges, the dream and purpose of education will not be fulfilled. Nowadays the system of education has assumed the character which involves more students' participation and student centric which is highly enabled through the application of various educational technologies. Edu - digital skills is considered prerequisite for all teachers teaching for nursery to doctorate scholars. 21st century school curriculum has been enriched to meet the demands of world requirements of quality. Communication, collaboration, critical thinking, problem solving, creativity, invention, information and technology literacy and self direction will facilitate the achievement of aims and objectives of education. Teachers of 21st century are expected to equip themselves with modern technology application in teaching and learning process. A paradigm shift has happened to meet the demands of gen y and z learners which require innovative, explorative and interesting approach in teaching and learning. The curriculum will need withstand the futuristic vision for the global scenario. At this juncture the teachers of today should be enthusiastic to update their knowledge and skills forever in order to keep young to the youngest generation whom they meet and it may also be emphasized greatly as the professional ethics. This study has been attempted to assess the knowledge and skills of teachers in the field of information and communication technology which a teacher necessarily possess in the digital world.

Teacher is an ideal personality whose knowledge and skill play a major role in the development of the nation to the global standard education in general and tapping the potentialities of students to the maximum extent in particular. Teachers are expected to learn forever to withstand the innovations in teaching and updating the knowledge and widen the clarity of the conceptual framework of the subject of specialization too. Unless and until the teachers prepared to meet the requirements and challenges, the dream and purpose of education will not be fulfilled. Nowadays the system of education has assumed the character which involves more students' participation and student centric which is highly enabled through the application of various educational technologies. Edu - digital skills is considered prerequisite for all teachers teaching for nursery to doctorate scholars. 21st century school curriculum has been enriched to meet the demands of world requirements of quality. Communication, collaboration, critical thinking, problem solving, creativity, invention, information and technology literacy and self direction will facilitate the achievement of aims and objectives of education. Teachers of 21st century are expected to equip themselves with modern technology application in teaching and learning process. A paradigm shift has happened to meet the demands of gen y and z learners which require innovative, explorative and interesting approach in teaching and learning. The curriculum will need withstand the futuristic vision for the global scenario. At this juncture the teachers of today should be enthusiastic to update their knowledge and skills forever in order to keep young to the youngest generation whom they meet and it may also be emphasized greatly as the professional ethics. This study has been attempted to assess the knowledge and skills of teachers in the field of information and communication technology which a teacher necessarily possess in the digital world.

Educational Digital Skills

It is mentioned that in order to thrive in a digital economy, students will need digital age proficiencies. It is important for the educational system to make parallel changes in order to fulfill its mission in society, namely the preparation of students for the world beyond the classroom. Therefore, the educational system must understand and embrace the following 21st century skills within the context of rigorous academic standards.

The 21st Century Literacy Summit (2002) contends that "the explosive growth of technology in every aspect of society offers us a unique opportunity to engage our citizens in economic and civic life" The report further states that to take advantage of this opportunity, we must continually acquire and develop new knowledge and skills. Summit participants noted "Information and communication technologies are raising the bar on the competencies needed to succeed in the 21st century, and they are compelling us to revisit many of our assumptions and beliefs" The sheer magnitude of human knowledge, world to technology necessitates a shift in our children's education - from plateaus of knowing to continuous cycles of learning. Therefore, policymakers and educators alike must define 21st century skills, highlighting the relationship of those skills to conventional academic standards. As they do so, they must also recognize the need for multiple assessments to measure these skills within the context of academic standards, evaluating their application to today's technological and global society.

Technological Literacy

Demonstrate a sound conceptual understanding of the nature of technology systems and view themselves as proficient users of these systems. Understand and model positive, ethical use of technology in both social and personal contexts. Use a variety of technology tools in effective ways to increase creative productivity. Use communication tools to reach out to the world beyond the classroom and communicate ideas in powerful ways. Use technology effectively to access, evaluate, process and synthesize information from a variety of sources. Use technology to identify and solve complex problems in real-world contexts have been considered as Technological Literacy

Information Literacy

Before Accessing Information one should determine what is known and what is needed for problem solving, identify different sources of information, including text, people, video, audio, and databases and prioritize sources based on credibility and relevance. When Accessing Information one need identify and retrieve relevant information from sources and use technology to enhance searching. Revise information-gathering strategies that prove to be in effective when understands how information retrieved does or does not address original problem, evaluate information in terms of credibility and know what are the social, economic, political, legal, and ethical issues that may impact it to facilitate to use technology for evaluation. After Information is extracted, using retrieved information to accomplish a specific purpose, present information clearly and persuasively by using a range of technology tools and media and evaluate the processes and products of these activities have here been considered essential to assure one to be Literate in information.

Global Awareness

Global awareness is knowledge about the connectedness of the nations of the world historically, politically, economically, technologically, socially, linguistically, and ecologically and understand that these interconnections of positive benefits and negative consequences too. The ability to recognize, analyzes, and evaluates major trends in global relations and the interconnections of these trends with both their local and national communities. Participate in the global society by staying current with international news and by participating in the democratic process.

Objectives of the Study

To find the level of Edu-digital skill among school teachers and find whether there is significant different exist among them in relation to their personal variables such as sex, Age, Educational Qualification, Area of Residence, Management of the Institution, Subject of Specialization and the Location of the School.

Research Question

What is the level of educational digital Skills of School Teachers? Is there any Significant Difference Exists among them with respect to their Personal Variables?

Research Methodology

A Normative Descriptive Method of study has been attempted to assess the level of Educational Digital Skills among the School Teachers in Namakkal District.

Population, Sample and Sampling Technique of the Study

All teachers who teach in school education are the population of the study and the sample of the study has been chosen from teachers work in Namakkal district only and the sample was taken by stratified random sampling technique which consists of 250.

Tools and Technique of Data Collection

A tool consisted of 24 items related to some basic skills necessary for adopting computer enabled teaching technology, using internet connection which will benefit students to gain knowledge, understand the concept better, improve the critical thinking, problem solving ability, creativity and to enhance their communication skill and appropriate application of the knowledge gained for the betterment of himself and to the society. The scope of this study extent all teachers who teach in the classroom from kindergarten to plus two levels. The questionnaire has dimensions of using the computer for retrieving useful information via internet, knowledge about various search engines, and preparation of effective PowerPoint materials, video clippings, software package application, audio recording, connecting to virtual classroom and the facilities to publish the students works in internet. Knowledge and the application of MS word, Excel format, mobile for teaching and learning purpose and the ability to set ready LCD, mike and arrange show in the smart classroom and the application of social media in education have also been taken for assessing.

Scoring Procedure & Statistical Tools Used

Questionnaire used in the study has five point scale of the level of skill of the respondents in relation to their digital skill hence it has five options of known very well, known, moderately known, known little and Unknown which scored as 5, 4,3,2 and 1 respectively.

SPSS package has been used to analyze the data and the percentage analysis and the differential analysis have been used to describe and infer the details pertaining to the research question formulated for the study.

Table -1: An Analysis of Edu Digital Skills among Teachers in Namakkal District

Items	Very well Known		Well Known		Moderately Known		Known Little		Unknown		Total
	F	%	F	%	F	%	F	%	F	%	
Information Retrieval	41	16.4	59	23.6	62	24.8	75	30	13	5.2	250
Power point preparation	52	20.8	67	26.8	53	21.2	60	24	18	7.2	250
Efficient use of Windows operating system	35	14	48	19.2	75	30	81	32.4	11	4.4	250
Connecting to the Online Teaching of World Classroom	15	6	20	8	39	15.6	116	46.4	60	24	250
Skill in make it work well of LCD mike screen view	15	6	26	10.4	77	30.8	114	45.6	18	7.2	250
Knowledge about E learning material preparation	21	8.4	15	6	27	10.8	129	51.6	58	23.2	250
Account in social networking sites like Face-book, twitter	22	8.8	36	14.4	74	29.6	12	4.8	106	42.4	250
Using of videos and computer games in teaching	19	7.6	29	11.6	55	22	85	34	62	24.8	250
Application of Virtual classrooms and chat rooms in teaching and learning	13	5.2	18	7.2	17	6.8	56	22.4	146	58.4	250

Items	Very well Known		Well Known		Moderately Known		Known Little		Unknown		Total
Application of documentary film in deliverance of the instructional objectives	51	20.4	60	24	41	16.4	31	12.4	67	26.8	250
Using of web-Camera in virtual interaction	16	6.4	41	16.4	27	10.8	71	28.4	95	38	250
Application of white Board in teaching	25	10	16	6.4	19	7.6	43	17.2	147	58.8	250
Safety and security issues in using webmail	17	6.8	39	15.6	90	36	70	28	44	17.6	250
Security Challenges in instant messaging	15	6	35	14	78	31.2	98	39.2	24	9.6	250
Application of iPod and tables in teaching	11	4.4	23	9.2	67	26.8	80	32	69	27.6	250
Application of Video conferencing for teaching and learning	32	12.8	24	9.6	71	28.4	90	36	33	13.2	250
Application of YouTube	49	19.6	86	34.4	55	22	62	24.8	38	15.2	250
Application of Flicker & Picasa	19	7.6	25	10	62	24.8	104	41.6	40	16	250
Application of mobile phone for transferring data of video	21	8.4	27	10.8	80	32	90	36	32	12.8	250
Application of mobile phone for transferring data of voice	22	8.8	33	13.2	76	30.4	81	32.4	38	15.2	250

Items	Very well Known		Well Known		Moderately Known		Known Little		Unknown		Total
Application of mobile phone for transferring data of text	187	74.8	46	18.4	3	1.2	9	3.6	5	2	250
Assessment of students performance through online	25	10	52	20.8	58	23.2	105	42	10	4	250
Application of learning Management System - LMS	11	4.4	21	8.4	37	14.8	57	22.8	15	6	250
Application of Video-recording	17	6.8	26	10.4	51	20.4	78	31.2	78	31.2	250

Majority of teachers have necessary in Skill and knowledge in the application of MS office, Mobile technology in teaching and learning, information retrieval system from online resource centre but the majority teachers have moderate and least knowledge about e-content preparation, application of social media, and security issues in web mails, various learning management system and efficient use of ICT in teaching

Table -2: Significance of Difference in Edu-Digital Skill of Teachers

Demographic Variables	P Value	.Level of Sig
Sex	0.153	NS
Area of Residence	0.104	NS
Location of the School	0.214	NS
Teaching Experience	0.098	NS
Educational Qualification	0.521	NS
Management of the School	*0.021	S
Subject of Specialization	**0.001	S

There is no significant difference exist among the respondents in their Educational digital skill in relation to their personal variables of Sex, Area of Residence, Location of the School, Teaching Experience and their educational qualification. But the statistical report of analysis shows that there is significant difference exist among the sample in relation to their management of the school and their subject of specialization.

Educational Implications

Teacher Education curriculum should emphasize the ICT enabled education in B.Ed program

Workshops need to be conducted for B.Ed program in the practical application of ICT and training program can be organized for E- content preparation

Orientation and Refresher courses for the teachers in schools should be conducted frequently to enable teachers to facilitate them in the efficient use of ICT in teaching and learning environment

Collaborative Approach should be made in integrating ICT in education

Conclusion

Teachers are the forerunner of all developments and growth of the nation and the world; they play a significant role in bringing desirable outcome in the world with their adaptability and their ever learning behavior of updating knowledge and skills in any field. No technology can replace the teacher in any period of time but the teacher needs possess skills in the application of technology which facilitate desirable educational outcome in the field of education.

References

Felix.A & Jahitha Begum (2011) "An Awareness of E-resources related to ICT and Education among M.Ed Students and M.Phil Scholars" ICT in teaching and learning, APH Publishing Corporation, New Delhi, p.169

Nagarajan .K (2009) "Educational Innovations and Management" Ram Publishers, Chennai. Pp.135-185.

Natchimuthu.K (2012), "Need of E-Content Development in Education Today" APH Publication Corporation, New Delhi. P.76.

Rangarajan. P & Senthilnathan.S (2012) "Teacher Educators Attitude towards E Learning" Edutracks, Vol.No.12 No.1 pp. 21-32.

www.educatorstechnology.com/2012/06/33-digital-skills-every-21st-century.htm

http://www.educatorstechnology.com/2013/07/the-8-digital-skills-students-need-for.html

❐

28.

Implications of Multimedia in Teaching Economics with Special Reference to Higher Secondary Students in Chennai

Introduction

The computer has revolutionized the whole society overwhelmingly inclusive of all human activities especially those of education. The computer is changing the total educational system namely, content, methodology, learner participation learning process, teacher roles, curricular implication etc. "The computers are very powerful instructional media that enhance quality of instruction". By programming the subject of study in computers, teaching and learning become full of contexts and situations. The student can take his own time to learn the contents because they are individualized instructional situation. The performance of the student in instruction as well as in test will automatically record in the computer. The present study aims to find out the implications of multimedia in teaching economics with special reference to higher secondary education in Chennai. A samples of 155 samples selected randomly were studied. A questionnaire method of survey was used to find out the implications of multimedia in teaching economics. The data were collected by using questionnaire as an instrument. Primary data were collected by conducting direct structured interview using questionnaire. All the respondents were asked the same questions in the same fashion and they were informed the purpose of study. t-test, ANOVA and Correlation analysis were applied to test the hypotheses. The findings and observations are the result and outcome of the interpretations made during the study of analysis.

In 1965, Lorence settler and Danieal Davis[5] developed most complicated teaching process in which computer was used for presenting instruction in place of teacher. They divided the teaching process of the computer in two parts.

Pre-tutorial phase

Tutorial phase.

In the first phase, computer assisted instruction is given to the pupils to achieve the specific objectives on the basis of his entry behaviour. In the second phase instructing material is presented accordingly. The pupil is evaluated. After presenting the instruction, computer also controls it. It also provides reinforcement to the pupils.

In the modern age, the use of computers in the field of education, made in the following areas.

All the researches do all analytical tasks with the help of computers in the research work.

- Computers are also used in educational guidance and counseling.
- Remedial teaching of the pupils is also done by the computers.
- Computers help in sought for preparing the results of the examinations.

Learning with aid of computer through computer, aided instruction, computer simulation etc. It is a self learning strategy in teaching learning process. Students learnt their subjects at their own pace.

Internet is worldwide computer network that contains a large collection of information which could be made available to you on your computer. The person having internet connection can retrieve any information on individual interest. Purves, A.C.[6] (1998) says that, the internet is the abbreviation of inter network system. The internet is the name for a vast, worldwide system consisting of people, information and computers. It is also described as a network of networks because these are more than one lakh readily accessible through the Internet. Internet is the largest and most complete learning tool for a group of people with varied educational background and interests. Teachers, students, businessmen and other educators can share ideas instantly across vast distances. For scientific and research community, internet is an essential and indispensable tool. Through Internet scientist can gain and enjoy instant access to the world's most advanced research facilities and discuss their research problems with others, working in the same field.

Review of Literature

Coyne, Margaret Ann[17], Ed.D., (2006), in their paper "Emerging literacy Assisted parents to scaffold the emerging literacy skill of their pre-school-aged children through the used of electronic storybooks", reported that, that importance of parents reading to their young child is well supported by research (Health, 1986). However, Edwards (1989) found that parents whose own literacy skills are emerging have difficulty supporting the emerging literacy skills of their young children through storybook reading.

The development of a new paradigm, Universal Design for Learning (UDL) (Meyer & Rose, 1998 and 2002) provides a framework for the use of computer technology to support learning. Drawing on Vygotsky's (1978; 1986) socio constructive theory of learning and the latest advances in the neurosciences, UDL investigates how technology can support diverse learners. This study examined whether UDL –based technology might help parents who are themselves emerging readers support their children's literacy development.

When parents use of targeted storybook reading behaviours increased if their children's pre-intervention scores on language measures were below age-level, the children's scores on post-intervention measures improved to age-level or above. In addition, the children's scores on measures of story retelling and print knowledge improved.

BEABVIS C.$_{18}$, Deakin University, Literacy and the new technologies in the middle years. (2006) This paper explores young people's textual engagements with electronic and other forms of popular culture, and the changing nature of literacy in the context of COM modification, mass marketing and the new technologies. Building on school based studies exploring computer games in the classroom and the Poke on phenomenon, it examines ways in which popular texts are read, and narrative and generic elements incorporated into the curriculum and into students' spoken and written texts. Drawing on Green's model of cultural, critical and opal dimensions of (technological) literacy, it examines issues of literacy and culture, identity and critique for teachers and students in the middle years, and their implications for constructions of literacy and curriculum.

BERRY L. and CHAPMAN E,$_{19}$ University of Sydney Effects of Background Information and Audiovisual Presentation Modes on Students' Attention Styles and Enjoyment in Listening to Unfamiliar Music.(2006) Research has indicated that students typically do not enjoy or engage with unfamiliar pieces of music. This is discouraging and puzzling to music educators who whish to introduce their students to a diverse range of musical genres. This study explored the effects of two factors on students' initial reactions to an unfamiliar Shakuhachi piece. Using a 2 by 2 crossed-factor design, 438 students in grades 9-11 were assigned at random to listen to the piece in either audio-only or audiovisual form, and with or without verbal background information.

Results indicated that while the provision of information significantly ($p<0.05$) increased students' enjoyment of the music and their interest in hearing more of the same kind of music, it had no effect on their listening attention styles (e.g., focusing on the melody or idiomatic details of the piece). Conversely, use of the audiovisual presentation mode significantly impacted on one aspect of students' attention styles (focus on idiomatic details) and perceived familiarity with the piece, but had only a marginally significant effect on their enjoyment or interest.

Implications of these results for the introduction of unfamiliar music to high school students will be discussed.

BLACKMORE J., JOHNSON R., WARREN W.[20], (2006) States that the potential of new learning technologies for transforming teaching and learning, and indeed the organization of schooling. Much has also been written about teacher responses to new learning technologies-how they resist, ignore, or innovate. A number of recent reports indicate a gap between policy, practice and the capacity of organizations to provide the conditions and resources sin schools to creatively use new learning technologies. Few of these discourses draw upon theories of educational change, in particular those which relate to the dissonance between attitudes and feelings about radical change, and how it impacts on teacher work identity with respect to learning technologies. Much of the literature has focused upon the technical aspects, the hardware and software, but not the 'warm ware', so critical to sound pedagogical practice. This paper draws from the Learning in New Environments Research Group action research project, a pilot study in a large metropolitan secondary college, which is exploring the social implications of new learning technologies for changing relations between students, between teachers and students, between teachers and between family and school. The paper draws from the first round of data collection from the teachers in an ongoing action research project in a region with a high level of socio-economic and cultural diversity.

It draws on concepts of Lieberman's notion of learning networks and Wenger's notion of communities of practice, as well as past research on the reception of gender equity reform in educational organizations, which focuses upon emotional aspects of professional work identity and organizational change.

Joseph Kacharayll[25] (2006) – "Suitability of colleges for Web Bases Learning" reported that Web based learning environment is expensive to establish, government and private managements should take necessary steps to provide adequate infrastructure facilities in colleges for web based learning. A proper utilization of available human resources would help improve web based learning. In order to overcome technical limitation, training has to be given to both teachers and learners to create flexible and uninterrupted learning environment. The training of material designers should be especially focused upon. Most of the colleges have not properly utilized the available web resources in their teaching learning strategies. There is only nominal technical support and assistance from technical staff and from government and private managements at the institutional level for web based learning. The author collected sample for the survey of 152 college lecturers was obtained through random sampling.

Objectives

- To find the effect on learning competency of the students by using Multi media for teaching economics
- To find the active participation of the teachers in using multi media for teaching economics.
- To find how the teaching of economics has been efficiently improved using the multi media.
- To find the importance of computers and internet in teaching economics.

Methodology

The investigator, for the present study adopts the survey method of research. It is a procedure in which data is systematically collected from a population through some form of direct solicitation such as face to face interview, questionnaire or schedule. The survey is extensive and cross sectional dealing with the relatively large number of cases of a particular time and yielding statistics that are abstracted from particular cases. It is the method of investigation which attempts to describe and interpret what exists at present in the form of conditions, practices, process, trends, effects, attitudes, and beliefs. Using this method the investigator had gathered information measure the Effect of Multi Media Aids in teaching economics for Higher Secondary Students in Chennai.

Sample

For the present study 155 Higher Secondary Students in Chennai.

Data Collection

Primary data, required for the present research work were collected by conducting direct interviews using questionnaire. All the respondents were given sufficient information about the study. These respondents were provided with the same questionnaires. They were also informed that they have to answer in the same fashion.

Statistical Tools for Analysis

The following tools statistical tools were used for the analysis of data. t-test, one way ANOVA and correlation analysis is used for the present study.

Analysis and Interpretation

Table 1: Six wise distribution of "t" value between the boys and girls of the higher secondary economics students using multimedia resources in their schools

Dimensions	Boys N = 55		Girls N = 100		Calculated value of "t"	Level of significance at 5% level
	Mean	S.D	Mean	S.D		
Working knowledge of computers	79.42	8.17	80.42	8.68	0.71	NS
Knowledge about internet	78.15	9.51	76.88	9.80	0.91	NS
Knowledge using A.V. Aids	79.76	7.48	76.26	10.79	2.37	S
Preparation of computer based study materials	76.40	7.97	74.77	11.04	1.06	NS
Assignment and project	81.75	6.31	78.35	10.18	2.56	S
Interaction with others through web	395.47	28.53	386.5	42.77	1.56	NS

(At5% level of significance, the table value of "t" is 1.96)

It is refereed from the above table that there is a significant difference between boys and of Higher Secondary Students of economics group in there, Knowledge in using A.V. Aids and Assignment and project but there is no significant difference between Male and Female Higher Secondary students of economics group in their Working knowledge of computers, knowledge about internet, Preparation of computer based study materials, interaction with others through web.

Table – 2 : Area wise distribution of "t" value between the urban and rural higher secondary economics students using multimedia resources in their schools

Dimensions	Urban N = 55		Rural N = 100		Calculated value of "t"	Level of significance at 5% level
	Mean	S.D	Mean	S.D		
Working knowledge of computers	79.42	8.17	80.42	8.68	0.71	NS
Knowledge about internet	78.15	9.51	76.88	9.80	0.91	NS

Knowledge using A.V. Aids	79.76	7.48	76.26	10.79	2.37	S
Preparation of computer based study materials	76.40	7.97	74.77	11.04	1.06	NS
Assignment and project	81.75	6.31	78.35	10.18	2.56	S
Interaction with others through web	395.47	28.53	386.5	42.77	1.56	NS

(At 5% level of significance, the table value of "t" is 1.96)

It is referred from the above table that there is no significant difference between urban and rural Higher Secondary Students of economics group in there, Knowledge in using A.V. Aids, Assignment and project, Working knowledge of computers, Knowledge about internet, Preparation of computer based study materials, Interaction with other through web.

Table – 3: "F" value among the boys and girls of Higher Secondary economics Group Students in Using Multimedia resources

Dimensions	df= 2,152			Calculated "f" Value	Remarks at 5% Level
	Source of variation	Sum of squares	M.S.V		
Working knowledge of computers	Between With in	118.75 11110.63	59.38 73.10	0.81	NS
Knowledge about internet	Between With in	7.94 14650.81	3.97 96.39	0.04	NS
Knowledge in using A.V. Aids	Between With in	23.44 15123.38	11.72 99.50	0.12	NS
Preparation of computer study materials	Between With in	155.56 15619.63	77.78 102.76	0.76	NS
Assignment and project	Between With in	164.39 12793.88	82.19 84.17	0.98	NS
Interaction with others through web	Between With in	216.00 23034.00	108.00 1515.39	0.07	NS

(For 2,152 df. At 5% level of significance, the table value of "f" is 3.06)

It is inferred from the above table that there is no significance difference among the boys and girls of Higher Secondary economics group students in using Multimedia resources in the Higher Secondary schools of Chennai.

Table – 4: "F" value among the Rural and Urban Higher Secondary Students of economics Group in Using Multimedia source in Chennai

Dimensions	df= 2,152			Calculated "f" Value	Remarks at 5% Level
	Source of variation	Sum of squares	M.S.V		
Working knowledge of computers	Between With in	39.50 11189.88	19.75 73.62	0.27	NS
Knowledge about internet	Between With in	394.39 14264.50	197.16 93.85	2.10	NS
Knowledge in using A.V. Aids	Between With in	130.31 15016.50	65.16 98.79	0.66	NS
Preparation of computer study materials	Between With in	444.44 153330.75	222.22 100.86	2.20	NS
Assignment and project	Between With in	364.69 12593.56	182.32 82.85	2.20	NS
Interaction with others through web	Between With in	5628.00 224924.00	2814.00	1.90	NS

(for 2,152 df.at 5% level of significance, the table value of "f" is 3.06)

It is inferred from the above table that there is no significance difference among the Rural and Urban Higher Secondary students of economics group in using Multi media resource in the Higher Secondary Schools of Chennai.

Table – 5: "F" value among the Higher Secondary Students of economics Group in Using Multimedia source in Government and Private Higher Secondary Schools in Chennai

Dimensions	**df= 2,152**			**Calculated "f" Value**	**Remarks at 5% Level**
	Source of variation	**Sum of squares**	**M.S.V**		
Working knowledge of computers	Between With in	39.50 11189.88	19.75 73.62	0.27	NS
Knowledge about internet	Between With in	394.39 14264.50	197.16 93.85	2.10	NS
Knowledge in using A.V. Aids	Between With in	130.31 15016.50	65.16 98.79	0.66	NS
Preparation of computer study materials	Between With in	444.44 153330.75	222.22 100.86	2.20	NS
Assignment and project	Between With in	364.69 12593.56	182.32 82.85	2.20	NS

Interaction with others through web	Between With in	5628.00 224924.00	2814.00	1.90	NS

(For 2,152 df. at 5% level of significance, the table value of '' is 3.06)

It is inferred from the above table that there is no significance difference among the Government and Private Higher Secondary students of economics group in using Multimedia resource in the Higher Secondary School of Chennai

Table – 6 : The Correlation value between the Male and Female Higher Secondary Students in using multimedia resources in the Higher Secondary Schools of Chennai

Category	?X	?X²	?Y	?Y²	?XY	Calculated	Remarks
Boys	683	8595	545	5495	6775	.68	NS
Girls	1199	14757	970	9584	11740	.425	S
Total	1882	23354	1515	15079	18515	.325	S

(Table value of Correlation Co-efficient at 5% level of Significance is 0.161)

It is inferred from the above table that there is no significant relationship between the rural and high secondary economics group boys in using multimedia resources and there is a significant relationship between rural and urban high secondary economics group girls in using multimedia resources.

Findings

There a significant difference among the higher secondary commence group students of boys and girls, higher secondary commence students of government and private schools, higher secondary commence group students of rural and urban schools, in their interest towards learning commence through multimedia resources in Chennai.

There is significant difference among the higher secondary economics group students in their levels of using multimedia shows moderate knowledge except interaction with others through web and no significant difference in low of using multimedia except interaction with other through web and no significant difference in higher level knowledge of using multimedia.

There is no significant difference among the higher secondary economics group boys in their level of using multimedia shows moderate knowledge and higher level of using multimedia and there is a significant difference low of using multimedia at the area of assignment and project, interaction with others though web.

There is no significant difference among the secondary economics group girls in all the levels of using multimedia resources. There is no significant difference among the higher secondary economics group students of government school in their level of using multimedia shows moderate knowledge and there is a significant difference in low level of interaction with others though web and shows significant difference in higher level of in knowledge about internet, knowledge in using AV aids and in the preparation of computer based study materials.

There is no significant difference among the higher secondary economics group students of private school in their level of using multimedia shows moderate knowledge and higher level knowledge of using multimedia and there is a significant difference in low level of using multimedia at the area of working of computer and in interaction with others though web.

There is no significant difference among the higher secondary economics group of rural school in their level of using multimedia shows moderate knowledge and there is a significant difference in low level of preparation of computer in high level of using multimedia at the is a significant difference in high level of using multimedia at the area of working knowledge of computer and in interaction with others with through web.

There is no significant difference between boys and girls or higher secondary students of economics group in their, knowledge in using A.V aids and assignments and project but there is no significant differences between male and female higher secondary of economics group in their working knowledge of computers, knowledge about internet, preparation of computer based study materials with others thought web.

There is no significant difference between urban and rural higher secondary of economics in their, knowledge in using A.V aids, assignment and project, working knowledge of computer knowledge about internet preparation of computer based study martial interaction with others web.

There is no significant difference among the Male and female higher secondary schools of economics group in using multimedia resource in the Higher secondary schools of Chennai.

There is no significance difference among the Rural and urban higher secondary students of economics group in using Multimedia resource in the higher secondary of Chennai.

There is n no significant difference among the Government and private Higher Secondary students of economics group in using Multimedia resource in the higher schools of Chennai.

There is no significant relationship between the Rural and urban high secondary group boys in using multimedia resources and there is a significant relationship between Rural and Urban high secondary economics group girls in using multimedia resources.

The research overwhelmingly demonstrates that usages of multimedia will definitely improve the quality of teaching economics in higher secondary classes.

The research found that the students are actively involved in learning part if the multimedia is introduced in classroom teaching.

The research shows the students are highly motivate towards the subject by using multimedia teaching aids and they are attracted more and improve their understanding and memory power in various economics topics like advertising, banking, etc. While using multimedia resources.

It is concluded that there is a positive effect of using multimedia aids in the economics achievement of the students in economics in Chennai.

Conclusion

The present study aims to find out the implications of multimedia in teaching economics with special reference to higher secondary. The researcher framed objectives and hypotheses on the basis of the above context. The research was carried out in 155 samples based randomly. A questionnaire constructed by R was used to collect the relevant data. After collecting the data they were analyzed using statistical tools such as t-test, ANOVA and Correlation analysis. The result concluded that students have average implications of multimedia in teaching at Higher Secondary level.

Reference

Beavis C. (2006), popular culture, textual practice and identify and identify: literacy and the new technologies, in the midde years

Berry l. And Chapman e, (2006); Effect of Background Information and Audiovisual Presentation Modes on Students' Attention style and enjoyment listening to Unfamiliar Music.

Blackmork j., Johnson R., Warren W. (2006), A handbook of Education Technology.

Bruce B.C (2004); Diversity and critical social engagement: How changing technologies enable new modes of literacy in changing circumstances. IN D.E. Alvermann (E.d), Adolescents and illiteracies in a digital world (pp. 1-18). New York: Peter Lang publication.

Chisamore, chris (2006), Multimedia and Education today.

Coyne, Margaret Ann (2006), Emerging Literacy: Assisting Parents to scaffold the emerging literacy skills of their preschool aged children through the use of electronic story books.

Lanksherar, C and Knoble, M (2003); New literacies: changing Knowledge and classroom learning. Philadelphia: Open university press.

Lewis, C and Finders, M. (2004); implied adolescents and implied teachers; A generation gap for new times. D.E Alvermann (Ed.), Adolescents and literacies in adugital world (pp.101-113).New York: peter Lang publishing.

❒

29.

Effectiveness of Blended Learning Programme in Teaching Biology at Higher Secondary School Students

Introduction

The technology is an integral part in the lives of young people who are direct beneficiaries of the educational process. This was often made argument for the need to develop learning methods that use modern technology in the formative and educational. By such methods students are responsible for their own learning, on which they themselves have control and manage it according to their interests and needs. The specialists' researches reveal that the methods which combine the traditional education with the modern technologies (*blended learning*) have increased the effectiveness. Blended Learning is a strategy which integrates the teaching learning process with different learning environments like face-to-face, online, social networking etc. Its rapid growth has been facilitated by the Internet and other emerging technologies like cloud computing, social networking etc. This paper provides a view about the effectiveness of blended learning programme in teaching biology at higher secondary school students

The recent research in science education has focused on instruction that is specific science content, specific instructional strategies and how they are related to biology learning contexts and instructional outcomes. In the present scientific and technological age, the conventional teaching methods are not sufficient to arouse interest among the students and do not meet up to the intellectual, psychological and emotional needs of the students in the new millennium. The methods of teaching biology need to be changed.

In a vast country like India, enormous work is now being done in the field of education but it is still not possible to equip each and every higher and higher secondary school with all the facilities for teaching biology in the near future. Most of the higher secondary schools, both in rural and urban area are suffering from lack of modern science laboratories. They need equally advanced gadgets to support their education. Technology enables students get a live vision of life's aspects and scientific factors. Any diagram can be explained in detail with 3d effect, it helps the student to understand the lesson clearly. Keeping in mind the investigator felt it appropriate to use blended learning for the teaching of the concepts in biology topics included in the XI standard biology syllabus (Tamil Medium).

Blended Learning

Blended learning provides platform to attract the senses of the learner for easy and happy learning. Blended learning is a programme which integrates teaching learning process with different leaning environment. Its rapid growth facilitated by the internet and other emerging technology cloud computing and social networking. "Blended learning is the thoughtful fusion of face-to-face and online learning experiences. The basic principle is that face-to-face oral communication and online written communication are optimally integrated such that the strengths of each are blended into a unique learning experience congruent with the context and intended educational purpose."

Blended learning – an instructional practice that combines teaching methods from both face-to-face instruction and online learning, gives to educational institutions new approaches and strategies for addressing the challenges they face and for taking advantage of the exciting new learning opportunities that are now available.

Blended learning does not exclude the traditional learning methods, but adds new and modern methods as: IT tools (email, web, chat, online conferences, e-learning platforms), workshops, individual project groups, practical demonstrations, etc.

Objectives of the Study

The objectives of the study as follows:

- To find out the effectiveness of blended learning programme for the teaching of biology at higher secondary level.
- To compare the effectiveness of blended learning programme in the teaching of biology with conventional method of teaching biology.

Hypotheses of the Study

The following null hypotheses have been formulated.

- There is no significant difference between the experimental group and control group in the achievement of biology at pre test level.

- There is no significant difference between the experimental group and control group in the achievement of biology at posttest level.
- There is no significant difference between the pretest and posttest in the achievement of biology for the experimental group.
- There is no significant difference between the pretest and posttest in the achievement of biology for the control group.

Sample

The sample of the study consists of 100 students studying in XI standard under State Board syllabus at perambalur district. The sample includes both boys and girls.

Tools Used

The following tools had been used for the present study:

An achievement test in biology constructed and validated by the investigators. Blended learning programme was developed by the investigator for the teaching of the concepts in biology topics included in the XI standard biology syllabus.

The progrmme was arranged logically based on the psychological principles of learning. Experimental design was adopted. For the experimentation pretest was conducted and sample was divided into two groups. The students of the experimental group were taught with the blended learning progrmme and the control group through the conventional method. After the treatment period the posttest was administered. The collected data were subjected to statistical analysis and the results obtained were interpreted.

Testing of Hypotheses

Hypothesis 1: There is no significant difference between the experimental group and control group in the achievement of biology at pre test level.

The't' test applied to test the significance of difference between the mean achievement test scores of the experimental group and control group of pretest level.

Table -1: Mean Achievement Test Scores of the Experimental Group Compared with that of the Control Group at Pretest level

Groups	N	Mean	S.D	't' value	Level of Significance at 0.05 level
Experimental	30	20.43	2.09	0.46	Not significant
Control	30	19.63	1.87		

The table indicates that the 't' value is not significant at 0.05 level. The students of the experimental group do not differ significantly from the students of the control group in the mean achievement test scores at pre test level.

Hypothesis 2: There is no significant difference between the experimental group and control group in the achievement of biology at posttest level

Th 't' test applied to test the significance of difference between the mean achievement test scores of the experimental group and control group of posttest level.

Table -2: Mean Achievement Test Scores of the Experimental Group Compared with that of the Control Group at Posttest level

Groups	N	Mean	S.D	't' value	Level of Significance at 0.01 level
Experimental	30	36.40	3.96	15.08	significant
Control	30	20.10	5.14		

The table indicates that the 't' value is significant at 0.01 level. Hence there is there is a significant difference between the two groups. As indicated by the mean value, it can be concluded that the students of the experimental group fared better in the achievement test than the students of the control group. This shows that learning with the help of blended learning programme will increase the achievement of the students better than learning through the conventional method.

Hypothesis 3: There is no significant difference between the pretest and posttest in the achievement of biology for the experimental group.

The 't' test applied to test the significance of difference between test scores of the pretest with that of the posttest for the experimental group.

Table -3: Mean Achievement Test Scores of Pretest Compared with that of the Posttest for the Experimental Group

Groups	N	Mean	S.D	't' value	Level of Significance at 0.01 level
Experimental	30	20.43	2.07	20.52	Significant
Control	30	37.40	3.96		

Table 3 indicates that the't' value is significant at 0.01 level. Hence, it could be concluded that there is a significant difference between the mean achievement test scores of the pretest and posttest for the experimental group. The higher mean value in the posttest shows that the students fared better in the posttest than in the pretest. This shows that the blended learning programme has helped the students to score more in the posttest.

Hypothesis 4: There is no significant difference between the pretest and posttest in the achievement of biology for the control group.

The 't' test applied to test the significance of difference between the mean achievement test scores of the pretest with that of the posttest for the control group.

Table-4: Mean Achievement Test Scores of Pretest Compared with that of the Posttest for the Control Group

Groups	N	Mean	S.D	't' value	Level of Significance at 0.05 level
Experimental	30	19.76	1.87	0.034	Not significant
Control	30	20.00	5.06		

Table 4 indicates that the 't' value is not significant at 0.05 level. Hence, it could be concluded that there is no significant difference between the mean achievement test scores of the pretest and posttest for the control group.

Findings of the Study

There is no significant difference between the experimental group and control group in the achievement of biology at pretest level.

There is a significant difference between the experimental group and control group in the achievement of biology at posttest level. The students leaning with the help of blended learning programme fared better in biology than in students learning through the conventional method.

There is a significant difference between the mean achievement test scores of the pretest and posttest for the experimental group. This shows that the blended learning programme has helped the students to score more marks in the posttest.

There is a significant difference between the mean achievement test scores of the pretest and posttest for the control group. This shows that the conventional method of teaching will not help the students to score more marks in the posttest.

Conclusion

In the field of education is not possible to equip the teaching leaning in higher and higher secondary level because most of the higher secondary schools suffering from lack of modern methods of teaching, they still follow the conventional method of teaching in higher secondary level. This should be change in the modern era; they should follow the blended learning methods in their teaching learning methods because it supports the education department well in advance.

Reference

Barbour Michael, et al, (2012), *Online and Blended Learning: A Survey of Policy and Practice of K-12 Schools Around the World*, available at http://www.inacol.org/cms/wpcontent/uploads/2012/11/iNACOL_IntnlReport2011.pdf

Rogers Carl (1983), *The Interpersonal Relationship in the Facilitation of Learning*, London: Rutledge

The Oxford Group (2013), *Blended Learning—Current Use, Challenges and Best Practices*, report 2013, available at http://www.kineo.com/m/0/blended-learning-report-202013.pdf (accessed July 2013)

30.

Awareness of Educational Media among Higher Secondary Teachers of Thiruvannamalai District and Their Perception of Media Based Education

INTRODUCTION

Perception refers to "the way in which man senses or becomes immediately aware of his environment". Although knowledge about the world is gained through the senses, sensory impressions themselves are not enough to given a suitable understanding of the object perceived. It is the brain that receives and interprets them, which then become organized into meaningful understanding. Thus any given perceptual event is the result of multiple sensory messages. Perceptual events do not occur in isolation, they are continuous. As result of constant sensory stimulation, experiences are arranged and rearranged, shuffled and reshuffled, selected and reselected and organized into a convenient combination of patterns. This process finally leads the formation of concept. In general, understanding of the things and events of the world is based on sensory experiences and the physical objects, as the human beings known them are products of their own sensory perceptions. The present study aims to find out the awareness of educational media among Higher Secondary teachers of Thiruvannamalai district and their perception of media based education. A samples of 200 samples selected randomly were studied. A questionnaire method of survey was used to find out the awareness of educational media among Higher Secondary teachers. The data were collected by using questionnaire as an instrument. Primary data were collected by conducting direct structured interview using questionnaire. All the respondents were asked the same questions in the same fashion and they were informed the purpose of study. t-test, One way ANOVA analysis, correlation analysis were applied to test the hypotheses. The findings and observations are the result and outcome of the interpretations made during the study of analysis. The result found that the average level of awareness of educational media among Higher Secondary teachers.

"Audio – visual aids are the different types of tools that appeal to the senses of learning and vision and are used in classroom for presentation of abstract information". Almost every educational reformer has expressed deep concern over excessive use of words that carry the shadow of meaning but not the substance. Several educationists have suggested making education realistic. About three centuries ago, Comenius (1976) prepared first "visualized" text book which contained some 150 pictures. "let the pictures be a source of delight to the children and let them become familiar with them before they enter school" was his theory. Later Rousseau (1712-1778) criticized the teaching of his days and condemned the liberal use of words by teachers. According to him the teaching process must be directed to the learner's natural curiosity. Rousseau's theory was put into action by Pestalozzi (1756-1827) in his 'object method'. His idea was to base instruction on sense perception. Although attempts on the use of concrete aids were made sporadically, intensive development in audio – visual education has been going on successfully of using motion films and by 1929 sound films was produced. Today it has been proved beyond doubt by research and classroom experience that audio-visual aids can contribute effectively in learning. These materials may be used to convey meaning without complete dependence on verbal symbols or language. Some audio-visual activities like filed trip, demonstrating an experiment etc. are in the nature of process or experience. Some like motion film or filmstrip need a projector to handle it. Some others like chart need no equipment and can be directly used. Experiences of this type will be classified under visual category. Magnetic tape or disc recordings belongs to audio category, hence 'a-v' aids designated in common usage means both process and material things.

The present era is an information technology era. Now-a-day the students are more aware of latest technological advancement. In olden days, teachers generally used oral method of teaching as well as they used black board for writing purpose. But these things were not given much more concentration to the students. Teachers faced a lot of problems to create attention among the students.

Number of researchers found that in comparing, Audio and Video method of teaching will attract the students as well as to motivate the students to concentrate more. Based on the concept, the present researches focus to know the teachers awareness educational media.

In the present technological world, a lot of Audio Visual aids are designed and used by the teachers to teach the subjects effectively. Generally, computers, Television, LCD's (Liquid Crystal Display) and OHP (over Head Projector) are the common educational media used by the teachers for teaching. Computers play an important role to access any kind of latest information within a short time as well as any individual can search any type of information throughout the globe. It is very easy to learn new informative technique when compared to the traditional methods. Efforts are also very less using this technique. Both teachers and students are able to know up to date information easily. Considering all this advantages educational media are very important for students and teachers to learn.

Even though teachers used these aids but there is a necessity to measure the teachers awareness of educational media and their perception of media based education. Only by knowing the teachers can enhance their method of teaching. In this concept, the present research title is significant and needed for the study.

REVIEW OF LITERATURE

Rama and Kumar (2007) described in detail, various dimensions of LAN to internet in education through educational media. They pointed out the local area network (LAN) to provide the concept of integrated learning, system where by a central file server can provide random access and interactivity in learning WAN promote the concept of integrated learning system where by a central file server can provide random access and interactivity in learning. Wide Area Networks (WAN) concept would be needed for multi campus as inter institutional environment when internet and intranet faculties would be needed larger band width, fiber optic lives for the internet and intranet enable to transmit full video broad casting. Internet provides information and instructional services within organization. An internet would be capable of communication between the organization faculty, library students and other seminars, transforming sessions, research presentation, guest lectures, silent development course of orientation programmes and can be held of interests since the www is accessible through the internet only if may be installed to extend seminar, short and long term courses along with a variety of extracurricular activities in addition.

Kumar (2007) reported that the recent innovation in information technology have revolutions the mean of instruction within and outside institution. LAN (Local Area Network) brought in the concept of integrated learning system where by a central file servers can provide random access and interactivity in learning. The internet and intranet enable them to transmit full view broad casting. Intranets provide information and instructional services within organization.

Bansal and Chaudhary (2008) found that interactive radio has a great potential to support learning at a distance. Being an easily accessible and cost effective medium, IGNOU (Indira Gandhi National Open University) now started an interactive radio project for the students of management and bachelor preparatory programme. The objective of the project was to interact within the students in their own language and share experiences with them the effectiveness interactive radio instruction was evaluated and reported in this paper. The students appreciated interactive radio sessions as effective inputs to accomplish the course objectives. Besides students enrolled with other institutions and enlightened public also participated in the session. The study revealed that student's participation in the interactive radio sessions was higher than the teleconferences and face to face personal contact sessions. The project can be replicated in other areas also, with systematic planning, implementation and monitoring.

Shivanekar (2008) reported that powerful computer networks enabling access to the data bases may however turn information into a real utility after an integrated service of e-mail and conferencing, advertising and news, information access to a range of key database and so on. To link every school in the nation, every public library, every university and every other educational or cultural institution to one massive communication network meeting all the communication and information differentiate needs of all the members may be called education utility.

Jamtshio (2008) discussed the distance education course for in service primary at the National Institute of Education (NIE) in Samtse, Bhutan. It is the fast and the only distance education, teacher have same syllabus and appear for the same term-end examination. The distance learners attend compulsory residential contact programme. The distance education programme needs systematic planning and monitoring to impart knowledge and skills to the teachers.

Baheerathan M, (2008) studied the awareness of educational media among the teachers of mathematics at high school level in Tanjavur district. He reported that the internet awareness among the students of mathematics at high school level is not sufficient. Also he found that the gender of the teachers and the locale and the management of the schools where they are working caused no significant difference in respect of their awareness of educational media.

Singh (2008) took up a study to see the effectiveness of educational media in teaching mathematics. He found that students significantly higher than those taught through the conventional method.

Jeyamani (2009) developed a computer assisted instruction (CAI) package in physics for class XI students. The experimental group received, CAI and after the experiment it was found that the experimental group performed better on the post test. The differences were insignificant in terms of sex and medium of instruction.

Gunawatdena (2009) discussed the use of technology for quality improvement in the distance education programme. The study is based on data gathered for teacher education programmes, which has implication for other open universities too.

Huang and Aloi (2010) investigated the impact of using interactive video in teaching general biology. Biology undergraduate students using a computer-assisted interactive videodisc system which included dissection simulations performed significantly better than students who had not used the computer-aided instruction.

Kalimuthu (2010) developed a video programme on environmental pollution in biology for higher secondary students and investigated whether students in higher secondary schools, who are taught environmental pollution in biology by the video method, achieve more than those who are taught by the traditional method. The major findings were that the higher secondary students taught through the video programme learnt more of the concepts on environmental pollution than those who were taught by the lecture method. The higher secondary students improved their performance in environmental pollution after viewing the video programme.

Wagh (2011) developed a multi-media instructional system for remedial measures for class VIII students, in fractional numbers. The multi-instructional system contains charts, flash cards, film-strips, audio-cassettes, assignments, and a self-learning programme. The results revealed that the Traditional Instructional System (TIS) and the (MIS) remedial approaches both helped students in improving their performance on all the six computational skills in fractional numbers.

Beerman, Brown and Evans (2011) found that there was a significant benefit of new technologies, as opposed to traditional texts, and hence it is better to allow students to learn in their own style and at their own pace. An additional argument is that CD-ROM provides media and visually rich material that is more likely to correspond effectively with students' individual learning styles.

Senthil Kumar K, (2011) studied the educational media knowledge of higher secondary chemistry students. He found that the media knowledge possessed by the first year higher secondary students is not high. Also he reported that, the girls have relatively high media knowledge when compared to boys in general.

OBJECTIVE

To find out the awareness of educational media among Higher Secondary teachers of Thiruvannamalai District and their perception of Media based Education of the entire and its sub samples.

METHODOLOGY

The methodology adopted for the study is explained in detail. The sampling technique, size of the sample, variables of the study, description of the tool used and administration of tool are elaborated.

METHOD OF DATA COLLECTION

The investigator personally distributed the questionnaires to each member of the randomly selected sample. They were requested to answer the items in the booklet as per the instructions provided at the beginning of each questionnaire. Confidentiality of response was assured. The questionnaires were collected by the investigator from the teachers. The responses were scored as per the scoring key of the respective questionnaire. Then the results were tabulated, analysed and discussed.

Sample : The investigator prepared a representative random sample of Higher Secondary teachers in different schools at Thiruvannamalai District. A sample of 200 teachers was finally selected.

Data Collection

Primary data, required for the present research work were collected by conducting direct interviews using questionnaire. All the respondents were given sufficient information about the study. These respondents were provided with the same questionnaires. They were also informed that they have to answer in the same fashion.

STATISTICAL TOOLS FOR ANALYSIS

The following tools statistical tools were used for the analysis of data. t-test, ANOVA analysis and correlation analysis.

ANALYSIS AND INTERPRETATION

Table 1: Showing Mean, SD and F-test for respondent about educational media awareness among Higher Secondary teachers on the basis of Academic qualification

Academic qualification	N	Mean	SD	F-value	Level of Significance
M.A. B.Ed.	54	72.26	9.37	3.24	0.01
M.Sc. B.Ed.	48	72.89	8.84		
M.Com. B.Ed.	98	69.00	7.08		
Total	200	71.78	8.58		

Hypothesis : Teachers do not differ in their educational media awareness among higher secondary teachers on the basis of Academic qualification.

The calculated F-value (3.24), which is significant at 0.01 level, confirms that there is a significant difference in their educational media awareness among higher secondary teachers on the basis of Academic qualification. Hence the stated hypothesis is rejected.

Table 2: Showing Mean, SD and t-test for respondent about educational media awareness among Higher Secondary teachers on the basis of Designation

Designation	N	Mean	SD	t-value	Level of Significance
PG Teachers	132	72.08	9.22	2.34	0.01
BT Teachers	68	69.33	5.18		

Hypothesis: Teachers do not differ in their educational media awareness among higher secondary teachers on the basis of Designation.

The calculated t-value (2.34), which is significant at 0.01 level, confirms that there is a significant difference in educational media awareness among higher secondary teachers on the basis of Designation. Hence the stated hypothesis is rejected. So PG Teachers have high level of educational media awareness than BT teachers.

Table 3: Showing Mean, SD and F-test for respondent about educational media awareness among Higher Secondary teachers on the basis of Type of Institution

Type of Institution	N	Mean	SD	F-value	Level of Significance
Govt.	58	70.31	4.09	3.42	0.01
Govt. Aided	68	71.30	9.56		
Self-Financing	74	74.29	9.75		
Total	200	71.78	8.58		

Hypothesis : Teachers do not differ in their educational media awareness among higher secondary teachers on the basis of Type of Institution.

The calculated F-value (3.42), which is significant at 0.01 level, confirms that there is a significant difference in their educational media awareness among higher secondary teachers on the basis of Type of Institution. Hence the stated hypothesis is rejected.

Table 4: Showing Mean, SD and F-test for respondent about educational media awareness among Higher Secondary teachers on the basis of Teaching Experience

Teaching Experience	N	Mean	SD	F-value	Level of Significance
Below 10 years	67	69.20	9.64	3.62	0.01
11 – 20 years	88	71.75	4.19		
Above 20 years	45	75.00	8.60		
Total	200	71.78	8.58		

Hypothesis : Teachers do not differ in their educational media awareness among higher secondary teachers on the basis of Teaching experience.

The calculated F-value (3.62), which is significant at 0.01 level, confirms that there is a significant difference in their educational media awareness among higher secondary teachers on the basis of Teaching experience. Hence the stated hypothesis is rejected.

Table 5: Showing Mean, SD and F-test for respondent about media perception evaluation among Higher Secondary teachers on the basis of Academic qualification

Academic qualification	N	Mean	SD	F-value	Level of Significance
M.A. B.Ed.	54	92.42	9.69	3.42	0.01
M.Sc. B.Ed.	48	92.24	9.24		
M.Com. B.Ed.	98	99.00	8.24		
Total	200	91.81	7.24		

Hypothesis : Teachers do not differ in their media perception evaluation among higher secondary teachers on the basis of Academic qualification.

The calculated F-value (3.42), which is significant at 0.01 level, confirms that there is a significant difference in their media perception evaluation among higher secondary teachers on the basis of Academic qualification. Hence the stated hypothesis is rejected.

Table 6: Showing Mean, SD and t-test for respondent about media perception evaluation among Higher Secondary teachers on the basis of Designation

Designation	N	Mean	SD	t-value	Level of Significance
PG Teachers	132	92.26	9.48	2.22	0.01
BT Teachers	68	98.42	5.36		

Hypothesis: Teachers do not differ in their media perception evaluation among higher secondary teachers on the basis of Designation.

The calculated t-value (2.22), which is significant at 0.01 level, confirms that there is a significant difference in media perception evaluation among higher secondary teachers on the basis of Designation. Hence the stated hypothesis is rejected. So BT Teachers have high level of media perception evaluation than PG teachers.

Table 7: Showing Mean, SD and F-test for respondent about media perception evaluation among Higher Secondary teachers on the basis of Type of Institution

Type of Institution	N	Mean	SD	F-value	Level of Significance
Govt.	58	90.24	4.29	3.92	0.01
Govt. Aided	68	91.29	9.29		
Self-Financing	74	94.65	9.36		
Total	200	91.81	7.24		

Hypothesis : Teachers do not differ in their media perception evaluation among higher secondary teachers on the basis of Type of Institution.

The calculated F-value (3.92), which is significant at 0.01 level, confirms that there is a significant difference in their media perception evaluation among higher secondary teachers on the basis of Type of Institution. Hence the stated hypothesis is rejected.

Table 8: Showing Mean, SD and F-test for respondent about media perception evaluation among Higher Secondary teachers on the basis of teaching Experience

Teaching Experience	N	Mean	SD	F-value	Level of Significance
Below 10 years	67	99.22	9.24	3.94	0.01
11 – 20 years	88	91.24	5.29		
Above 20 years	45	95.21	7.21		
Total	200	91.81	7.24		

Hypothesis : Teachers do not differ in their media perception evaluation among higher secondary teachers on the basis of Teaching experience.

The calculated F-value (3.94), which is significant at 0.01 level, confirms that there is a significant difference in their media perception evaluation among higher secondary teachers on the basis of Teaching experience. Hence the stated hypothesis is rejected.

The above table shows correlation between educational media awareness and media perception evaluation among Higher Secondary teachers. Result shows that there is a positive and significant correlation between educational media awareness and media perception evaluation.

Suggestions

The following suggestions are arrived from the research findings. Research found that use of educational media will contribute more in student's achievement. Also the result reveals that use of awareness educational media increases the memory power, concentration. Further it sharpens the intelligence. Apart from that it reduces misconception in learning. So, the present research suggested that in all schools and colleges, the students advised to use of educational media compulsory. The education department forms a rule for that and advises the educational institutions make a step to establish separate infrastructure for this one. Also the Government take a step to use media based teaching effectively students in their academic. This will definitely help the students to be a good learner imbibing the concepts.

Conclusion

The present study awareness of educational media among Higher Secondary teachers of Thiruvannamalai district and their perception of media based education. For that the researcher framed some objectives. On the basis of objectives, a questionnaire is framed. After framing the questionnaire, these are circulated to the selected samples. 200 samples were selected randomly. The responses were collected and coded using computerised. To test the hypotheses and characteristics of the data, some standard statistical tools were used. The statistical tools such as t-test, F-ratio and correlation were used. From the analysis the result concluded that the Higher Secondary teachers have favourable of educational media and their perception of media based education.

REFERENCE

- Agostinho, Hedberg and Lefoe (2008), "Advanced Educational Technology", New Delhi : Knishka Publishers distribution.
- Baheerathan M, (2008) "Teach the Internet in a week". New Delhi: Prentice Hall of India Private Limited.
- Bansal and Chaudhary (2008) "The Internet invasion of how wills the teachers educator cope" New Delhi: Journal of higher education".
- Beerman, K., Brown, G., & Evans, M. (2011). Interactive CD study modules in food science and Human Nutrition: Assessing Technology-Enhanced study programs. *Journal of Educational Multimedia and Hypermedia, 7(4): 365-374.*
- Charag (2011), "Practice Experiences of CD-Rom based language learning", British Journal of Educational technology, vol.30, page 153-175, Oxford Blackwell.
- Coneia (2010), "Computer and language learning", International Journal, page no 15-68.
- Fetterman (2008), Asia and the Pacific programme of educational in Innovation for development (APEID), page 15-82 UNESCO Regional offices for education in Asia and the Pacific.
- Gunawatdena (2009), "Quantitative Techniques and Operations Research" Thiruvananthapuram : Yamuna publications.
- Hexel, Marcellus and Berwoull (2008). "The concept and problem of Networking in educational research" The experience of Ernesa, Networking in educational research. Proceeding of the Boleswa Education Research Symposium, University of Swaziland.
- Huang, S. D., & Aloi, J. (2010). The impact of using interactive video in teaching general biology. *The American Biology Teacher, 53(5): 281-284.*
- Jamtshio (2008) "Living in the information age" Vadodara: Premise and Implication for school education programme, Challenges in School Education.
- Jeyamani (2009). "The concept and problem of Networking in educational research" The experience of Ernesa, Networking in educational research. Proceeding of the Boleswa Education Research Symposium, University of Swaziland.
- Johnson (2009), "Education, Its Philosophy, Psychology and Technology" Thrissur : Breeze publications.
- Jonasson (2008), "Mastering the Internet", USA: International Journal of Information Technology and Communication.

- Kalimuthu, T. (2010). Developing a video programme on environmental pollution in biology for higher secondary students. *Fifth Survey of Research in Education, Vol. II, p.1377.*
- Koeppen and Andre (2011), "Quantitative Techniques and Operations Research" USA: Yamuna publications.
- Kumar (2007) "A Study of Utilisation of Internet by the Students of Higher Education", M.Ed Dissertation, Annamalai University.
- Lee (2009), "Third survey of researcher in education and development", Baroda.
- Medina (2011) "Cognitive and Affective Attitude of Teachers Towards Computer", Experiments in Education, 30 (2), pp.7-12.
- Rama and Kumar (2007) "Cognitive and Affective Attitude of Teachers Towards Computer", Experiments in Education, 30 (2), pp.7-12.
- Senthil Kumar K, (2011): "New Approach to Information Technology Education", Compendium on Information Technology on Science Education.
- Shivanekar (2008). "Introduction of Educational Technology", New Delhi, Sterling Publishers Pvt. Ltd.
- Singh (2008) "Introduction to educational technology, Sterility Publishers", New Delhi : Private Limited.
- Stefansdottir (2007) "The Internet Complete Reference; Second Edition", New Delhi: Tata McGraw-Hill Company Limited".
- Teles and Rylands (2011) "Living in the information age" Vadodara: Premise and Implication for school education programme, Challenges in School Education.
- Wagh, S. K. (2011). Development of a multimedia instructional system for remedial measures in fractional numbers. *Fifth Survey of Research in Education, Vol. II, pp.1299.*

❐

31.

Relevant Effectiveness of Computer Based Multimedia Learning Material

Introduction

Performance and behavioural outcome of the student is important aspects in school education here performance refers knowledge uplifted from the course of study. Behaviour outcome refers to social behaviour like responsible co-operation. Now a day complete is using in the entire field for the various purpose. In our education computer is used for giving instruction, administration and research. CAT, programmed instruction, PSI all is innovations in educational field to improve the performance. So the researcher has as her rightly chosen the study of the relevant effectiveness of computer based multimedia learning material on performance and behaviour outcome of high school students. The present study to find out the relevant effectiveness of computer based multimedia learning material on performance and behaviour outcome in Tindivanam Town. A samples of 100 respondents selected randomly were studied. A questionnaire method of survey was used to find out the effectiveness of computer based multimedia learning material on performance and behaviour outcome. The data were collected by using questionnaire as an instrument. Primary data were collected by conducting direct structured interview using questionnaire. All the respondents were asked the same questions in the same fashion and they were informed the purpose of study. T-test, One Way ANOVA and Correlation analysis was applied to test the hypotheses. The findings and observations are the result and outcome of the interpretations made during the study of analysis. The result found that there is a significant difference between traditional method and computer method of teaching.

Multimedia refers to any computer-mediated software or interactive application that integrates text, color, graphical images, animation, audio sound, and full motion video in a single application. Multimedia learning systems consist of animation and narration, which offer a potential venue for improving student understanding. Multimedia programme is an integral part of the educational technology. As a technique, it offers a high potential in application at different stages of education for the purpose of enhancing the teaching and learning processes, as is evident from the experience of developed countries.

The integration of multimedia technology into the communication environment has the potential to transform the students from passive recipients of information to active participants in a media-rich learning process. The introduction of multimedia or any other computer-based information technology is not intended to substitute a presenter. This new technology is intended to provide the presenter with a powerful tool that can greatly enhance communication by delivering a multisensory experience. With interactive multimedia technology, a teacher can communicate with the students by means of a presentation that becomes more than message-it becomes an active, exciting experience in a multisensory environment to create a multisensory experience. Multimedia reaches users in many different ways, enabling them to retain more knowledge and increase their understanding.

There are 4 steps in learning like attention, rehearsal, encoding and retrieval. A well designed multimedia application demands the simultaneous attention of several senses through dual encoding or the process of appealing to more than one sense simultaneously. Dual encoding facilitates and enhances the rehearsal process. Multimedia helps retrieval by associating sound, text and images with the concept being presented. Using text, images, animation and sound simultaneously greatly improves the students' retention of the knowledge and directs the students' attention to classroom (Louis, 2001).

Multimedia consists of the combination of video and movie clips and sound, text and graphic files all controlled by a piece of software and a computer which is equipped with a sound card, a video card, a CD-ROM drive and speakers or headphone. Sometimes, there is also a videodisk player, which is controlled by the software.

Computer based multimedia delivers information in a variety of ways but achieves its greatest effectiveness through interaction. In the first case, music and informative knowledge combine to convey the message. In the second case, technology provides a more effective presentation wherein information, images and sounds are technically and aesthetically integrated, focusing on a single specific purpose. The ability of students to work independently and to receive instruction suited to their needs and learning styles is inherently attractive.

Review of Literature

Dalacosta et al. (2009) developed and studied the effectiveness of Multimedia **application with animated cartoons in teaching science in elementary**

education. The results of the study provide evidence that the use of animated cartoons significantly increases the young students' knowledge and understanding of specific science concepts, which are normally difficult to comprehend and often cause misconceptions to them.

Jian Hu et al. (2009) investigated the effects of introducing a software program, named the Dental 3D Multimedia System (D3DM), into the education of a group of junior dental students in their preclinical practice. One group received their training program in the traditional way, unassisted by 3D technology. The second group received their training program in the traditional manner, but also used the D3DM to supplement their education. The results showed that the D3DM-assisted group achieved higher scores and also indicated that the usage of 3D multimedia PC software had a positive impact on several aspects of subjects' performance.

Kanmani and Radha (2009) studied the Effectiveness of CAI package in basic electronics teaching. There was a significant difference between the control and the experimental group students in attainment of knowledge level, understanding level, and application level objective in the gain scores. Hence, the experimental group students were better than the control group students in attainment of knowledge level, understanding level, and application level objective in the gain scores. It was inferred from the finding that the experimental treatment is effective to the students.

Korakakis et al. (2009) made a study on the **"3D visualization types in multimedia applications for science learning for 8th grade students in Greece".** The aim of the study was to determine whether the use of specific types of visualization (3D illustration, 3D animation, and interactive 3D animation) combined with narration and text, contributes to the learning process in science courses. The results indicated that multimedia applications with interactive 3D animations as well as with 3D animations do in fact increase the interest of students and make the material more appealing to them.

She, Hsiao-Ching and Chen, Yi-Zen (2009) examined how middle school students constructed their understanding of the mitosis and meiosis processes at a molecular level through multimedia learning materials presented in different interaction and sensory modality modes. The dependent variables included subjects' pre-test, post-test, and retention-test scores, showing their understanding of mitosis and meiosis process at molecular level. The results of the study showed that the group which used multimedia learning material has a greater amount of visual attention and consistent with their long term retained learning than the group which did not use the same. This study adds empirical evidence of a direct correlation between the length of eye fixation behavior and the depth of learning. Moreover, it provides insight into the multimedia effect on students' cognitive process through the use of eye fixation behavior evidence.

Anboucarassy (2010) studied the effectiveness of Multimedia in Teaching

Biological Science to IX Standard students. The results of the study revealed that experiment group performed better than the control group due to the exposure of multimedia based learning. Thus multimedia helps the students to sustain their interest and also their retention power compared to the traditional method of teaching. The constant use of multimedia will make students understand more and achieve more in their academic achievement. Hence it was concluded that the multimedia approach is considered to be one of the best techniques for biology teaching at IX standard level.

Ponraj and Sivakumar (2010) studied the effectiveness of Computer-Assisted Instruction in Teaching Zoology in Relation to Learners' Personality. The major findings of the study indicated that achievement scores of experimental group students were higher than the control group students after the treatment.

Yusuf, Mudasiru and Afolabi, Adedeji (2010) investigated the effects of computer assisted instruction (CAI) on secondary school students' performance in biology. The findings of the study showed that the performance of students exposed to CAI either individually or cooperatively were better than their counterparts exposed to the conventional classroom instruction. Based on the research findings recommendations were made on the need to develop relevant CAI packages for teaching biology in Nigerian secondary schools.

Objectives

- To measure behaviour and performance of high school student.
- To assess effectiveness in performance of high school student
- To assess effective in behaviuoral outcome of the high school student.
- To assess effectiveness in traditional and multimedia method of teaching.
- To find out relevant effectiveness of computer based multimedia learning material on performance and behaviour outcome.

Hypothesis of the Study

High school students do not differ in their average level of relevant effectiveness of computer based on multimedia learning material on performance and behaviour outcome in traditional method and multimedia teaching of entire samples.

Respondents do not differ in their relevant effectiveness of computer based multimedia learning material on performance and behaviour outcome in pre test on the basis of groups.

Respondents do not differ in their relevant effectiveness of computer based multimedia learning material on performance and behaviour outcome in pre test on the basis of type of school.

Respondents do not differ in their relevant effectiveness of computer based multimedia learning material on performance and behaviour outcome in pre test on the basis of parent's education.

Respondents do not differ in their relevant effectiveness of computer based multimedia learning material on performance and behaviour outcome in pre test on the basis of parent's income.

Respondents do not differ in their relevant effectiveness of computer based multimedia learning material on performance and behaviour outcome in post test on the basis of type of school.

Respondents do not differ in their relevant effectiveness of computer based multimedia learning material on performance and behaviour outcome in post test on the basis of parent's education.

Respondents do not differ in their relevant effectiveness of computer based multimedia learning material on performance and behaviour outcome in post test on the basis of parent's income.

Methodology

The methodology adopted for the study is explained in detail. The sampling technique, size of the sample, variables of the study, description of the tool used and administration of tool are elaborated.

Sampling Technique

The random sampling techniques used in the present study. The survey should cover all the aspects of the subject selected of the study others are inferred from a study of a sample group carefully selected to be representative of the total population. At time, the survey describes a limited population which is the only group under consideration. It involves a clearly defined problem and defined objectives. It requires expert and imaginative planning. Careful analysis and interpretation of the data gathered and logical and skillful reporting of the findings. There are different findings such as social surveys, market surveys. The survey method is applied to the analysis of existing social conditions including educational conditions and to the analysis of public opinion. So in this present study, the investigator has used stratified disposition random sampling method.

Sample

Samples of 100 high school students selected randomly were studied in Tindivanam Town. Out of these high schools as many as 5 higher secondary schools have been chosen by appropriate method. All the available high school students studying in each of this selected high school were chosen as sample. Stratified disposition random sampling technique has been used in the selection of the sample.

Data Collection

Primary data, required for the present research work were collected by conducting direct interviews using questionnaire. All the respondents were given sufficient information about the study. These respondents were provided with the same questionnaires. They were also informed that they have to answer in the same fashion.

Tools used for the study

Development of effectiveness of multimedia programme and Scale by the investigator. The scale for measuring the high school student's effectiveness of multimedia towards science in the study. This scale has as many as 25 statements of which 3 point scale method.

Analysis and Interpretation

Table 1: Showing the Mean, Standard deviation of relevant effectiveness of computer based multimedia learning material on performance and behaviour outcome in pre and post test of entire samples

Groups	N	Mean	SD	r value
Pre test	100	14.79	2.69	0.346**
Post test	100	19.30	2.86	

Hypothesis: High school students do not differ in their average level of relevant effectiveness of computer based on multimedia learning material on performance and behaviour outcome in traditional method and multimedia teaching of entire samples.

The mean and standard deviation of relevant effectiveness of computer based multimedia learning material on performance and behaviour outcome scores of entire samples are 14.79 and 2.69 in pre test and 19.30 and 2.86 in post test. The mean score of all categories are lay in between ($M \pm 1\sigma$) value. So it is concluded that average level of relevant effectiveness of computer based multimedia learning material on performance and behaviour outcome of entire samples.

Table 2: Showing the Mean, Standard deviation and t-test for relevant effectiveness of computer based multimedia learning material on performance and behaviour outcome on the basis of groups

Groups	Sample size	Mean	Standard Deviation	t-value	Level of Significance
Pre test	100	14.79	2.69	12.86	0.01 (Significant)
Post test	100	19.30	2.86		

Hypothesis: Respondents do not differ in their relevant effectiveness of computer based multimedia learning material on performance and behaviour outcome in pre test on the basis of groups.

The calculated t-value (12.86), which is significant at 0.01 level, confirms that there is a significant difference between relevant effectiveness of computer based multimedia learning material on performance and behaviour outcome on the basis of groups. So the null hypothesis is rejected and alternate hypothesis is accepted. Therefore it is concluded that pre test and post test groups differ in their effectiveness of computer based multimedia learning material on performance and behaviour outcome.

Table 3: Showing mean, standard deviation and t-value for traditional method among the high school student on the basis of type of school

Sl. No	Type of school	Sample size	Mean	Standard Deviation	t-value	Level of Significance
1	Government	75	14.73	2.71	0.37	0.716 (Not Significant)
2	Aided	25	14.96	2.67		

Hypothesis: Respondents do not differ in their relevant effectiveness of computer based multimedia learning material on performance and behaviour outcome in pre test on the basis of type of school.

The calculated t-value (0.37), which is not significant, confirms that there is a no significant difference between relevant effectiveness of computer based multimedia learning material on performance and behaviour outcome in pre test on the basis of type of school. So the null hypothesis is accepted and alternate hypothesis is rejected. Therefore it is concluded that government and aided school groups do not differ in their pre test score.

Table 4: Showing mean, standard deviation and t-value for traditional method among the high school student on the basis of parents education

Sl. No	Parents education	Sample size	Mean	Standard Deviation	F-value	Level of Significance
1	School	86	14.82	2.75	0.58	0.560 (Not Significant)
2	Under graduate	8	14.13	2.03		
3	Post graduate	6	14.21	2.44		
	Total	100	14.79	2.69		

Hypothesis: Respondents do not differ in their relevant effectiveness of computer based multimedia learning material on performance and behaviour outcome in pre test on the basis of parents education.

The calculated F-value (0.58), which is not significant, confirms that there is a no significant difference between relevant effectiveness of computer based multimedia learning material on performance and behaviour outcome in pre test on the basis of parents education. So the null hypothesis is accepted and alternate hypothesis is rejected. Therefore it is concluded that different parents education students groups do not differ in their pre test score.

Table 5: Showing mean, standard deviation and t-value for traditional method among the high school student on the basis of parents income

Sl. No	Parents income	Sample size	Mean	Standard Deviation	F-value	Level of Significance
1	Below Rs.50,000	70	14.51	2.53	1.56	0.215 (Not Significant)
2	Rs.50,000 – 2,00,000	24	15.50	3.09		
3	Above Rs.2,00,000	6	16.00	2.65		
	Total	100	14.79	2.69		

Hypothesis: Respondents do not differ in their relevant effectiveness of computer based multimedia learning material on performance and behaviour outcome in pre test on the basis of parents income.

The calculated F-value (1.56), which is not significant, confirms that there is a no significant difference between relevant effectiveness of computer based multimedia learning material on performance and behaviour outcome in pre test on the basis of parents income. So the null hypothesis is accepted and alternate hypothesis is rejected. Therefore it is concluded that different parents income students groups do not differ in their pre test score.

Table 6: Showing mean, standard deviation and t-value for multimedia method among the high school student on the basis of type of school

Sl.No	Type of school	Sample size	Mean	Standard Deviation	t-value	Level of Significance
1	Govt.	75	18.75	2.91	4.33	0.01 (Significant)
2	Aided	25	20.96	1.93		

Hypothesis: Respondents do not differ in their relevant effectiveness of computer based multimedia learning material on performance and behaviour outcome in post test on the basis of type of school.

The calculated t-value (4.33), which is significant at 0.01 level, confirms that there is a significant difference between relevant effectiveness of computer based multimedia learning material on performance and behaviour outcome in post test on the basis of type of school. So the null hypothesis is rejected and alternate hypothesis is accepted. Therefore it is concluded that aided school students (20.96) scored higher mean value than government school students (18.75).

Table 7: Showing mean, standard deviation and t-value for multimedia method among the high school student on the basis of parents education

Sl. No	Parents education	Sample size	Mean	Standard Deviation	F-value	Level of Significance
1	School	86	19.34	2.87	3.19	0.01 (Significant)
2	Under graduate	8	16.75	3.01		
3	Post graduate	6	20.12	2.63		
	Total	100	19.30	2.86		

Hypothesis: Respondents do not differ in their relevant effectiveness of computer based multimedia learning material on performance and behaviour outcome in post test on the basis of parents education.

The calculated F-value (3.19), which is significant at 0.01 level, confirms that there is a significant difference between relevant effectiveness of computer based multimedia learning material on performance and behaviour outcome in post test on the basis of parents education. So the null hypothesis is rejected and alternate hypothesis is accepted. Therefore it is concluded that different parents education students groups differ in their post test score.

Table 8: Showing mean, standard deviation and t-value for multimedia method among the high school student on the basis of parents income

Sl. No.	Parents income	Sample size	Mean	Standard Deviation	F-value	Level of Significance
1	Below Rs.50,000	70	19.11	2.64	3.29	0.01 (Significant)
2	Rs.50,000 – 2,00,000	24	20.04	3.24		
3	Above Rs.2,00,000	6	16.00	4.58		
	Total	100	19.30	2.86		

Hypothesis: Respondents do not differ in their relevant effectiveness of computer based multimedia learning material on performance and behaviour outcome in post test on the basis of parents income.

The calculated F-value (3.29), which is significant at 0.01 level, confirms that there is a significant difference between relevant effectiveness of computer based multimedia learning material on performance and behaviour outcome in post test on the basis of parents income. So the null hypothesis is rejected and alternate hypothesis is accepted. Therefore it is concluded that different parents income students groups differ in their post test score.

Findings

High school students differ in their average level of relevant effectiveness of computer based on multimedia learning material on performance and behaviour outcome in traditional method and multimedia teaching of entire samples.

- Respondents differ in their relevant effectiveness of computer based multimedia learning material on performance and behaviour outcome in pre test on the basis of groups.
- Respondents do not differ in their relevant effectiveness of computer based multimedia learning material on performance and behaviour outcome in pre test on the basis of type of school.
- Respondents do not differ in their relevant effectiveness of computer based multimedia learning material on performance and behaviour outcome in pre test on the basis of parents education.
- Respondents do not differ in their relevant effectiveness of computer based multimedia learning material on performance and behaviour outcome in pre test on the basis of parents income.
- Respondents differ in their relevant effectiveness of computer based multimedia learning material on performance and behaviour outcome in post test on the basis of type of school.
- Respondents differ in their relevant effectiveness of computer based multimedia learning material on performance and behaviour outcome in post test on the basis of parents education.
- Respondents differ in their relevant effectiveness of computer based multimedia learning material on performance and behaviour outcome in post test on the basis of parents income.

Conclusion

In the present study, the researcher arrive the following conclusion based on the findings. In the present study, science students have relevant effectiveness of computer based multimedia learning material on performance and behaviour outcome of high school students in Tindivanam Town when compared with other students. The researcher framed objectives and hypotheses on the basis of the above context. 100 samples were selected randomly. A standard questionnaire was used to collect the relevant data. After collecting the data they were analyzed using statistical tools such as t-test and ANOVA in the both groups (pre and post test). The result concluded that the all the science students of average level of relevant effectiveness of computer based multimedia learning material on performance and behaviour outcome.

References

- Anboucarassy, B. (2010). Effectiveness of Multimedia in Teaching Biological Science to IX Standard students. EDUTRACKS, 9(5): 37-38.
- Annaraja, P., & Jenitha Rani, J. R. (2003). Development of Visual Basic based CAI package in Commerce and its effectiveness on Achievement in Commerce. Research and Reflections on Education.
- Balasubramanian, N., & Jayaraman (2001). Relative Effectiveness among Different Modes of Computer Based Instruction. Experiments in Education, 29(2): 9-13.
- Chang, Chun-Yen (2002). The impact of different forms of multimedia CAI on students' science achievement. Innovations in Education and Teaching International, 39 (4): 280-88. Retrieved March 20, 2010
- Dalacosta, K., Kamariotaki-Paparrigopoulou, M., Palyvos, J.A., & Spyrellis, N. (2009). Multimedia application with animated cartoons for teaching science in elementary education. Computers & Education, 52(4): 741-748. Retrieved March 20, 2010
- Dawson, M. E., Skinner, S., & Zeitlin, A. (2003). Rules of Engagement: Proceed with Caution when Integrating Multimedia learning Tools into Existing Course Formats. Electronic Journal of Science Education, 7(4). Retrieved March 21, 2010
- Diseko, R. & Van Der Westhuizen, D. (2006). The Design and Development of a multimedia Tutorial for facilitation constructivist Learning among Nursing Science students: A Design experiment. Proceedings of World Conference on Educational Multimedia, Hypermedia and Telecommunications 2006, pp. 493-499. Retrieved March 20, 2010
- Garnett, P., Hackling, M., & Oliver, R. (1997). An Interactive Multimedia Package Designed to Improve Beginning Students' Understanding of Chemical Equations. UniServe Science News, Vol. 8, pp. 18-21. Retrieved March 21, 2010
- Jian Hu, Hao Yu, Jun Shao, Zhiyong Li, Jiawei Wang & Yining Wang (2009). Effects of dental 3D multimedia system on the performance of junior dental students in preclinical practice: a report from China. Advances in Health Sciences Education, 14(1): 123 – 133. Retrieved March 20, 2010
- Junaidu, Sahalu (2008). Effectiveness of multimedia in learning & teaching data structures online. Turkish Online Journal of Distance Education-TOJDE, 9(4), Article 7. Retrieved March 21, 2010
- Kadhiravan, S., & Suresh, V. (2001). Effect of Computer-assisted Instruction on Self-regulated Learning. Perspective in Education, 18(3): 161-169.
- Kanmani, M., & Radha, M. (2009). "Effectiveness of CAI package in basic

electronics teaching", Journal of All India Association for Educational Research, 21(1): 47-50.

- Korakakis, G., Pavlatou, E.A., Palyvos, J. A., & Spyrellis N. (2009). 3D visualization types in multimedia applications for science learning: A case study for 8th grade students in Greece. Computers & Education, 52(2): 390-401. Retrieved March 21, 2010
- Liao, Yuen-kuang & Chen, Yu-wen (2007). The Effect of Computer Simulation Instruction on Student Learning: A Meta-analysis of Studies in Taiwan. Journal of Information Technology and Applications, 2(2): 69-79. Retrieved March 21, 2010
- O'Day, Danton H. (2007). The value of Animations in Biology Teaching: A Study of Long – Term Memory Retention. Journal of CBE - Life Science Education, 6(3): 217-223. Retrieved March 20, 2010
- O'Day, Danton H. (2007). The value of Animations in Biology Teaching: A Study of Long – Term Memory Retention. Journal of CBE - Life Science Education, 6(3): 217-223. Retrieved March 20, 2010
- Ozmen, Haluk (2008). The influence of Computer-Assisted Instruction on students' conceptual understanding of chemical Bonding and Attitude toward chemistry: A case for Turkey. Computers and Education, 51(1): 423-438. Retrieved March 21, 2010
- Ponraj, P., & Nellaiyapen, N. O. (2008). CAI in teaching Zoology. Research and Reflections on Education, 6(2): 18-21.
- Ponraj, P., & Sivakumar, R. (2010). Computer-Assisted Instruction in Zoology in Relation to Learners' Personality. EDUTRACKS, 9(6): 34-37.
- Prinz, A., Bolz, M., & Findl, O. (2005). Advantage of three dimensional animated teaching over traditional surgical videos for teaching ophthalmic surgery: a randomised study. British Journal of Ophthalmology, 89(11): 1495-1499. Retrieved March 21, 2010
- Pryor, Caroline R., & Bitter, Gary G. (2008). Using multimedia to teach in-service teachers: Impacts on learning, application, and retention. Computers in Human Behavior, 24 (6): 2668-2681. Retrieved March 20, 2010
- Rotbain, Y., Marbach-Ad, G., & Stavy, R. (2008). Using a computer animation to teach high school molecular biology. Journal of Science Education and Technology, 17(1): 49-58. Retrieved March 21, 2010
- Segers, E., & Verhoeven, L. (2002). Multimedia support of early literacy learning. Computers and Education, 39(3): 207-221. Retrieved March 20, 2010
- She, Hsiao-Ching & Chen, Yi-Zen (2009). The impact of multimedia effect on science learning: Evidence from eye movements. Computers & Education, 53(4): 1297-1307. Retrieved March 20, 2010
- Thilaka Suresh (2000). Instructional strategy change on the achievement

in biotechnology and attitude towards science among higher secondary school students. Journal of All India Association for Educational Research, 12(3 & 7): 14-19.

- Venkataraman, S. (2008). Relative effectiveness among selected modes of CAI in physics in relation to learner's personality. Unpublished Doctoral Dissertation, Annamalai University. Chidambaram.
- Vernadakis, N., Zetou, E., Tsitskari, E., Giannousi, M., & Kioumourtzoglou, E. (2008). Student attitude and learning outcomes of multimedia computer-assisted versus traditional instruction in basketball. Education and Information Technologies, 13(3): 167-183.
- Victor, Adeosun Olufemi (2008). Relative effects of three Multi-Media Instructional Packages on Nigerian student's achievement in Social Studies. Pakistan Journal of Social Sciences, 5 (5): 415 – 420. Retrieved March 20, 2010
- Yusuf, Mudasiru O., & Afolabi, Adedeji O. (2010). Effects of Computer AssistedIinstruction (CAI) on Secondary School students' performance in biology. TOJET: The Turkish Online Journal of Educational Technology, 9(1): 62-69. Retrieved March 21, 2010.

❐

32.

Perception of Prospective Teachers on Designing Learning

Introduction

Teaching and learning process in the 21st century has undergone a vast change from the narrow and teacher – centric method to a more liberal and student – centric one. Research studies on student's characteristics, teacher characteristics, learning environment both at the school and home, role of parents, peer group, nature and demand of the curriculum, mode of transaction of curriculum and assessment reveals the continuous changing process of teaching and learning. Of course the development of science and technology over a period of hundreds and thousands of years dramatically changed the process of teaching and learning with reference to individual and social demands, national and global demands from localization of education to globalization of education, from face to face mode of education to distance mode of education, from stereo type of learning to multimedia approach of learning etc. Therefore it is evident that there are host of factors that determine the effectiveness of teaching and learning. Among them, the classroom environment is the basis and foremost important one that facilitate for the smooth transaction of curriculum in such a manner to make the learning less hard, joyful, unforgettable and concrete one.

Learning Environment - Concept and Meaning

Learning environment means the support system that organize the condition in which human learn best system that accommodate the unique learning needs of every learner and support the positive human relationship needed for effective learning. The learning environment are the physical spaces, tools and learning communities that encourage and enable students and educators to attain the skill – set that the future century requires. This includes a number of important elements such as the physical environment, a school's daily operations including scheduling course and available activities, technology infrastructure, school culture, community involvement and school leadership.

Learning Environment - Definition

According to MC Robbie, Roth and Lucus (1997), "The nature of the classroom learning environment and psycho – social interactions can make a difference in how the students learn and achieve their goals". As cited by Khine and Chiew (2001) from Wilson (1996), "Classroom learning environment refers to a space on a place where learners and teachers interact with each other and use a variety of tools and information resources in their pursuit of learning activities". B.Wilson. (1996) remarks, learning environment is a place or community where people can draw upon resources to make sense out of things and construct meaningful solutions to problems".

Need for the Study

In the emerging trend of classroom context of the digital age, students leaning cannot be restricted and completed with just making them to sit in the classroom and listening to the teachers. But learning is a continuous process and has no limits, as referred by the researchers learning includes so many aspects and more connected with cognitive, affective and phycho-motor domains.

Classroom environment is the most important basis for effective transaction of teaching and learning process. It is determined by innumerable factors such as the physical environment of the classroom, learning resources, opportunities to explore the learning possibilities, interactions between students, interactions between teachers and students, learners' behavior, teachers' behaviour. However the traditional learning environment of the classroom has been thoroughly modified in the modern age of science and technology, especially by the application of digital technology. In this context, the educational administrators, curriculum framers, teachers, parents, students and other stakeholders of education should know the expectations of the learners, either in face to face mode of education or open distance learning. Hence the researcher felt the need for a study on the learning environment at different levels of education.

Statement of the Problem

The problem identified by the investigator is entitled as "Perception of Prospective Teachers on Designing of Learning Environment of Tomorrows Classroom".

Operational Definition of Key Terms

1. **Perception:** In this research, perception refers to the B.Ed students ability or capacity to perceive the future classroom learning environment based on the

total score obtained by them, on the Learning Environment Inventory, a self-developed five-point rating scale.

2. **Prospective Teachers:** In this study, this refers to the B.Ed., students undergoing the course of study during the academic year 2013 – 2014.

3. **Designing of Learning Environment:** In this investigation, this refers to the total score obtained by the subjects of the study on the Perception of designing Classroom Learning Environment Inventory a self-developed five- point scale.

4. **Tomorrows Classroom:** In this study, it refers to the future classroom environment.

Objectives of the Study

The researcher intended to carry out the present study with the follow objectives.

- To find out the nature of perception of prospective teachers on the designing of learning environment of tomorrows classroom.
- To develop a suitable tool to study the perception of prospective teachers on the designing of learning environment of tomorrows classroom.
- To find out the significant difference in the perception of prospective teachers on the designing of learning environment of tomorrows classroom with respect to gender.
- To find out the significant difference in the perception of prospective teachers learning environment of tomorrows classroom with respect to subject group.
- To find out the significant difference in the perception of prospective teachers on the designing learning environment of tomorrows classroom with respect to educational qualification.

Hypotheses

- The present study is planned to be carried out with the following hypotheses.
- The nature of perception of prospective teachers on the designing of learning environment of tomorrow's classroom.
- There is no significant difference in the perception of prospective teachers on the designing
- Learning environment of tomorrow's class room with respect to gender.
- There is no significant difference in the perception of prospective teachers on the designing of learning environment of tomorrow's class room with respect to subject group.
- There is no significant difference in the perception of prospective teachers on the designing of learning environment of tomorrow's class room with respect to educational qualification.

Methodology

The present study is conducted to a randomly selected 100 prospective teachers (i.e B.Ed students) from five different Colleges of Education, Chennai city, who are undergoing the B.Ed., Course during the academic year 2013 -2014.b To collect data from the selected sample an Information Schedule' was used in addition to a self -made five-point scale, 'Perception of Designing Classroom Learning Environment Inventory', which includes five dimensions with four items under each dimension thus making into 20 statements altogether. All the 20 statements are positive in nature the maximum possible score is 100 and the minimum will be 20. The tool was validated by test-retest method. The statistical techniques such as descriptive analysis and differential analysis are used.

Table 1: Designing of Learning Environment as perceived by the B.Ed Students

Variable	No. of Samples	Level	Frequency	Percentage
Perception of Designing of Learning Environment of Classroom	100	Poor	3	3.00
		Average	33	33.00
		High	64	64.00
		Total	100	100.00

Inference

From the above table, it is observed that majority of the B.Ed., students have shown high level of perception of designing of learning environment of tomorrows classroom (64.00%), about one third them (33.00%), have shown average level of perception of designing of learning environment and the remaining students (3.00%), have shown poor perception.

Table 2: Mean, Standard Deviation, Critical Ratio on Perceived Learning Environment of B.Ed students with regard to gender.

Variable	Gender	N	Mean	SD	Critical Ratio	Level of Significance
Physical Aspects	Male	20	17.85	2.834	2.534	0.05
	Female	80	18.92	1.281		
Social Aspects	Male	20	16.60	2.210	2.200	0.05
	Female	80	17.68	1.888		
Instructional Aspects	Male	20	17.75	1.970	2.127	0.05
	Female	80	18.59	1.464		
Teacher Characteristics	Male	20	17.05	2.328	2.484	0.05
	Female	80	18.12	1.554		
Student Characteristics	Male	20	17.00	2.991	3.055	0.01
	Female	80	18.72	2.044		
Overall Perception of Learning Environment	Male	20	92.90	4.471	1.551	N.S*
	Female	80	90.35	6.987		

*Not significant at 0.05 level.

Inference

From the above table, it is noted that there exist no significant difference on the overall perception of designing of learning environment of tomorrow's classroom among the B.Ed student with regard to gender at 0.05 level. However, the male and female teacher-trainees significantly differ on the perception of learning environment dimensions – Physical Aspect, Social Aspect, Instructional Aspects and Teacher Characteristics at 0.05 level. They also significantly differ on the dimension-Student Characteristics at 0.01 level. In these aspects, the female students have more mean score, when compared to the male students. But, in the case of overall perception of designing of learning environment, the male teacher-trainees have more mean score than the female teacher- trainees.

Table 3: Mean, Standard Deviation, Critical Ratio on Perceived Learning Environment of B.Ed students with regard to subject group

Variable	Subject	N	Mean	SD	Critical Ratio	Level of Significance
Physical Aspects	Arts	39	19.21	1.06	2.322	0.05
	Science	61	18.39	2.01		
Social Aspects	Arts	39	17.33	1.96	0.507	N.S*
	Science	61	17.54	2.02		
Instructional Aspects	Arts	39	18.38	1.74	0.176	N.S*
	Science	61	18.44	1.52		
Teacher Characteristics	Arts	39	17.64	1.88	1.214	N.S*
	Science	61	18.08	1.69		
Student Characteristics	Arts	39	18.36	2.55	0.071	N.S*
	Science	61	18.39	2.24		
Overall Perception of Learning Environment	Arts	39	89.41	6.03	1.77	N.S*
	Science	61	91.79	6.86		

*Not significant at 0.05 level.

Inference

From the above table, no significant difference is noted that on the overall perceived learning environment of tomorrow's classroom and also in all its dimensions except on the dimension of Physical Aspects. In Physical Aspects, the arts group B.Ed students have more mean score (M= 19.21) when compared to the science group B.Ed (students (M= 18.39).

Table 4: Mean, Standard Deviation, Critical Ratio on Perceived Learning Environment of B.Ed students with regard to educational qualification.

Variable	Educational Qualification	N	Mean	SD	Critical Ratio	Level of Significance
Physical Aspects	UG	81	18.72	1.84	0.071	N.S*
	PG	19	18.68	1.25		
Social Aspects	UG	81	17.27	2.02	1.98	0.05
	PG	19	18.26	1.66		
Instructional Aspects	UG	81	18.36	1.68	0.797	N.S*
	PG	19	18.68	1.20		
Teacher Characteristics	UG	81	17.85	1.84	0.674	N.S*
	PG	19	18.16	1.46		
Student Characteristics	UG	81	18.43	2.02	0.456	N.S*
	PG	19	18.16	3.52		
Overall Perceived Learning Environment	UG	81	90.52	6.91	1.07	N.S*
	PG	19	92.32	5.13		

*Not significant at 0.05 level.

Inference

From the above table, no significant difference is noticed at 0.05 level, on the perceived learning environment of tomorrow's classroom and also in all its dimensions expect the dimension of Social Aspects at 0.05 level among the B.Ed students with regard to educational qualification. In Social Aspects, the B.Ed students with post graduate qualification have more mean score (Mean = 18.26) when compared to the students with under graduate qualification (Mean = 17.27).

Major Findings of the Study

Majority of the B.Ed students involved in this study express more perception, on the designing the learning environment of tomorrows class room.

The B.Ed students do not differ significantly on the overall perception of designing the learning environment of tomorrow's classroom at 0.05 level with regard to gender. But they differ significantly on the entire five dimension – Physical Aspects, Social Aspects, Instructional Aspects, Teacher Characteristics and Student Characteristics. In all these dimensions the female students have more mean score when compare to the male students.

No significant difference is noticed among the B.Ed students on the overall perception of designing of learning environment of tomorrow's classroom and also in all its dimensions except the dimension the Physical Aspects with regard to subject group at 0.05 level. Further they significantly differ at 0.05 level on the dimension – Physical Aspects. In which, the Arts group student have more mean score (M=19.21) when compare to the Science group students (M=18.39).

No significant difference is noted among the B.Ed students on the overall perception of designing the learning environment of tomorrow's classroom and also in all its dimensions except the dimension of Social Aspects with regard to educational qualification at 0.05 level. In the dimension of Social Aspects the post graduate students have more mean score when compared to the undergraduate students.

Educational Implication

The present study reveals high level of perception of prospective teachers (B.Ed students) on designing of the learning environment of tomorrows classrooms. Accordingly the new class room atmosphere for effective teaching and learning need to be created with the help of all stakeholders of education. Even though the B.Ed male and female students did not differ significantly on the overall perception of designing the learning environment, the female students have high level of perception as compared to the male students. Therefore the male students need to be given necessary orientation to make use of the classroom environment for effective learning. Though the B.Ed students of Arts and Science group of optional subject did not differ significantly on the overall perception of designing the learning environment of tomorrows classroom, the students of Arts group need to be given necessary inputs on the importance of favourable transaction of teaching learning process. Further the B.Ed students with U.G and P.G qualification although did not differ significantly on the designing of the learning environment of tomorrows classroom they need to realize that suitable learn environment is the basis for the curriculum transaction at all levels of education.

Suggestions for Further Study

- The researcher has recommended the following for further research.
- This study may be extended to school and other college students.
- This study may be extended to the teachers of all levels of education.
- This study may be conducted to more number of samples.
- The area of the study may be extended to other places.

Conclusion

Learning environment plays an important role infringing total success of all activities at all levels of education. As the classroom environment is determined by many factors, the B.Ed students who are the future architects of modern India needs to have a thorough knowledge and mind set to create conducive atmosphere to accomplish the teaching and learning process a successful one.

References

- Androw M. Colman (2001). A Dictionary of Psychology. New York: Oxford University Press.
- Erkenberg, Jorma. (1995). Complex technology – based learning environment, Automating Instructional Design: computer based development and delivery tool, (245-264). NATU AS1 Series.
- Magbool Ahmed (2008). Comprehensive Dictionary of Education. New Delhi: Atlontic Publishers & Distributers.
- Torsten Husen(Eds) (1994). The International Encyclopedia of Education. (Second Edition). Great Britain: Pergamon.

❐

33.

Awareness of Flip Teaching among School Teachers in and Around Madurai District

Introduction

The Flip classroom is the latest learning model to have taken the teaching and training world by storm. The investigator adopted the survey method and target population was the school teachers who are teaching in various boards such as Matriculation and CBSE in and around Madurai district. The size of the sample of the present study is 60 school teachers. The self made check list was used in the study and it consists of 20 items. Statistical technique used are Calculating mean value,‘ t’ test. The Findings are there is no Awareness of flip teaching among school teachers in and around Madurai District and there is no significant difference in the awareness of flip teaching among school teachers with regard to the gender and Board of Institution.

“A Quality education has the power to transform societies in a single generation, provide children with the protection they need from the hazards of poverty, labor exploitation and disease and give them the knowledge, skills and confidence to reach their full potential”. India needs multi-dimensional and broad based quality education to maintain its leader ship in the 21st century. Therefore India should show the concern over the quality in education as the education in India is not competitive in terms of the quality with other countries. The FLIP classroom is the latest learning model to have taken the teaching and training world by storm.

In a flipped classroom content normally delivered in lectures is covered by students in their own time, often through the use of video or readings. Face-to-face time is used for activities where the focus is on learning through experience. It allows teachers and trainers to flip through concepts, which in turn gives them more time to interact with students instead of lecturing. This is also known as backwards classroom, reverse instruction, flipping the classroom and reverse teaching. The flip classroom is ideal for adult education and training, where students are more self-motivated and focused. This model of learning compliments training objectives which are 'actionable' rather than passive objectives like 'awareness or comprehension'.

Significance of the Study

This study is undertaken to find out the awareness of flip teaching among school teachers in and around Madurai District. This study gave them the clear knowledge about Flip teaching is a form of blended learning in which students learn new content online by watching video lectures, usually at home, and what used to be homework (assigned problems) is now done in class with teachers offering more personalized guidance and interaction with students, instead of lecturing. This is also known as backwards classroom, flipped classroom, reverse teaching, and the Thayer Method

Background of the Study

This study was done in and around Madurai city. The need of today is quality of education. If the quality is maintained in all the above we can produce professionally skillful students who are going to the meet the future global citizens. So it is necessary to have innovative teaching methods or alternative methods in imparting knowledge among the students. The traditional pattern of teaching has been to assign students to read textbooks and work on problem sets outside school, while listening to lectures and taking tests in class.

Traditionally, the teacher engages with the students who ask questions — but those who don't ask tend to need the most attention. "We refer to 'silent failers,' " said one teacher, claiming that flipping allows her to target those who need the most help rather than the most confident. Flipping changes teachers from "sage on the stage" to "guide on the side", allowing them to work with individuals or groups of students throughout the session. The Investigator wanted to know whether there is awareness of flip teaching among school teachers in and around Madurai District

Objectives of the study

To measure and find out whether there is awareness of flip teaching among school teachers in and around Madurai District

To enable the teachers to sensitize the today's need to turn towards the flip teaching and classrooms.

Hypotheses

Awareness of flip teaching among school teachers in and around Madurai District are high

There is significant difference in the awareness of flip teaching among school teachers with regard to the board of institution. [Matriculation and CBSE]

There is significant difference in the awareness of flip teaching among school teachers with regard to the gender. [Male & Female]

Methodology used

The survey method was taken and target population is the school teachers who are teaching in various boards such as Matriculation and CBSE in and around Madurai district. The size of the samples of the present study is 60 teachers.

Tool Construction

The self made check list was used to find out whether there is awareness of flip teaching among school teachers in and around Madurai District. The checklist had 20 items

Administration of the Tool

The photocopies of the check-list were distributed to the teachers of four educational institutions in and around Madurai. The filled in questionnaires were corrected analyzed and interpreted.

Statistical Technique Used

Table shows the number of teachers from four schools

S.no	Name of the school	Institution	Total no	F	M
1)	S.S.V.Sala	Matriculation	15	15	-
2)	Le Chatlier	Matriculation	15		15
3)	PVK Academy	CBSE	15	8	7
4)	Vellammal	CBSE	15	7	8
		Total	60	30	30

Hypothesis: 1

Awareness of flip teaching among school teachers in and around Madurai District are high

Table Showing the Mean Value

Name of the school	Total no	Sex		Board	Over All Mean
		Female	Male		
S.S.V.Sala	15	15	-	Matriculation	7.5
Le Chatlier	15		15	Matriculation	9
PVK Academy	15	8	7	CBSE	8.5
Vellammal	15	7	8	CBSE	9.5

It is inferred from the above table that there is no Awareness of flip teaching among school teachers in and around Madurai District .All the mean scores indicated that they are less than the theoretical mean (10). Still there were no innovative teaching methods were followed to reach the global standard as well as to improve the low achievers.

Hypothesis: 2

There is significant difference in the awareness of flip teaching among school teachers with regard to the board of institution. [Matriculation and CBSE]

Table showing the difference between the variables

S.No	Variable	Mean	Std.dev	't'	Significance at 0.5 level
1	Matriculation	8.25	0.50	0.93	No Significant
2	CBSE	9	0.74		

It is inferred from the above table that the't' value is 0.93 is lesser than the't' value 1.96 at 0.5 level of significance. So the research hypothesis is rejected. The result indicated that there is no significant difference in the awareness of flip teaching among school teachers with regard to the board of institution. [Matriculation and CBSE]

Hypothesis: 3 : There is significant difference in the awareness of flip teaching among school teachers with regard to the gender. [Male & Female]

Table showing the difference between the variables

S.NO	Variable	mean	Std. dev	't'	Significance at 0.5 level
1	Female	8.5	1.25	0.98	No Significant
2	male	9	0.57		

It is inferred from the above table that the't' value is 0.98 is lesser than the't' value 1.96 at 0.5 level of significance. So the research hypothesis is rejected. The result indicated that there is no significant difference in the awareness of flip teaching among school teachers with regard to the gender. [Male & Female]

Hypotheses Verification

There is significant difference in the awareness of flip teaching among school teachers with regard to the board of institution. [Matriculation and CBSE] is rejected.

There is significant difference in the awareness of flip teaching among school teachers with regard to the gender. [Male & Female] is rejected.

Delimitation

The samples are taken from only from four schools in and around Madurai area and also restricted to the variable that is type of institution and gender alone. In this study the Investigator use only mean and'‘t’ test as the statistical treatment .This was also delimitation.

Scope of the Study

This study can highlight the need for the alternative, creative, student friendly, user friendly and innovative methods of teaching. The flip classroom is the latest learning model to have taken the teaching and training world by storm. The flip teaching models are being incorporated by teachers of all subjects, for students of all ages. This mode of learning is now slowly making inroads into the teaching and training in India. The flip classroom is ideal for adult education and training, where students are more self-motivated and focused. This model of learning compliments training objectives which are ‘actionable’ rather than passive objectives like ‘awareness or comprehension’.

Suggestion for the Future

- We can take more schools for the study
- We can take so many variables
- We can also use extend all the boards of schools in future.

Educational Implications

This Study revealed that there is a need for considering another scenario where in students has already gone through a video lecture on the second conditional at their own time. They can rewind, pause and repeat the lecture as many times as they want. Additionally, they do graded exercises to practice the concept and take up an assessment to check their proficiency. Both the learner and the facilitator now know what to focus on and the class is much more productive for the learner. The facilitator only has to provide solutions for problem areas. Flip training can help overcome the constraints and make learning a focused and productive experience for the learner.

❐

34.

Attitude of Prospective Teachers towards Blended Learning

Introduction

The rapid advancement in information technology (IT) has made remarkable changes in the traditional educational systems. It adopts modern technology and pedagogical techniques in teaching-learning process and creates an innovative learning environment that motivates the students for better learning. Such a system of learning is mainly based on internet services which facilitate active learning. It disseminates different types of information needed for the holistic development of an individual. Blended learning has emerged as an effective method of learning to meet the needs of students' learning styles. The growth of blended learning environments in education has emphasised the need for better ways of describing and recognising good teaching that promotes student learning in these environments. Blended learning combines online components with the conventional face-to-face components that optimize best practices in teaching and learning through synchronous and asynchronous learning environments.

Blended learning

Blended learning is viewed as a pedagogical approach that combines the effectiveness and socialization opportunities of the classroom with the technologically enhanced active learning possibilities of the online environment rather than a ratio of delivery modalities. Graham (2006) opined, "Blended learning is a face-to-face instruction combined with computer-mediated instruction, delivery media, and web-based technologies to facilitate interactive and reflective higher-order learning". According to him, blended learning is designed with the use of synchronous and asynchronous web-based technologies, such as chat rooms, wikis, threaded discussions, virtual classrooms, instant messaging, conferencing tools, bulletin boards, computer conferencing, blogs, etc. Blended Learning is a blanket term for an approach, and provides the following types learning environment for students. These are:

- full provision of module related documents in electronic format
- regular formative assessment with feedback
- opportunities to learn from each other collaboratively
- electronic personal development planning,
- the opportunity to submit all appropriate summative assessments electronically,
- face to face interactive learning
- Need and significance of the study

Most of traditional class room teaching-learning process fails to engage the young learners actively to construct the knowledge. The knowledge is transferred monotonously and their needs, interests and attitudes have never taken into account. Hence a face to face combination of classroom element with the online instruction, popularly referred Blended learning has become the alternative that gains popularity among educators. So far several studies reported that the provision of blended learning courses is highly appreciated and positively rated by the students. The UCF data reveals that blended learning was effective and could lead to higher student success rates in specific academic disciplines (Dziuban et al., 2004). In addition faculty seems to be very satisfied with teaching either blended or online as long as they received training and academic support (Schroeder & Oakley, 2005). Research by Garrison and Kanuka (2004) posited that blended learning was not only an acceptable methodology but a transformative one for higher education. Hiltz and Turoff (2005) also strongly support the view that the introduction of asynchronous learning networks to campus courses would be a critical breakthrough in improving learning. McCombs & Vakili (2005) reached a similar conclusion because blended learning can lead to a more learner-centered education environment. Prospective teachers are they would be teachers to shape the young minds of future society, through active learning methodology. Blended learning would cater the needs of the young mind. Hence the present investigators made an attempt to study the attitude of prospective teachers towards blended learning.

Objectives

- To study the attitude of prospective teachers towards blended learning
- To study the significant difference in the attitude scores of prospective teachers towards blended learning with respect to Gender, locality, subjects of study and educational qualification.

Hypotheses

There existed no significant difference in the attitude scores of prospective teachers towards blended learning with respect to Gender, locality, subjects of study and educational qualification.

Methodology

The Normative survey method was used to collect data. The Sample consisted of prospective teachers who undergo B.Ed course in colleges of education in Kanyakumari District. The sample size was 200. Simple random sampling technique was used to collect the data. Blended Learning Attitude Scale (BLAS) constructed and validated by the investigators, was used as tool for collecting the data. The tool possessed adequate content and face validity. The reliability of the tool was found to be 0.72. It consisted of 40 items with the responses namely Strongly Agree (SA), Agree (A), Undecided (UD), Disagree (D) and Strongly Disagree (SD). The scoring was done by using a scoring key. The scores were 5, 4,3,2,1, for SA, A, UD, D, and SD respectively for the positive items and was reversed for the negative items. Statistical techniques such as Percentage analysis and t test were used for data analysis.

Results and Discussion

Table 1 level of attitude of prospective teachers towards blended learning

Variable	Low		Moderate		High	
	number	percentage	number	percentage	number	percentage
Attitude	28	14	78	39	94	47

It is inferred from the table1 47% of prospective teachers shows high favourable attitude towards blended learning.

Table2 Significance of difference in the mean scores of attitude towards blended learning of prospective teachers on the basis of gender, locale, medium of learning and educational qualification

subsample	Group	Mean	SD	N	t	p	sig.level
Gender	Male	117.08	12.02	92	3.05	0.00	0.01
	Female	123.26	16.51	108			
Locale	Rural	118.17	13.17	102	2.19	0.03	0.05
	Urban	122.76	16.27	98			
Subject of study	Arts	117.71	15.70	87	2.24	0.03	0.05
	Science	122.50	13.99	113			
Educational qualfn.	UG	121.50	13.98	113	1.16	0.58	N.S
	PG	119.00	16.01	87			

From the table2 it is clear that t- values are 3.05, 2.19, 2.24 ($p<0.05$) are significant at 0.05 level with df 198 respectively for gender, locality and subject of study. It means that there is significant difference in the mean Attitude scores of prospective teachers on the basis of locale, medium of learning and their educational qualification. Further the mean scores indicated that the female prospective teachers possessed more favourable attitude that their male counterparts. Urban prospective teachers possessed more favourable attitude that their rural counterparts. And Science prospective teachers who possessed more favourable attitude that their Arts counterparts. Hence the null hypotheses were rejected. But undergraduate and post graduate prospective teachers do not differ significantly in their attitude towards blended learning.

Major findings

- The prospective teachers showed more favourable attitude towards blended learning.
- There existed significant difference in the mean Attitude scores of prospective teachers on the basis of locale, medium of learning and their educational qualification.
- Female prospective teachers possessed more favourable attitude towards blended learning that their male counterparts.
- Urban prospective teachers possessed more favourable attitude that their rural counterparts.
- Prospective teachers who belong to science subject possessed more favourable attitude that their Arts counterparts.
- Undergraduate and post graduate prospective teachers do not differ significantly in their attitude towards blended learning.

Educational implications

- Teacher Educators could be given adequate training to use blended learning
- Teacher Education courses and syllabus could be redesigned
- Extensive training, Seminars and workshop could be organised for prospective teachers and provide hands on experience to use this type learning

References

- Albrecht, B. (2006). Enriching student experience through blended learning. *ECAR Research Bulletin,* 12.
- Bersin, J. (2003). What works in blended learning? Retrieved April 27, 2014 from http://www.learningcircuits.org/2003/jul2003/bersin.htm
- Carman, J. M. (2005). Blended learning design: Five key ingredients. Retrieved April 27, 2014 from http://www.agilantlearning.com/pdf/Blended%20Learning%20Design.pdf

- Cook, K., Owston, R. D., & Garrison, D. R. (2004). Blended Learning Practices at COHERE Universities. (Institute for Research on Learning Technologies Technical Report No. 2004-5). Toronto, ON: York University. Dziuban, C. D., Hartman, J. L., & Moskal, P. D. (2004). Blended learning. ECAR Research Bulletin, Retrieved on April 27,2014fromhttp://net.educause.edu/ir/library/pdf/erb0407.pdf
- Graham, C. R. (2006). *Blended learning systems: Definition, current trends, and future directions*. In C. J. Bonk and C. R. Graham (Eds.), *Handbook of Blended Learning: Global Perspectives, Local Designs*. San Francisco: Pfeiffer Publishing.

❒

35.

Effectiveness of Continuous and Comprehensive Evaluation of Science

Introduction

"Education is an admirable thing, but it is well to remember from time to time that nothing that is worth learning can be taught" – Oscar wilde.

Education is not a static but a dynamic process which develops the child according to changing situations and times. It always induces the individual towards progress. It reconstructs the society according to the changing needs of the time and place of the society. The role of the education is countless for a perfect society and man. It is essential for every society and nation to bring holistic happiness and prosperity to its individuals.

Science Education and CCE

Science, as a subject is universal and knows no boundaries. It almost revolutionaries human life and proved indispensable for existence of man. Now, supremacy of science has been established in every field. Science Education deals with sharing of science content and process with individuals who are not considered traditionally to be member of the scientific community.

NCF 2005 envisioned a vastly different system built upon entirely new foundations that would actually make the teachers the primary evaluator of the students. This system advocates Continuous and Comprehensive Evaluation (CCE), G.O No. 143 School Education (U2) dated: 19.09.2011 decided to introduce

CCE from the academic year 2012 – 13 for the standards I to VIII initially and for standard IX in 2013 – 14 and for standard X in 2014 – 15. It is a system of School based evaluation.

Continuous: Regularly & Periodicity in the assessment.

Comprehensive: Holistic assessment of Learners growth and development (Both scholastic and Co- scholastic aspects).

Evaluation: Assessment of the student's attitude, aptitudes and life skills in addition to scholastic areas.

Scholastic Assessment: Evaluation of all academic subjects as spread over the entire learning. Physical Education is considered as an integral part of this.

Co- Scholastic Assessment: Asses life skills, Attitude &Values, Wellness & yoga and Co- Curricular Activities.

CCE focus on

- Holistic development of a learner.
- Assessment in scholastic and co- scholastic areas.
- Bring out strength and weakness of learners.
- Providing feed back to the teacher.

CCE Ensures

- Not to label the learners as slow, poor intelligent etc.
- No comparisons between learners.
- No negative statements about the learners.

Objectives

- To compare the mean pre and post test scores of control group.
- To compare the mean pre and post test scores of Experimental group
- To compare the mean pre test scores of control and Experimental groups.
- To compare the mean post test scores of control and Experimental groups.
- To compare mean post test scores of boys and girls of Experimental group.

Hypotheses

- There is no significant difference between pre and post test scores of control group.
- There is no significant difference between pre and post test scores of experimental group.
- There is no significant difference between pre test scores of control and experimental groups.
- There is no significant difference between post test scores of control and experimental groups.
- There is no significant difference in the mean post test scores of boys and girls of experimental groups.

Methodology

In this present study the investigator applied Experimental research as a method. For this study VIII standard Science, unit IV (III Term) which consists of **"Light and Sound"** is taken. Twenty objective type questions were taken from above said lesson for pre and post tests. For the Experimental group 10 marks were allotted for FA (a) activities such as Collections, Preparation of Albums, Mind map, Drawing, Experiments, Making Model, etc. FA (a) Activities were conducted and scored with the help of concerned Science Teacher as per guidelines given by the SCERT. For FA (b) investigator prepared objective type questions, marks are converted into 10 marks (ie. Twenty marks converted into ten). This method studies describes and interprets what will be exists in future.

Population

The population consisted of students studying VIII standard in middle schools situated in Gobichettipalayam block of Erode District.

Sample

The sample for the present study consists of 160 VIII standard students studying in middle schools in Gobichettipalayam block Erode district. The sample was selected by using simple random sampling technique. The sample was further divided into two groups Control group and Experimental group. Each group consists of 80 samples.

Tools Used

Achievement Test (Objective type Questions) in the lesson "Light and Sound" VIII standard - III term - IV Unit) constructed and validated by the investigator.

FA (a) Activities for Science Subject as per the guidelines of SCERT.

Statistical Techniques

Arithmetic mean, Standard Deviation and't' test were used for this study.

Ho 1: There is no significant difference between pre and post test scores of control group.

Table 1: Mean, SD and 't' Value of Control group students in achievement of Science (Pre & Post Test).

S.No	Test	N	Mean	SD	't' Value	Level of Significance at 0.05
1	Pre Test	80	10.05	3.95	2.16	Significant
2	Post Test	80	11.37	3.77		

The mean Achievement score of control group students in pre test and post test are found to be 10.05 and 11.37 respectively. In order to find out the significant mean difference between pre test and post test of control group students in their achievement score in science, the investigator calculated 't'value, which is found to be 2.16. It is significant at 0.05 level. Hence the framed hypothesis is rejected. It is inferred that control group students differ significantly in their pre test and post test achievement scores in the lesson light &Sound. It is improved in their post test. So, we it inferred that there is a gain in their post test performance. Even though there is no treatment to control group there is an improvement in their performance in the lesson light &Sound which may be due to the exposure gained in their pre test and time.

Ho 2: There is no significant difference between pre and post test scores of Experimental group.

Table 2: Mean, SD and 't' Value of Experimental group students in achievement of Science (Pre & Post Test).

S.No	Test	N	Mean	SD	't' Value	Level of Significance at 0.05
1	Pre Test	80	14.28	2.87	11.62	Significant
2	Post Test	80	18.23	1.39		

The mean Achievement score of Experimental group student in pre test and post test are found to be 14.28 and 18.23 respectively. In order to find out the significant mean difference between pre test and post test of control group students in their achievement score in the lesson light &Sound, the investigator calculated 't'value, which is found to be 11.62. It is significant at 0.05 level. Hence the framed hypothesis is rejected. It is inferred that experimental group students different significantly in their pre test and post test achievement scores in the lesson light &Sound. The achievement of experimental group students is more in their post test. So it may inferred that there is a gain in their post test performance compared to pre test. It may be due to the treatment given to the experimental group after the pre test.

Ho 3: There is no significant difference between pre test scores of control and experimental groups.

Table 3: Mean, SD and 't' Value of Control & Experimental group students in achievement of Science (Pre Test).

S.No	Group	N	Mean	SD	't' Value	Level of Significance at 0.05
1	Control	80	10.05	3.95	7.69	Significant
2	Experimental	80	14.28	2.87		

The Mean Score of control and experiment group students in pre test are found to be 10.05 and 14.28 respectively. In order to find out the significant mean difference between control and experimental group of pre test scores in the lesson light &Sound, the investigator calculated 't' value, which is found to be 7.69. It is significant at 0.05 level. Hence the framed hypothesis is rejected. It is inferred that control and experimental group students differ significantly in their pre test. Before the treatment, the experimental group students scored more than the control group student.

Ho 4: There is no significant difference between post test scores of control and experimental groups.

Table 4: Mean, SD and 't' Value of Control & Experimental group students in achievement of Science (Post Test).

S.No	Group	N	Mean	SD	't' Value	Level of Significance at 0.05
1	Control	80	11.38	3.77	15.15	Significant
2	Experimental	80	18.23	1.39		

The Mean Score of control and experiment group students in post test are found to be 11.38 and 18.23 respectively. In order to find out the significant mean difference between control and experimental group of post test scores in the lesson light & Sound, the investigator calculated 't' value, which is found to be 15.15. It is significant at 0.05 level. Hence the framed hypothesis is rejected. It may infer that the experimental group student's performance is good in Science particularly in the unit IV. CCE enhance effective learning and also creates scientific attitude and knowledge.

Ho 5: There is no significant difference in the mean post test scores of boys and girls of experimental groups.

Table 5: Mean, SD and 't' Value of Experimental group boys & girls students in achievement of Science (Post Test).

S.No	Gender	N	Mean	SD	't' Value	Level of Significance at 0.05
1	Boys	42	9.28	4.23	0.44	Not Significant
2	Girls	38	8.95	4.93		

The Mean Achievement Score of boys and girls of experiment group students in post test are found to be 9.28 and 8.95 respectively. In order to find out the significant mean difference between boys and girls of this group in the lesson light & Sound, the investigator calculated 't' value, which is found to be 0.44. It is not significant at 0.05 level. Hence the framed hypothesis is accepted. It is inferred that boys and girls scores of experimental group students differ significantly in their post test.

Findings

- There is a significant difference in pre test and post test scores of control group.
- There is a significant difference in pre test and post test scores of experimental group on effectiveness of CCE of Science subject among VIII standard students.
- There is a significant difference of pre test scores of control and experimental group among VIII standard students.
- There is a significant difference of post test scores of control and experimental group on effectiveness of CCE of Science subject among VIII standard students.
- There is no significant difference of boys and girls in post test of experimental group.

Conclusion

It is concluded from the analysis of data, the experimental group students showed better in the post test. It may be due to the FA (a) activities, which promotes for their better understanding. The achievement score of control group students is less than experimental group. The study recommended the new evaluation procedures to improve the student's achievement and also an effective mode of teaching- learning.

From the findings, we can infer that evaluation is all pervasive assessment of all the aspects of the educative process. Both the method of teaching and evaluation were become objective based, which brings about greater correlation between what is taught and what is tested. Evaluation is not a secret process as the students will be quite aware of the objectives of teaching and testing. To be quite successful in their profession, the teachers must acquaint themselves thoroughly with new evaluation procedures.

References

- Continuous and Comprehensive Evaluation, general guidelines for upper primary classes VI – VIII prepared by State Council of Educational Research and Training (2012), Chennai.
- Kola. Aina Jacob (2013) "Importance of Science Education to National Development and Problems Militating Against its Development." American Journal of Educational Research 1.7:225-229
- National Policy on Education (with modifications undertaken in 1992). National Council of Educational research and Training. Retrieved 10 December 2012.
- Omosewo, E.O. Views of physics teachers on the need to train and retain Physics teachers in Nigeria. Africa Research Review, 3 (1), 314 – 325.
- Tamizh Selvan.T & Babu. R (2014) "Effectiveness of Blended Teaching

of Tamil Subject among High School Students." Journal of Educational Research and Extension. Vol.51(1) - Jan- March.

- Tamil Nadu School Education department, Chennai. Science Text book (III Term) for VIII Standard.

❒

36.

Effectiveness of Multimedia Programme in Perceiving Human Anatomy among Higher Secondary Students

Introduction

Research work is being continuously done in the field of science and also in the related teaching methods and materials. In order to keep pace with the development of science, the need for new instructional strategies was greatly felt. One such innovative teaching strategy, called multimedia programme, has been chosen and studied by the investigator in this research work. Upgrading Biology curriculum by introducing Human anatomy demands a change in the instructional strategy. The need for developing an instructional strategy for teaching Human anatomy and physiology is very important to make the teachers and students aware of the scientific principles that govern the advances being made in medicine. The functions of the internal organs of human body can be easily explained through a multimedia programme. This also saves the use of expensive chemicals and sophisticated instruments which are beyond the reach of higher secondary schools. In schools, the required equipment to explain the human anatomy is not available. In this situation, the working mechanism of internal organs can be explained by a multimedia programme, which when used as an instructional strategy will make the task of learning human anatomy easier, effective and less expensive. The present study aims to find out the effectiveness of multimedia programme in perceiving human anatomy among higher secondary students in Tindivanam. A samples of 100 higher secondary students selected randomly were studied. A questionnaire method of survey was used to find out the effectiveness of multimedia programme in perceiving human anatomy. The data were collected by using questionnaire as an instrument. Primary data were collected by conducting direct structured interview using questionnaire. All the respondents were asked the same questions in the same fashion and they were informed the purpose of study. Mean, SD, and t-test analysis was applied to test the hypotheses. The findings and observations are the result and outcome of the interpretations made during the study of analysis. The result found that majority of the higher secondary students satisfied about multimedia programme.

In view of growing importance of science education, old concepts of science teaching have therefore, rather become completely outmoded and an entirely new ethos and approach to science curriculum have come into existence. Moreover, unprecedented development of scientific research, new discoveries, and new methods of investigation, in the early twentieth century, has created a need and urge to examine and reorganize science teaching programmes at all levels in schools. Institutions are functioning in an era of rapidly emerging new technologies. Some of them, like information and communications technology, have fuelled a veritable explosion of rising expectations everywhere. When such is the pace of developmental processes, it becomes fairly imperative on the part of the students not only to possess sound knowledge and understanding of fundamental concepts, but also to understand and appreciate the ramifications of various developments in the field of science and technology, especially in the context of their future career. The situation underscores the significance of research in science education and it is time for the educationists to evolve a proper and appropriate strategy for teaching science.

At the Higher Secondary level, the science subject is divided into Physics, Chemistry, Botany, and Zoology according to Tamil Nadu State Board syllabus. Zoology deals with the life history, distribution, structure, reproduction, and importance of animals including Homosapiens, the human beings. 'Human anatomy' is one of the units of the Zoology subject. Human anatomy is the branch of anatomy devoted to the structure of the human body. In general the study of human anatomy helps the students to do their higher studies in Medicine, Physiotherapy, Nursing, Degree courses like B.Sc., Zoology, and Microbiology etc. Apart from acquiring the technical knowledge, it is necessary for human beings to know and control their own systems of their body for healthy life. Hence the investigator has selected the unit "human anatomy" to teach through multimedia programme for the higher secondary students in the present investigation.

An instructional or teaching strategy refers to a pattern of teaching act that serves to attain certain goals and to guard against others. An instructional strategy is a purposefully-conceived and determined plan of action. It also occupies a central position in formal education. Instructional strategies aim at establishing relationship between teaching inputs and learning outputs, mainly in terms of realizing the learning outcomes. Instructional strategies include teaching methods, approaches and techniques.

Methods of instruction may be teacher-centered such as Historical method, Biographical method, Lecture method, Lecture-demonstration method or pupil-centered method which includes group methods such as project method, discussion, seminar and workshop. The pupil-centered methods also include individual methods such as programmed instruction, Computer Aided Instruction, Instructional Modules and Multimedia packages.

Review of Literature

Chang, Kuo-En et al. (2008) studied **the effects of learning support in simulation-based physics learning.** The results of the study revealed that the outcome for learning about the basic characteristics of an optical lens was significantly better for simulation-based learning than for laboratory learning.

Djeassilane (2008) investigated the effect of computer aided instruction (CAI) in enhancing the academic achievement of higher secondary students in commerce. The findings of the study showed that the computer aided instruction was effective in helping the students of the experimental group to perform better in the post-test. It proved the effectiveness of the computer aided instruction in commerce developed by the investigator. And also it was found that the experimental students had more favourable attitude towards computer assisted instruction.

Garnett, Hackling and Oliver (2009) developed an interactive multimedia package to improve students' understanding of the particulate basis of chemical reaction, and their ability to interpret chemical equations and solve problems based on equations. The study showed that Interactive multimedia provided learners with access to a rich information source and appropriate activities to promote learning and understanding.

Junaidu, Sahalu (2009) studied effectiveness of multimedia in learning & teaching data structures online. This paper explores and reports on the importance of creating multimedia-rich course content and the important role that animations can play in creating a successful online learning experience. Results indicated that students consistently perform much better in questions requiring application of material taught in carefully animated algorithms. These results should carry over to other educational environments.

Liao, Yuen-kuang C., Chang, Huei-wen and Chen, Yu-wen (2009) compared the effects of computer applications (i.e., computer-assisted instruction, computer simulations, and Web-based learning) versus traditional instruction on elementary school students' achievement in Taiwan. The results suggest that computer application instruction is more effective than traditional instruction for elementary school students in Taiwan.

O'Day, Danton (2010) studied on "using animations to teach biology: past & future research on the attributes that underlie pedagogically sound animations". Multiple technical resources (commonly referred to as multimedia) are currently used by many instructors to communicate difficult topics and concepts to their students in meaningful ways. Various sources have shown that animations are more effective than static sequential images. This study evaluated how animations can be and have been used as effective teaching and learning tools in biology and what more needs to be done to understand their true value.

Ozmen, Haluk (2010) studied on "The influence of CAI on students' conceptual understanding of chemical Bonding and attitude towards chemistry: A case for Turkey". The results of this study suggested that teaching-learning of topics in chemistry related to chemical bonding can be improved by the use of computer-assisted teaching materials.

Ponraj and Nellaiyapen (2010) investigated the effectiveness of CAI in teaching Zoology. The major finding of the study showed that the experimental group performed better than the Control group in the post-test. The results of the study revealed that experimental method of teaching is more effective than the traditional method of teaching the topic 'Nucleus' in Zoology.

Pryor, Caroline and Bitter, Gary (2010) used multimedia to teach in-service teachers and studied its impacts on learning, application, and retention. The study found that the video modeling in the module was effective in helping teachers learn, and discourse strategies were learned, applied, and retained.

Rotbain, Marbach-Ad and Stavy (2011) used a computer animation to teach high school molecular biology. The achievements of the experimental group were compared with those of a control group. Analysis of the post-test showed that the mean score of the experimental group was significantly higher than the mean score of the control group.

Venkataraman (2011) prepared software packages (CAI) for XI standard physics and studied the effectiveness of it's among selected modes of CAI in physics in relation to learners' personality. The results of the study showed that the CAI is effective with different modes. Computer Assisted Instruction shows significant difference in the achievement of different instructional objectives. Further Computer Assisted Instruction enhances the retention of the learnt content.

Vernadakis et al. (2012) examined the effect of multimedia computer-assisted instruction (MCAI), traditional instruction (TI), and combined instruction (CI) methods on learning the skill of shooting in basketball. Additionally, a comparison of the students' attitudes towards the MCAI and TI methods was made. Students took pre-, post-, and retention written test covering techniques and rules of the games. Post-test results indicated no significant differences between the groups concerning the written test. Nevertheless, the attitude test scores of the CI group were more favourable to MCAI method than the TI method. Retention test results showed that groups retained the knowledge acquisition. However, the combined method of instruction tended to be the most effective for cognitive learning.

Victor, Adeosun Olufemi (2012) investigated the relative effects of three multi-media instructional packages on Nigerian students' achievement in social studies. The purpose was to determine which of the combinations of videotape recording presentation, pictures and the chalk and talk method; the combination of audiotape recording presentation, pictures and the chalk and talk method and the combination of pictures and the chalk and talk method. The study revealed that the combination of pictures and the chalk and talk method was most effective among the packages tested in the learning of social studies.

Objectives

- To develop a Multimedia Programme for the unit of Human anatomy from XI standard Zoology subject in order to teach the higher secondary students.
- To find out the effectiveness of Multimedia Programme in teaching Human anatomy among higher secondary students.

Methodology

The methodology adopted for the study is explained in detail. The sampling technique, size of the sample, variables of the study, description of the tool used and administration of tool are elaborated.

Sample

A samples of 100 higher secondary students in selected randomly were studied in Tindivanam Town.

Data Collection

The present study aims at developing and using Multimedia programme for perceiving human anatomy for higher secondary students to enable them to understand the concepts very easily through individualized instructional technique. It is maintained that the Multimedia programme may reduce monotony in the classroom by bringing out real life situations and motivate them for self-study and provides opportunities for individual pace and ability.

The study intends to develop a multimedia programme for human anatomy for XI standard Zoology subject prescribed by Tamil Nadu State Board Syllabus and find out the effectiveness of the Multimedia programme through experimentation in perceiving human anatomy among the higher secondary students. The study provides scope for the development and use of many Multimedia programmes in the concerned discipline as well as other disciplines for the benefit of learners of different categories. Hence the multimedia programme can be used as an individualized instructional technique for the students of different categories in the science subjects as well as other subjects.

Analysis and Interpretation

Performance of control group students between the pre test and post test in human anatomy.

The Mean, Standard Deviation and Co-efficient of Variation were computed for the control group students in their performance in human anatomy between the pre test and post test.

Table 1: Distribution of Mean, Standard Deviation and Co-efficient of Variation on the performance of control group students between the pre test and post test in human anatomy

Group	N	Mean	S.D	CV
Pre test	100	42.69	13.60	31.86
Post test	100	52.46	13.28	25.31

The Co-efficient of Variation of the pre test and post test for the control group students was found to be 31.86 and 25.31, which reveals that the control group students are more consistent in their performance in human anatomy in the post test than the pre test. It reveals that the control group students have improved in their performance in human anatomy in the post test than the pre test.

To find out the significance of the difference between the control and experimental group students in their performance in human anatomy in the pre test, the 't' test was used.

Table 2: Distribution of 't' value between the control and experimental group students in their performance in human anatomy in the pre test

Group	N	Mean	S.D	't' value	Level of Significant
Control	100	42.69	13.60	0.17	p>0.05
Experimental	100	43.31	12.59		

There is no significant difference between the control and experimental group students in their performance in human anatomy in the pre test.

The obtained 't' value 0.17 is not statistically significant since it is less than the table 't' value 1.96 for 50 df at 0.05 level of significance. Hence the null hypothesis is accepted. It shows that there is no significant difference between the control and experimental group students in their performance in human anatomy in the pre test. It is therefore concluded that both control and experimental group students have the same level of performance in human anatomy in the pre test.

To find out the significance of the difference between the control and experimental group students in their performance in human anatomy in the post test, the 't' test was used.

Table 3: Distribution of 't' value between the control and experimental group students in their performance in human anatomy in the post test

Group	N	Mean	S.D	't' value	Level of Significant
Control	100	52.46	13.28	14.38	$p<0.05$
Experimental	100	92.81	5.31		

There is no significant difference between the control and experimental group students in their performance in human anatomy in the post test.

The obtained 't' value 14.38 is statistically significant since it is greater than the table 't' value 1.96 for 50 df at 0.05 level of significance. Hence the null hypothesis is rejected. It shows that there is significant difference between the control and experimental group students in their performance in human anatomy in the post test. It is therefore concluded that the experimental group students performed significantly better in human anatomy than that of control group students in the post test.

To find out the significance of the difference between the pre and post test mean scores of control group students in the performance in human anatomy, the 't' was used.

Table 4: Distribution of 't' value for the pre and post test mean scores of control group students in the performance in human anatomy

Group	N	Mean	S.D	't' value	Level of Significant
Pre test	100	42.69	13.60	2.62	$p<0.05$
Post test	100	52.46	13.28		

There is no significant difference between the pre and post test mean scores of control group students in the performance in human anatomy.

The obtained 't' value 2.62 is statistically significant since it is greater than the table 't' value 1.96 for 50 df at 0.05 level of significance. Hence the null hypothesis is rejected. It shows that there is significant difference between the pre and post test mean scores of control group students in the performance in human anatomy. It is therefore concluded that the control group students have improved in their performance in human anatomy in the post test.

Suggestions

The present study aims at developing and using Multimedia programme for perceiving human anatomy for higher secondary students to enable them to understand the concepts very easily through individualized instructional technique. It is maintained that the Multimedia programme may reduce monotony in the classroom by bringing out real life situations and motivate them for self-study and provides opportunities for individual pace and ability.

Conclusion

The study intends to develop a multimedia programme for human anatomy for XI standard Zoology subject prescribed by Tamil Nadu State Board Syllabus and find out the effectiveness of the Multimedia programme through experimentation in perceiving human anatomy among the higher secondary students. The study provides scope for the development and use of many Multimedia programmes in the concerned discipline as well as other disciplines for the benefit of learners of different categories. Hence the multimedia programme can be used as an individualized instructional technique for the students of different categories in the science subjects as well as other subjects.

The present study reveals that the experiment group students who used multimedia programme performed significantly better than that of the control group students who did not use, which implies that the multimedia programme has tremendous impact upon the performance in human anatomy than the students learning through traditional method. This proves the effectiveness of the multimedia programme in human anatomy developed by the investigator.

The present study reveals that the performance of the control and experimental group students in the post test is significantly higher than the pre test. But the performance of the experimental group students in the post test is more significantly higher than the post test performance of control group students. Thus, it proves the supremacy of the multimedia programme over traditional method.

References

- Chang, Kuo-En; Chen, Yu-Lung; Lin, He-Yan; Sung, Yao-Ting (2008). **Effects of learning support in simulation-based physics learning. Computers & Education,** 51(4): 1486-1498..
- Djeassilane, N. (2008). Effect of computer aided instruction (CAI) in enhancing the academic achievement of higher secondary students in commerce. Unpublished Doctoral Dissertation, Alagappa University, Karaikudi.
- Garnett, P., Hackling, M., & Oliver, R. (2009). Designing interactive multimedia materials to support concept development in beginning chemistry classes.
- Junaidu, Sahalu (2009). Effectiveness of multimedia in learning & teaching data structures online. Turkish Online Journal of Distance Education-TOJDE, 9(4), Article 7. Retrieved March.
- Liao, Yuen-kuang C., Chang, Huei-wen & Chen, Yu-wen (2009). Effects of Computer Applications on Elementary School Students' Achievement: A Meta-Analysis of Students in Taiwan. Computers in the Schools, 24(3-4): 43-64. Retrieved.
- O'Day, Danton H. (2010). Using animations to teach biology: past & future research on the attributes that underlie pedagogically sound

animations. The American Biology Teacher, 70(5):274-278. Retrieved March 20.

- Ozmen, Haluk (2010). The influence of Computer-Assisted Instruction on students' conceptual understanding of chemical Bonding and Attitude toward chemistry: A case for Turkey. Computers and Education, 51(1): 423-438. Retrieved March.
- Ponraj, P., & Nellaiyapen, N. O. (2010). CAI in teaching Zoology. Research and Reflections on Education, 6(2): 18-21.
- Pryor, Caroline R., & Bitter, Gary G. (2010). Using multimedia to teach in-service teachers: Impacts on learning, application, and retention. Computers in Human Behavior, 24 (6): 2668-2681. Retrieved March.
- **Rotbain, Y., Marbach-Ad, G., & Stavy, R. (2011). Using a computer animation to teach high school molecular biology. Journal of Science Education and Technology, 17(1): 49 – 58.** Retrieved March.
- Venkataraman, S. (2011). Relative effectiveness among selected modes of CAI in physics in relation to learner's personality. Unpublished Doctoral Dissertation, Annamalai University. Chidambaram.
- Vernadakis, N., Zetou, E., Tsitskari, E., Giannousi, M., & Kioumourtzoglou, E. (2012). Student attitude and learning outcomes of multimedia computer-assisted versus traditional instruction in basketball. Education and Information Technologies, 13(3): 167-183.
- Victor, Adeosun Olufemi (2012). Relative effects of three Multi-Media Instructional Packages on Nigerian student's achievement in Social Studies. Pakistan Journal of Social Sciences, 5 (5): 415 – 420. Retrieved March.

❐

37.

Usage of Internet for Education Purpose among Arts and Science College

INTRODUCTION

Education plays an important role in building a creative society. Due to the revolutionary changes in the field of telecommunications and Information Technology, educational institutions may be transformed from "teaching centers" to "centers of learning resources". Language is a tool for communication, and the system of language is learned for the purpose of communication (Clark, 1978). Internet is also a tool for effective communication among the several developments in Information and Communication Technology. The usage of Internet, social network, you tube; etc will stimulate the creativity among the users. Usage of internet for hi-tech innovative learning will develop the creativity of the students.

NEED AND SIGNIFICANCE OF THE STUDY

Developing a creative society is the worldwide objective in education. Internet learning allows the learners to have more control over their own learning to think creatively, analytically, critically and to work collaboratively. The role of internet communication mediums have increased in social and academic interpersonal communications(Huang,2010).However, the internet usage among the students for learning is considerably less due to lack of Internet facilities and skills. The purpose of using Internet has an impact upon the innovative learning of the students.

Student teachers are enrolled only from Arts and Science colleges. As a Teacher educator, to promote the hi-tech knowledge of student teachers, we should evaluate and know about the technology skill of students from Arts and Science colleges, so that we can plan hi- tech oriented curriculum for our student teachers. Hence the investigator feels the need to study the usage of Internet by students' population from Arts and Science colleges. The 'usage' is referred to as practical use of Internet application in day to day educational activities by Arts and Science College students. Five major Internet communication modes (i.e.websites, e-mail, social network, YouTube and blogs) were considered in this study.

OBJECTIVES

1. To find out the level of Internet usage by the students of Arts and Science colleges.
2. To find out whether there is significant differences in the usage of Internet by the students of Arts and Science colleges in terms of the variables namely
    1. Gender
    2. Subject of study group
    3. Location of college
    4. Nature of the college
    5. Annual income of Parents.

HYPOTHESES

The level of Internet usage among the students of Arts and Science colleges is high.

There is significant difference in the usage of Internet among the students of Arts and Science colleges in terms of

1. Gender
2. Subject of study group
3. Location of the college
4. Nature of the college
5. Annual income of Parents.

SAMPLE

A sample of 160 Arts and Science college students belonging to five colleges in Madurai in Tamil Nadu was selected for the study. Samples were selected by **proportionate stratified representative** sample techniques. To achieve the objectives of the study **survey method** of the research was used.

TOOL USED

he tool consisted of 30 statements under 5 dimensions anchored with 5-point rating scale [often, as and when needed some time, Rarely, Never] to indicate the level of acceptance of students. The minimum and maximum scores of the scale were 30 and 150 respectively. The tool was finalized with consultation of the teacher educators and research experts. Reliability and validity of the tool was established.

DATA COLLECTION PROCEDURE

The purpose of the study was explained to the students and ample time was given to go through the tool and doubts were clarified while administrating the tool.

i) Mean

No of Samples	Theoretical Mean	Calculated Mean
160	90	92.59

ii) Mean Value under Dimension

S.No	Dimensions	Mean
1	Websites	23.41
2	e-mail	21.26
3	Social network	19.48
4	You tube	19.43
5	Blogs	9

iii) Level of Significance:

S. No	Variables	Category	N	Mean	S D	't' Value	0.05 level of Significance
1	Gender	Male	80	92.96	11.92	2.054	Significant.
		Female	80	89.13	11.63		
2	Subject of study group	Computer science	80	91.45	10.62	1.973	Significant
		Other subjects	80	88.23	10.02		
3	Nature of the college	Aided	80	93.213	10.93	1.720	Not Significant
		Self Finance	80	90.362	11.02		
4	Location of the college	Urban	80	91.62	11.73	1.909	Not Significant
		Rural	80	88.11	11.52		
5	Annual income of Parents	Above 3 lakhs	75	93.97	90.14	1.984	Significant
		Below 3 lakhs	85	11.65	12.81		

FINDINGS

- The mean value of Internet usage among the students of Arts and Science College is **high.**
- The results obtained from mean value of different dimensions show that the majority usage of internet is through **Websites** and least usage is through **Blogs.**
- There is **significant difference** between **male and female** students of Arts and Science colleges in the usage of Internet for educational purposes. The result is in favour of **male group.**
- There is **significant difference** between **computer science and other subject group** students of Arts and Science colleges in the usage of Internet for educational purpose. The result is in favour of computer science group students.
- There is **no significant difference** between the students of **Aided and Self finance** Arts and Science colleges in the usage of Internet for educational purpose.
- There is no **significant difference** between students of **Rural and Urban** Arts and Science colleges in the usage of Internet for educational purpose.
- There is **significant difference** in the usage of Internet for educational purpose between the students of Arts and Science colleges whose parents' annual income is below and above Rs.3Lacks.The result is in favour of students whose Parents' annual income is **above 3 lakhs**.

SUGGESTIONS FOR EDUCATIONAL IMPLICATION:

- From this research findings here are some suggestions for improving the usage of Internet.
- As Internet has become an integral part in today's education, well-equipped infrastructure such as computer lab with Internet facility is essential in every institution.
- The Internet usage payment in colleges should be providing at concession rate for the students.
- The syllabi should have some online based learning topics for students.
- All teachers should communicate with their students by using Internet mode.
- All major students other than computer science should learn ICT oriented courses in a compulsory manner.
- Parents should give opportunity to their children, [particularly female] for using Internet for their studies.
- To encourage on line communication, teacher should encourage the students to submit their assignments only through e-mail, blogs, etc
- The university should organize the technology oriented enrichment programmes for all students and teachers.

CONCLUSION

Only hi-tech knowledge can promote the creative society nowadays. Tremendous changes in education can occur through advanced technologies used inside the classroom. Only the teacher can develop the digital knowledge among students in all levels. Therefore the investigator suggests that apart from class room teaching, teachers should involve themselves in creative techno instruction and encourage the students to develop their software knowledge.

REFERENCES

- Jyotsna saxena,Manoj kumar saxena,Sandhya Gihar,ICT in Professional Education,A.P.H.Publishing corporation,2010,New DELHI.
- Kamatchi,ICT For Social Change,Edutracks,Vol.11-No.12,Aug,2012
- Parthasarathy,Ananthasayanum,Ravi,Usage of Internet Applications among B.Ed students,Edutracks,Vol.12-No.7,March,2013.

❐

38.

Students Attitude towards Audio-Visual Aids Used By the Teachers

Introduction

Audio Visual aids or Graphic aids are the form of visuals that are represented on plane surface. The subject matter areas that are represented in Audio Visual aids or Graphic aids are in an abridged and easily understandable form. They convey meaning mainly through relatively conventionalized symbols that are nearer to reality perceptually than verbal symbols. They secure the attention of the pupils by their attractive format and simplicity of layout. They convey the expected message by combination of visual and pictorial message made meaningful by suitable captions. Pictures and words blended in harmony deliver the required information. The idea conveyed by any graphic aid should be a single concept. The layout and words should not be complicated so as to puzzle the viewer and make him lose interest in the same. The statement "one good visual which can secure and maintain attention and educate the viewer in the desired area is worth a thousand words" is quite correct. Graphics could be truly considered as the shorthand language of the idea presented. The criteria for good graphics are that they should be simple, bold, legible, brief and have adequate margins. Graphics are only two-dimensional and should be carefully planned to offset the limitation. An Audio Visual aids or a graphic aid by eliminating non–essentials and by using bold symbolic representations with attractive portrayal should be able to create interest and secure the attention of the pupils. Since the message to be conveyed pertains to a single concept and hence brief, the viewer will not get perplexed on being exposed to the visual but will try to read and understand what is implied (visual and words).Audio Visual aids or a graphic aids could easily be prepared by and teacher using simple materials that are easily available and stored for future use. Making graphics should form an integral part of the teacher's preparation for teaching. Almost any material involving illustrations is basically graphic in nature. There can be an infinite variety of graphic materials. It is difficult to give a rigid list of these materials. The present study aims to find out the students attitude towards audio-visual aids used by the teachers in Coimbatore district. A samples of 100 respondents selected randomly were studied. An interview schedule method of survey was used to find out the attitude towards audio-visual aids. Primary data were collected by using a structured interview scheduled. All the respondents were asked the same questions in the same fashion and they were informed the purpose of study. ANOVA, t-test and regression analysis were applied to test the hypotheses. The data collected through questionnaires have been tabulated. The findings and observations are the result and outcome of the interpretations made during the study of analysis.

Graphs, Diagram, Posters, Maps, Comics, Cartoons, Charts, Globes, Display Board, Peg Boards, Hook and loop board, felt board, magnetic board, marker board, chalk board, bulletin board, models, Epidiascope, slight projector, over head projector (OHP), fields trips, excursion, exhibition, museums, radio, Television, Tape recorder, Video Caste Record VCR and Computers. By using audio visual materials in accessible process, materials givens objects changes in time, speed and space could easily be brought to the class. Audio visual aids can helps to imaginative teachers to solve the communication problems. It also helps to extend human experience. Use of audio visual aids results in greater acquisition of knowledge of facts and ensures longer retention of the information gained. It can provide effective substitutes for direct contact of students with environment-social and physical. It also adds an expected change in attitude and behaviour of the students. It can provide integrated experiences varying from abstract to concrete. It helps in to secure and retain to attention as well as develop the communication skills. It could be used to motivate and stimulate interest of students to gain further knowledge. Lastly, In a conventional teaching method teacher is the centre of attention and the primary sources of information.

An attitude is a mental state of readiness exerting directive or dynamic influence upon individual's response to all objects and situations with which it is related. Therefore if we can have some judgement about the attitude of an individual towards a specific thing or activity then we can have a fair idea as to whether the individual can be persuaded to participate in a particular thing or activity and whether he shall adopt it with interest and sincerity or not.

The attitude is the degree of positive or negative effect associated with some psychological objects namely institution, ideal, symbol, phrase, slogan, job or idea towards which people can differ with respect to positive or negative effect (Thurstone, 1946). The attitude is a dispositional readiness to respond to certain situations, persons, objects in a consistent manner which has been learnt and has become one's typical mode of response (Free Mann, 1950). According to Guild (1950) attitude is a tendency of individual to favour or not to favour some type of situation. The attitude may be considered as motivational perceptual states, which direct perceptions and predispose a person to act in accordance with perceptions (Allport, 1955). The attitudes are learnt pre-dispositions to respond positively to certain objects, situations, institutions, concepts or other persons (Aiken, 1979).

Review of Literature

Glee Harrah Cady and **Pat Mc Gregor (2005)** describe that "Internet is a network of network and the internet mostly connects network of computers".

Barry (2006) studied the relationship between student's perceptions of their science class room learning environment and attitude to four different scores of scientific information experiments, books, promote positive attitude towards experiment as a source of information, while less favorable environment promoted more positive attitude to the more authoritarian sources of information.

Schafer (2007) compared third and fourth grade students using ESS units with students using laid low science serious on classification skills, science achievements and science attitudes. No achievement or classification skill different were noted but ESS students had more favorable attitudes.

Williams (2008), "Attitude of high school pupils towards general science and its relationship with achievement and its subjects". In her study it is found to examine if there are any differences among the different groups of students such as boys and girls. Rural school pupil and Urban school pupils in respect of their achievement in science, attitude towards science and attitude forwards science education.

Martis Anandi (2009) developed the test on scientific attitudes (TOSA), taking the point of view that attitudes must be inferred from the behavior of students. They developed a multiple – choice format test. The developed behavioral definitions of eight attitudes: (1) critical mindedness, (2) suspended judgment (3) Respect for evidence (4) Honesty, (5) Objectivity, (6) Willingness to change opinions, (7) Open – mindedness and (8) Questioning attitude. The behavioral definitions to these eight attitudes were used to develop items.

Mohanty Ajay Kumar (2010) investigated attitudes towards education, critical thinking ability and specific effective behavious of (1) Students who had studied, the BSCS environmental models "Investing your Environment" (IYE), (2) Those students using one of BSCS biological science version and (3) Those studying models of Biology. He found that the ability of students who had experienced BSCS Biological science was significantly increased but no other differences were found among the students on any of the other variables.

Objective

The present study attempts to investigate the attitude towards Audio-visual aids used by the teachers.

Methodology

Methodology is an important aspect of any research work. There are different methods followed at various stages of any investigation. The details of methods followed in this study such as selection of tools, sample frame, collection of data, and analysis of data are involved in this research paper. The study has been designed with the student's attitude towards Audio-visual aids used by the teacher's achievement. The major aim of the present study is to determine the student's Audio-visual aids used by the teacher.

Method of data collection

The investigator personally distributed the questionnaires to each member of the randomly selected sample. They were requested to answer the items in the booklet as per the instructions provided at the beginning of each questionnaire. Confidentiality of response was assured. The questionnaires were collected by the investigator from the employees. The responses were scored as per the scoring key of the respective questionnaire. Then the results were tabulated, analysed and discussed.

Sample

A sample is a finite number of observations (or) cases in a particular universe of which it is a pat (Good 1952). The investigator prepared a representative random sample of students studying VIII & IX standard in different schools at Coimbatore District. A sample of 100 students was finally selected.

Hypothesis

Students have favorable attitude towards use of Audio Visual Aids in Coimbatore district school.

Nature of the Tool

The inventory contained general instruction for the students and information about bio data. In addition to that the specific instruction ware given to on the first page of the inventory. Space for collecting personal data like students name type of school, locality of the school, class, gender, community, religion, group, medium of instruction, birth order of the child and parental literacy.

Data Processing

The collected data were analysed using appropriate statistical techniques. The descriptive statistics such as mean and S.D, t-ratio were computed. In order to study the functional dependencies to indicate the likelihood of causal relationships between the variables, inferential statistical techniques of ANOVA and Percentage analysis were computed.

Analysis and Interpretation

Table 1: Showing Mean, SD and t-test for respondent about students attitude towards audio visual aids used by the teachers on the basis of type of the school.

Types of the school	N	Mean	SD	t-value	LS
Government	62	70.48	6.50	2.78	0.01
Private	38	73.30	10.33		

Hypothesis 1: Students do not differ in their student's attitude towards audio visual aids used by the teachers on the basis of types of the school.

The calculated t-value (2.78), which is significant at 0.01 level, confirms that there is a significant difference in student audio visual aids on the basis of type of the school. Hence the stated hypothesis is rejected. So government students have high level of audio visual aids than private school students.

Table 2: Showing Mean, SD and t-test for respondent about students attitude towards audio visual aids used by the teachers on the basis of locality of the school.

Locality of the school	N	Mean	SD	t-value	LS
Urban	74	72.24	8.11	1.07	NS
Rural	26	71.14	9.19		

Hypothesis 2: Students do not differ in their student's attitude towards audio visual aids used by the teachers on the basis of locality of the school.

The calculated t-value (1.07), which is not significant at 0.05 level, confirms that there is no significant difference in their audio visual aids on the basis of locality of the school. Hence the stated hypothesis is accepted.

Table 3: Showing Mean, SD and t-test for respondent about students attitude towards audio visual aids used by the teachers on the basis of Gender.

Gender	N	Mean	SD	t-value	LS
Male	74	70.97	7.41	1.85	NS
Female	26	72.90	9.89		

Hypothesis 3: Students do not differ in their student's attitude towards audio visual aids used by the teachers on the basis of gender.

The calculated t-value (1.85), which is not significant at 0.05 level, confirms that there is no significant difference in their audio visual aids on the basis of gender. Hence the stated hypothesis is accepted.

Table 4: Showing Mean, SD and t-test for respondent about students attitude towards audio visual aids used by the teachers on the basis of group.

Group	N	Mean	SD	t-value	LS
Arts	56	69.19	5.37	5.58	0.01
Science	44	74.58	10.37		

Hypothesis 4: Students do not differ in their attitude towards audio visual aids used by the teachers on the basis of group.

The calculated t-value (5.58), which is significant at 0.01 level, confirms that there is a significant difference in student audio visual aids on the basis of group. Hence the stated hypothesis is rejected. So science students have high level of audio visual aids than art students.

Table 5: Showing Mean, SD and F-ratio for students attitude towards audio visual aids used by the teachers on the basis of medium of instruction.

Medium of instruction	N	Mean	SD	F-ratio	LS
Hindi	50	70.20	9.64	6.49	0.01
English	30	71.75	4.19		
Kannada	20	75.00	11.60		
Total	100	71.78	8.58		

Hypothesis 5: Students do not differ in their attitude towards audio visual aids used by the teachers on the basis of medium of instruction.

The calculated F-ratio (6.49), which is not significant at 0.05 level, confirms that there is a significant difference in students attitude of audio visual aids on the basis of medium of instruction. Hence the stated hypothesis is rejected.

Table 6: Regression for student demographic characters and their attitude towards audio visual aids used by the teachers

Model Summary

Model	R	R Square	Adjusted R Square	Std. Error of the Estimate
1	436[a].	190.	159.	7.87

a. Predictors: (Constant)

ANOVA[b]

Model	Sum of Squares	df	Mean Square	F	.Sig
Regression	4189.756.	11	380.887	6.155	000[a].
Residual	17821.724	88	61.881		
Total	22011.480	99			

a. Predictors: (Constant)

b. Dependent variable

Coefficients[a]

Model	Unstandardized Coefficients		Standardized Coefficients	t	Sig.
	B	Std. Error	Beta		
Name of the school	58.979	4.376		13.477	.000
Type of the school	2.387	1.116	.139	2.139	.033**
Locality of the school	-1.000	1.005	-.058	-.995	.320
Class	-.500	1.046	-.028	-.478	.633
Gender	1.989	1.052	.115	1.891	.060
Community	-1.365	.422	-.190	-3.233	.001**
Religion	.757	.627	.068	1.208	.228
Groups	5.255	.947	.306	5.548	.000**
Medium of instruction	2.183	.649	.191	3.365	.001**
Birth order of the child	-9.11	1.032	-.001	-.009	.993
Parental literacy (Father)	-.143	1.003	-.008	-.143	.887
Parental literacy (Mother)	-.585	.955	-.033	-.612	.541

a. Dependent Variable: Attitude towards Audi visual aids

** Significant at 0.01 level

According to the regression result it is known that the demographic variables are influenced nearly 19 per cent to measure their attitude towards audio visual aids. This is proved by the obtained r square value (0.19).

Further the calculated F-value (6.15) also significant at 0.01 level. It indicates that there is a significant influence between students demographic characters and their attitude towards audio visual aids.

Also from the obtained t- values the demographic variables such as type of school, community, group studied and medium of instructions the students studied are significant at 0.01 level. So it is concluded that there is a significant difference regarding attitude towards audio visual aids on the basis of these variables.

Conclusion

Audio Visual aids or graphic aids are the form of visuals that are represented on plane surface. The subject – matter areas that are represented in Audio Visual aids or graphic aids are in an abridged and easily understandable form. They convey meaning mainly through relatively conventionalized symbols that are nearer to reality perceptually than verbal symbols. They secure the attention of the pupils by their attractive format and simplicity of layout. They convey the expected message by combination of visual and pictorial message made meaningful by suitable captions. Pictures and words blended in harmony deliver the required information. The idea conveyed by any graphic aid should be a single concept. The layout and words should not be complicated so as to puzzle the viewer and make him lose interest in the same. The statement "one good visual which can secure and maintain attention and educate the viewer in the desired area is worth a thousand words" is quite correct. Graphics could be truly considered as the shorthand language of the idea presented. The criteria for good graphics are that they should be simple, bold, legible, brief and have adequate margins.

Findings of the study

Based on the results that students do not differ in their audio visual aids on the basis of types of the school

From the calculation that students do not differ in their audio visual aids on the basis of locality of the school

Based on the results that students do not differ in their audio visual aids on the basis of gender

Based on the results that students do not differ in their audio visual aids on the basis of group

From the analysis that students do not differ in their audio visual aids on the basis of medium of instruction

Discussion

Audio visual aids a process of inward journey to unravel the hidden potentialities of a being. It helps an individual to develop ones personality. A systematic approach of Audio visual aids helps an individual to see the all around development at physical, mental, intellectual and emotional level. The practice of use of audio visual aids makes an individual perfect. It removes the unwanted elements in the mind of the learner. It improves concentration and brings mental stability. Audio visual aids are an essential tool for students to achieve higher score in their studies as if improves concentration, memory and skills. The present study clearly indicates and recommends the students to use of audio visual aids as to develop positive attitude towards everything in their life which helps to excel themselves in their studies. The entire study concluded reveals that the use of audio visual aids has high achievement and expressed more favourable attitude.

Educational Implications

Audio-visual aids are very important and useful aids for teaching. As well as it creates high interest among the students to learn the subjects. So, the department of education shall take a steps to implement the latest audio-visual aids to all the school and colleges for teaching purpose.

For self-learning, these type of aids are very helpful to the students. Also students are very much interested in using latest technologies such as computers and internet. In internet lot of facilities are there to learn new information with visual appearance. From that students are also get more interest to use that.
In the case of teaching, in older days teachers follow interactive methods and oral demonstration. But these are not creating much interest. In order to create interest and attention audio-visual aids are highly useful. So, the concerned educational institution tries to provide these facilities. So that teachers and students get benefited.

Suggestions

The following suggestions are arrived from the research findings. Research found that use of audio visual aids will contribute more in students achievement. Also the result reveals that use of audio visual aids increases the memory power, concentration. Further it sharpens the intelligence. Apart from that it reduces misconception in learning. Further due to use of audio visual aids the sensory expression would be more exercised. So, the present research suggested that in all schools and colleges, the students advised to use of audio visual aids compulsory. The education department forms a rule for that and advises the educational institutions make a step to establish separate infrastructure for this one. Also the Government take a step to use audio visual aids effectively students in their academic. This will definitely help the students to be a good learner imbibing the concepts.

Conclusion

The present study attempted to identify the students attitude towards audio-visual aids used by the teachers. For that the researcher framed some objectives. On the basis of objectives, a questionnaire is framed. After framing the questionnaire, these are circulated to the selected samples. 100 samples were selected randomly. The responses were collected and coded using computerised. To test the hypotheses and characteristics of the data, some standard statistical tools were used. The statistical tools such as t-test, F-ratio and correlation were used. From the analysis the result concluded that the students have positive attitude towards audio-visual aids used by the teachers.

References

- Glee Harrah Cady and Pat Mc Gregor (2005) "Internet is a network of network and the internet mostly connects network of computers". Journal of research in science teaching.
- Barry (2006) "Relationship between students perceptions of their science class room learning environment and attitude", Journal of Educational Research.
- Schafer (2007) vargo students science attitudes and self concept in science

as a function of rose specific pupil/teacher interpersonal compatibility", San Francisco, California, National association for research in science teaching.

- Williams (2008), "Attitude of high school pupils towards general science and its relationship with achievement and its subjects". Journal Community and Guidance.
- Martis Anandi (2009), in test on scientific attitudes (TOSA), taking the point of view that attitudes must be inferred from the behavior of students, Journal of All India Association for Educational Research, Vol.17, Nos. 1 & 2, March & June.
- Mohanty Ajay Kumar (2010), Attitudes towards education, critical thinking ability and specific effective behavious, Journal of all India Association for Educational Research,Vol.14, Nos.3&4.

❒❒❒